PEONIES

PEONIES

Jane Fearnley-Whittingstall

HARRY N. ABRAMS, INC., PUBLISHERS

Editor: Helena Attlee

Designer: Nigel Soper

Library of Congress Cataloging-in-Publication Data

Fearnley-Whittingstall, Jane.

    Peonies / by Jane Fearnley-Whittingstall.

    p.   cm.

    Includes bibliographical references (p.   ) and index.

    ISBN 0–8109–4354–9

    1. Peonies   I. Title

SB413.P4F425   1999

635.9'3362—dc21   99–25414

First published in the United Kingdom in 1999 by Weidenfeld & Nicolson, London

Text copyright © 1999 Jane Fearnley-Whittingstall

Design and layout copyright © 1999 Weidenfeld & Nicolson

Published in 1999 by Harry N. Abrams, Incorporated, New York

Printed and bound in Italy by Printer Trento Srl

Harry N. Abrams, Inc.

100 Fifth Avenue

New York, N.Y. 10011

www.abramsbooks.com

CONTENTS

BY THE SAME AUTHOR

GARDEN PLANTS MADE EASY, WEIDENFELD & NICOLSON, 1997.
GARDENING MADE EASY, WEIDENFELD & NICOLSON, 1995.
IVIES, CHATTO & WINDUS, 1992.
HISTORIC GARDENS, WEBB & BOWER, 1990.
ROSE GARDENS, CHATTO & WINDUS, 1989.

For Peter and Anne

One of a series of drawings commissioned in China by John Reeves of the British East India Company, showing a tree peony with the sought-after dark purple colouring.

INTRODUCTION

Travellers to China in the eighteenth century claimed they had seen a new kind of flower, like a gigantic rose, but without thorns. It was no exaggeration; they had seen peonies for the first time, flowers of spectacular beauty and sweet fragrance. This book tells their story. It starts before 600 BC and has not ended yet. It takes us from the Imperial courts of China and Japan to Empress Josephine's France, Edwardian England and twentieth-century America, tracing the history of a flower that has symbolized royalty and riches and inspired artists and poets as well as gardeners.

Peonies can be ranked among the few flowers known and loved by non-gardeners, and today they are enjoying a renaissance as garden plants. They are back in fashion because of the ease of their cultivation in a wide range of climates and the rich diversity of their lovely flowers. They include open, saucer-like single flowers, and doubles with hundreds of densely-packed petals, and there is every possible nuance in between. Colours range from yellow, cream and white through every shade of pink to lavender, crimson, maroon and nearly black. The shrubs known as tree peonies can be as tall as 3 m (10 ft) or as short as 90 cm (3 ft). Herbaceous peonies vary from 1.5 m (5 ft) tall and wide down to 45 cm (18 in). So there is a peony for almost any site in any garden.

The marvellous range of species and varieties – about 3,000 – to choose from is bewildering, and I aim to help readers choose the right peonies for their gardens and integrate them successfully with their planting design. But I have to own that there is a nettle to be grasped. The beauty of peonies is not in dispute, but their value as garden plants is sometimes questioned. Why, asks a sensible, practical gardener, should we grow plants that are in flower just for a week or two? The standard answer is that some peonies do flower for four weeks and longer, and by choosing carefully and planning for a succession of bloom you can have peonies in flower from mid-April until the end of July. My own answer is that it is precisely *because* their season is fleeting that we love peonies so much. The excitement begins with the spring thaw, when the first stubby shoots break through the ground. Anticipation gradually builds to a climax when the first flower bud opens, and is more keenly felt because we know that once each plant is in bloom we have only a few weeks in which to enjoy it.

In this respect the peony is on a par with the flowering cherry or the damask rose. It's flowering stirs the emotions as well as the senses and is something to celebrate. In China and Japan people flock to peony festivals in their thousands. Stall holders sell images of peonies painted on parchment and porcelain, and embroidered on silk; there are firework displays and lantern processions; gifts of peonies are exchanged as symbols of friendship and prosperity. In the West, the passion for peonies is communicated in less demonstrative ways, from grower to gardener, from one gardener to another and from gardener to garden visitor. This book is my own way of communicating my love for a beautiful plant with a romantic and fascinating history.

JANE FEARNLEY-WHITIINGSTALL
GLOUCESTERSHIRE 1999

The gap between East and West was bridged by images of peonies in Turkish arts and crafts. This Iranian tile reflects the Turkish influence

PART ONE

PEONIES IN THE PAST

CHAPTER 1

OUT OF THE WILDERNESS

WILD PEONY SPECIES IN FOUR CONTINENTS

…there, balancing rarely amid the brushwood, shone out to me
the huge expanded goblet of *Paeonia Moutan*, refulgent as pure
snow and fragrant as heavenly roses.

Reginald Farrer, *Gardener's Chronicle* VOL. 56 (1914).

THE STORY OF THE PEONY begins with peony species in the wild. As the tale
unfolds we will see how, seduced by their beauty, connoisseurs in China
brought them into cultivation and invested in hybridizing programmes to
produce larger, fuller flowers in an ever-widening range of colours. The work was
continued by twentieth-century plant breeders whose passion was the refinement of
earlier hybrids and the introduction of new flower shapes and colours. As a result of
their work many hundreds of highly-bred garden peonies are available today. But
they all have their origins in a few wild species.

Both wild and cultivated peonies belong to one of two types: herbaceous peonies
and tree peonies. The familiar garden peonies of Europe and North America are
herbaceous; their leaves wither and die in autumn and new shoots emerge from
beneath the ground every spring. The growth remains comparatively soft and sappy
all summer. The second category, misleadingly known as 'tree peonies' are
deciduous woody shrubs. They are not trees, being invariably multi-stemmed and
seldom growing taller than 2 or 2.5 m (6 or 8 ft). Many have beautifully shaped and
coloured leaves.

PREVIOUS PAGE: *Bee and Peony* by Ichimiosai, nineteenth century.

TOP: *A TREE PEONY:* 'L'Espérance' at the
National Trust's Hidcote Gardens, Gloucestershire.

ABOVE: *A HERBACEOUS PEONY: Paeonia lactiflora* 'L'Eclatante'
at Green Cottage, Lydney, Gloucestershire.

Hybrids and cultivated varieties of both tree and herbaceous peonies have flowers ranging from single to very full double, but the wild species from which they are bred all have single flowers with a simplicity of outline and purity of colour that give some of them great appeal as garden plants. Most have the bonus of attractive and healthy foliage.

Describing flowers can be a difficult challenge: throughout this book I avoid using technical terms as much as I can, but verbal descriptions of flowers and leaves inevitably refer to botanical parts. They are identified on the diagram opposite.

The history of peonies starts with geography: two rather insignificant species are native to America. The rest are distributed through the northern hemisphere from Europe to China and Japan via Siberia, the Caucasus and northern India. Exploration and research still throws up evidence from time to time prompting botanists to change their opinions as to which plants are genuine species. A change in name is often the result, which can be confusing to the gardener, especially when the changes have not filtered through to nurseries and other sources of supply. Allan Rogers unravels the complexities of *Paeonia* species and subspecies in the third chapter of his book *Peonies*, and I can recommend his account to readers who would like more technical details than I have space for here.

CHINA

Peonies have been cultivated in China for at least 1,500 years, initially probably for the medicinal qualities of their roots. By the sixth century AD Chinese civilization had reached the degree of sophistication at which flowers are appreciated for their beauty as well as their usefulness. The richness and diversity of China's native plants is truly amazing, but even among such *embarras de richesse* the startling size and lovely colouring of peony flowers made them prime candidates for introduction into the gardens and houses of ruling families, wealthy civil servants and merchants. Some of the most beautiful herbaceous peonies are to be found in China, including *P. lactiflora*, the parent of most garden hybrids and varieties. From this one simple flower come numberless permutations from single to very double, from white through every shade of pink to deepest black crimson. This Chinese peony has also contributed the precious gift of scent to its successors. China is also the unique home of the wild Moutan or tree peony from which all others are bred.

STAMENS   FILAMENTS

SEPAL

CARPELS

PETALS

BRACT

LEAF

PETIOLE

THE PARTS OF A PEONY

The tree peony *Paeonia delavayi*
with *Euphorbia characias* at Highdown, Sussex.

TREE PEONIES

Paeonia delavayi is found in pine forests in the Lijiang mountain range in North Yunnan province at altitudes of 3,050 to 3,650 m (10,000 to 12,000 ft) and was discovered by the French missionary Père Jean Marie Delavay in 1884. The rather bare stems can reach 1.75 m (5 ft 6 in). The flowers, appearing over a comparatively long period in late spring and early summer, vary in colour from darkest black maroon to a lighter blood red. It is a variable plant in cultivation as well as in the wild; a good form can be spectacular, but the flowers are often small and can be hidden among the leaves. Their dark colouring has made them important in the breeding of garden hybrids, and the much-dissected leaves make *P. delavayi* an attractive shrub, if a plant from a good strain can be obtained. The Royal Horticultural Society has given it an Award of Garden Merit. Although hardy to US Zone 5, it seldom flowers in climates colder than Zones 7 or 8.

Paeonia jishanensis was first found by the British collector William Purdom in Shaanxi Province in 1910. Originally thought to be a variety of *P. suffruticosa*, it grows to 1.2 m (4 ft). The flowers, borne singly in mid and late spring, have ten white petals, sometimes shaded pink towards the base.

Paeonia lutea is another of Père Delavay's 1884 discoveries, found on Mount Hea Chan Men in Yunnan and in the mountains above Dali at overlapping and slightly higher altitudes than *P. delavayi*. The plants are similar in some ways, and may be two forms of the same species. They can never be confused when in flower, for *P. lutea* lives up to its name with single flowers of bright, clear yellow. They have the bonus of a lemony scent but they share with *P. delavayi* a reluctance to flower in climates below Zone 7.

Paeonia lutea var. *ludlowii* is a fine form found near the Tsango gorges in south-east Xizang, Tibet in 1936 by the British plant hunters Frank Ludlow (a Londoner) and Major George Sherriff, a Scottish soldier. At 2.5 m (8 ft) tall by up to 4 m (13 ft) wide it needs a large garden to show off its great sculptural leaves and large yellow flowers. It flowers very well in New Zealand. It is quite hardy; although it may be cut to the ground by frost it will sprout again.

Paeonia ostii is now an endangered species. Named after the Italian botanist Dr Gian Osti, it comes from Gansu, Anhui, Shaanxi and Henan provinces in north China. It is a hardy shrub growing to 1.5 m (5 ft) with grey-brown bark, lance-shaped leaflets and, in mid-spring, flowers up to 15 cm (6 in) across, pure white sometimes faintly tinged with pink, without basal blotches. Like *P. jishanensis* it has purplish-red filaments, disc and style.

Paeonia potaninii is a compact shrub reaching 1 m (3 ft) at most. It grows in north-west Yunnan and west Sichuan. It was named in memory of the eminent Russian explorer and naturalist Grigori Potanin in 1921. It has the unique characteristic of spreading by underground stolons and bears attractive, deeply-divided leaves and quite small brownish-red flowers. There is a white-flowered form, *P. potaninii* 'Alba', and a highly desirable form with delicate yellow flowers which is called *P. potaninii trollioides*.

Paeonia rockii is a famous and very beautiful plant with a history that demonstrates the difficulties botanists experience in identifying and naming species. *P. rockii* or another almost identical tree peony reached Europe from China as a garden plant on Captain James Prendergast's ship *Hope* in 1802. It seems not to have been named. It was first recorded in the wild in 1914 when Reginald Farrer, the English plant hunter, writer and artist, described seeing it (see page 95) near the border between south Gansu and Shaanxi. It was not collected, but placed, from Farrer's description, as a form of *Paeonia suffruticosa*. Today plants previously described as members of this very variable species are thought to be crosses between four wild species identified and named by the distinguished Chinese botanist Professor Hong Tao and his colleagues in 1992. So *P. suffruticosa* no longer exists. Two of the 'new' species (*P. jishanensis* and *P. ostii*) are described above and a description of the third, *P. yananensis* follows below.

The fourth species identified by Hong Tao is *P. rockii*. It is the plant Farrer saw in 1914, rediscovered in 1926 growing in a Tibetan monastery in south west Gansu by the American collector Dr Joseph Rock. It is a leggy shrub about 2 m (6 ft) tall and nearly as wide. The fragrant flowers carried at the tip of each stem, are of stunning beauty, up to 16 cm (6 in) wide with white petals bruised at their bases with deep black-maroon blotches, surrounding a crown of golden-yellow anthers on purple and white stamens.

Rock's find was celebrated as *P. suffruticosa* 'Rock's Variety' or *P. s.* 'Joseph Rock', names considered correct until Professor Hong published his findings in 1992. It is now generally agreed that *Paeonia rockii* is a species in its own right. Whatever name

Paeonia lutea var. *ludlowii*, *P. delavayi*
and Kelways' seedling *P. delavayi* 'Coffee Cream'.

Paeonia rockii at Highdown, Sussex, one of the plants that Sir Frederick Stern raised from seed collected in China by Joseph Rock.

it goes under, it is lovely but not easy to grow or to propagate, and young plants are rare and expensive.

Paeonia suffruticosa is a species that is no longer recognized, as explained under *P. rockii* above. But 'suffruticosa' is a useful umbrella term for a group of tree peonies that have more in common with each other than they do with *P. delavayi* or *P. lutea*.

Paeonia yananensis is the remaining member of Professor Hong's quartet, from the arid hills of Yan'an district of Shaanxi Province. Yan'an is revered as the finishing point of the Long March and was the Communist headquarters in the war against Japan. The peony is only 40 cm (16 in) high with divided, rounded leaflets. The flowers are sometimes white, sometimes pale purplish rose with a dark red blotch at the base.

In addition to these Chinese species of tree peony, there are others likely to be universally accepted before long: *Paeonia qiui* is similar to *P. jishanensis* except for some differences in the leaves. *P. szechuanica* and *P. yunnanensis* were described in 1958 by the Chinese botanist Fang Wen-Pei, but are not yet familiar to botanists in the West.

HERBACEOUS PEONIES

Although the Moutan or tree peony has always been first favourite in China, herbaceous peonies come a close second; both kinds are valued and are collected for use as medicine as well as for their ornamental qualities, and are therefore increasingly rare in the wild.

Paeonia beresowskii, named by the Russian botanist Vladimir Komarov in 1921, is very similar to *P. veitchii* and grows in the same region, but it may be a separate species as the hybrids from each of the two plants have quite distinct characteristics. See under *P. veitchii*.

Paeonia lactiflora (*P. albiflora, P. chinensis*) is the ancestor of thousands of garden varieties and by far the most influential peony. It covers a vast area from Siberia and Mongolia to northern China and parts of Tibet. It's territory is steppe grassland and scrub and it is very hardy provided it grows in free-draining ground. The light green stems, flushed with red, reach 60 cm (24 in). They carry smooth, dark green leaves divided into lance-shaped leaflets. From early to mid-summer two or more white flowers up to 10 cm (4 in) across, bloom on each stem, hence the earlier name of

P. albiflora (white flower). The German explorer Peter Pallas gave it this name in 1788, forgetting he had named the same plant *P. lactiflora* (milk flower) in 1776. It is a strict botanical rule that the earliest name takes precedence, so in due course, to the consternation of those who had grown to know and love *P. albiflora*, it became *P. lactiflora*. It has contributed autumn colour to the leaves and scent to the flowers of many of its descendants. Roy Lancaster notes in *Travels in China* that this peony was still quite common in the wild in the Changbai Shan reserve in Jilin Province when he was there in 1984.

Paeonia mairei is not in cultivation but is known from herbarium specimens. It grows in the mountains of north Yunnan and west Sichuan. The plant reaches about 45 cm (18 in) and has rose-pink flowers about 10 cm (4 in) across, one to each stem in late spring and early summer.

Paeonia obovata is a native of mountain woodland and scrub in Siberia, China, Japan and Korea. The seeds of the first plants introduced to Europe were collected by E H Wilson in 1900 in Hupeh Province. The flower petals are shaped like the blunt end of an egg (obovate) and the flowers, up to 7 cm (3 in) wide, vary in colour from white to purplish red. The seeds are dark blue berries and the leaves continue to grow after the plant has flowered. In its white form (*P. obovata* var. *alba*) it holds the Royal Horticultural Society Award of Garden Merit.

Paeonia sinjiangensis is a native of the province of Xinjiang and was only discovered in 1979. It shares characteristics with *P. anomala* and *P. veitchii* but carries only one flower on each stem.

Paeonia veitchii was collected by E H Wilson for the Veitch nursery in London in 1907. It grows in grassland and scrub at 2,400 to 3,000 m (7,900 to 9,850 ft) in Gansu, Shaanxi and Sichuan Provinces. Like *P. anomala* (see below under 'Central Asia and Siberia') it has intricately cut leaves, but it differs in carrying two or more flowers to each stem, varying in colour from soft pink to magenta, in early summer. The height varies between 20 and 50 cm (8 and 20 in). The smaller *P. veitchii* var. *woodwardii* is more likely to be available as a garden plant. It is a brave little plant from windswept country grazed by yaks at 2,700 to 3,500 m (9,000 to 11,000 ft) near Zhoni in Gansu Province. Rabbits and deer have an aversion to peonies, and apparently the aversion is shared by yaks. The plants are just 30 cm (12 in) high with rose-pink flowers. *P. beresowskii* (see above) is very similar to *P. veitchii*.

'Lovely Rose', a hybrid between the species *P. lactiflora* and *P. peregrina*
introduced to the USA by A P Saunders in 1942,
growing in the RHS gardens at Wisley.

JAPAN

There are no tree peonies native to Japan but Chinese species were introduced by Buddhists from about AD 734. They are known there as *Botan* or *Bhotan*, and in due course many hybrids of great elegance and charm were developed in Japan. Comparatively few found their way to European and American gardens but recently there has been increased traffic between enthusiasts, passing in particular from east to west.

HERBACEOUS PEONIES

Paeonia japonica is native of the northern islands of Japan and was first described in 1910. It grows in the mountains at 950-1,300 m (3,120-4,260 ft) in forests of deciduous trees. This species is similar to *P. obovata* but smaller. The flowers are always white. In Japan it is called 'Yama-shakuyaku'.

　　Paeonia obovata Described under 'China' above.

THE HIMALAYAS

The rather harsh conditions that peonies seem to prefer are found on the lower slopes of the Himalayas from Afghanistan to southern Tibet, in areas where just enough shelter is provided by woodland or scrub.

HERBACEOUS PEONIES

Paeonia emodi must be a wonderful sight in the wild. It inhabits forest clearings in the mountains of Afghanistan, Kashmir and North Pakistan at altitudes of 1,500 to 3,200 m (4,260 to 6,230 ft), making handsome, leafy clumps about 75 cm (30 in) high. In late spring each stem carries between two and four large white flowers with yellow stamens, each flower up to 12 cm (5 in) wide. Though perfectly hardy, it is not easy to grow. The best chance of success is in semi-shade, protected from early morning sun.

　　Paeonia sterniana was collected by Frank Ludlow in the Tsangpo Valley in southeast Tibet at an altitude of about 9,500 ft (3,000 m). It is not unlike *P. emodi* but there is just one flower with white, tissue-paper petals to each stem. Blue seeds bursting out of bright red capsules add excitement in autumn. Unfortunately, it is not commercially available.

Paeonia emodi, a native of the Himalayas.

Paeonia sterniana. In autumn the seed capsules turn scarlet and then burst to reveal blue seeds.

Paeonia mollis at Kew Gardens, London.

Central Asia and Siberia

In this vast, mountainous region, the peony's eastern range is halted only by the Gobi Desert, demonstrating dramatically that, providing its prerequisite of good, free drainage is supplied, it will thrive in terrain inhospitable to equally robust species.

HERBACEOUS PEONIES

Paeonia anomala has an immense range stretching from the Ural mountains in Russia to the Pamir mountains in Central Asia, to the Tien Shan mountains in Kazakhstan and the Gobi Desert in Mongolia. *Anomala* means unusual, and refers to the finely divided leaves which turn orange brown in autumn. The plant is about 50 cm (20 in) high with single flowers from late spring to early summer from magenta red to crimson rose, the best being brilliant red with yellow stamens. The roots, which grow very large, are cooked and eaten by Mongol Tartars.

 Paeonia anomala var. *intermedia* is sometimes also known as *Paeonia hybrida* var. *intermedia*. This plant is more available in cultivation than the true species. It occupies the same range but wanders still further, from the Kola peninsula in northern Russia to the Altai mountains in Siberia.

 Paeonia daurica see *P. mascula* subsp. *triternata*.

 Paeonia lactiflora is described under 'China' above. Besides northern China it is found from Siberia to Mongolia.

 Paeonia mollis is of uncertain origin. Said to have been brought to Britain from Russia in the early nineteenth century, it has never been found in the wild. The flowers, appearing in late spring on short stems, may be red or white. It is a compact garden plant up to 45 cm (18 in) high with blue-green leaves.

 Paeonia obovata is described under 'China' above, its range extends to Siberia.

The Caucasus (Kavkaz)

The wild and remote Caucasus mountains range from the Black Sea to the Caspian Sea, and include the republics of Georgia, Armenia, Azerbaijan, and part of Ukraine. Majestic snowy mountains rise above fertile subtropical valleys and on their beautiful but harsh and windswept slopes some of the loveliest herbaceous peonies grow. They include those with yellow flowers, a trait that has so far resisted all the hybridizers' attempts to reproduce it in a double form.

Paeonia mlokosewitschii known to gardeners as 'Molly-the-Witch'.

HERBACEOUS PEONIES

Paeonia macrophylla is from the western Caucasus in Georgia at 800 to 1,000 m (22,625 to 32,280 ft). It is like *P. wittmanniana* (see below) with larger leaves of darker green, and white flowers tinged with yellow.

Paeonia mlokosewitschii 'or Molly-the-Witch', is named after Mlokosewitsch, the man who discovered it in the Valley of Lagodeki in the south-eastern part of central Caucasus, growing on sunny slopes and in hornbeam or oak forests. It grows to about 90 cm (3 ft). The dark green oval leaflets have red veins and edges; the cupped flowers, 10 cm (4 in) across, are a clear, soft shade of yellow. This is one of the earliest peonies to flower and everyone who sees it is bowled over by its beauty. The leaves colour up in the autumn. It is not easy to grow, especially in the USA, but it does well in the heavy soils of the Pacific North-west.

Paeonia tenuifolia the fern-leaved peony, is another deserving candidate for a place of honour in the garden. It has the fragile beauty of a large scale anemone or pasque flower and grows on steep hillsides in the Terek district of the Caucasus, in Ukraine to the north of the Black Sea and westwards into Transylvania. First mentioned in a European catalogue in 1757 and described by Carl Linnaeus in 1759, it was probably introduced to England in 1765 by William Malcolm. The ferny leaves are finely dissected, almost thread-like. They grow close together on stems from 30 to 60 cm (12 to 24 in) tall. It is the earliest peony to flower with scented, blood-red single flowers 6-7 cm (2.5 to 3 in) across with a boss of yellow stamens at the centre.

Paeonia wittmanniana is a close relation of *P. mlokosewitschii* and similar in appearance but the leaves are lighter green and the flowers paler yellow, sometimes white. The seeds are bright coral red. It grows in rocky slopes and alpine valleys in the Caucasus where Wittman the botanist travelled. A letter in the *Journal of Botany* (London) in 1842 reported its introduction via Count Worontzov's garden at Adsharia near Erzerum in the Crimea. Nothing further was heard of it until in about 1880 it was rediscovered in an Irish garden. Though hardy to Zone 4, it can be difficult to grow, but its hybrids are tougher. Lemoine crossed it with Chinese varieties to produce early-flowering peonies with large, fragrant single flowers in white, yellow, rose and salmon, with thick, luxuriant leaves such as 'Avant Garde', 'Le Printemps', 'Mai Fleuri' and 'Messagère'.

No. 926

Paeonia tenuifolia the fern-leaved peony,
from the 1806 volume of William Curtis' *Botanical Magazine*.

TURKEY AND ASIA MINOR

Some of the earliest peony species introduced into Western gardens come from this area which is comparatively accessible to travellers. The species have themselves tended to spill over from Turkey to Greece, Italy and northern Europe.

HERBACEOUS PEONIES

Paeonia kesrouanensis is native to Syria, the Lebanon and Turkey. It is very similar to *P. mascula* (see below). It was first discovered in 1936 at Kesrouan in western Lebanon by J Thiébaut.

Paeonia mascula subsp. *mascula* is the most widely distributed of a number of subspecies of the variable species *P. mascula*. It is found in southern Italy, Sicily, Greece, northern Iran, Iraq, Syria and Turkey. It also occurs in France and Germany, but it is not necessarily native in these countries. Colonies of the plant are sometimes found where there were once monastery gardens, so it may have been introduced for medicinal use. The word 'mascula' is not a description of the plant's male sex. It refers to heraldic Latin, where the word means 'like a mask' or 'lozenge-shaped'. A sprawling plant, from 60 to 90 cm (2 to 3 ft), in mid and late spring it bears rose-red flowers up to 13 cm (5 in) across. The leaves often colour well in autumn, turning pinkish yellow.

Paeonia mascula subsp. *arietina* was formerly thought to be a separate species, *P. arietina*. It grows in Eastern Europe, Crete, Armenia, Turkey and Syria. *Arietina* means ram-like, from the same Latin root as the zodiac sign Aries. It describes the plant's fruit, shaped like a ram's horn. Single, dark red (sometimes pink) petals surround bosses of creamy-yellow anthers on red filaments. They bloom from early to mid-summer and the leaves are divided into one to two-inch-wide segments. Several forms of this subspecies are available today, and the best of them are excellent garden plants.

Paeonia mascula subsp. *triternata* is another plant formerly treated as a separate species under the alternative names of *P. corallina* and *P. daurica*. It has been found on the Aegean islands, in Turkey, Romania, Siberia and Ukraine. It differs from other subspecies of *P. mascula* in the undulating margins of its leaves, which turn a warm orange-brown in autumn. It was originally sent to England from Siberia by John Bell in 1790 as *P. daurica*.

Paeonia mascula subsp.*mascula* at Highdown, Sussex.

Paeonia broteroi growing wild on the hills of
Serrania de Ronda, southern Spain

Paeonia turcica is found in pine forests in south-western Turkey. It is very like *P. kesrouanensis* and *P. mascula* (see above).

NORTH AFRICA

There are two herbaceous peonies in Africa, *Paeonia mascula* subsp. *atlantica* in the forests of Algeria, at altitudes between 1,250 and 2,000 m (4,500 and 6,500 ft.) and, in Morocco in the Atlas Mountains and southern Spain, a similar plant, *Paeonia mascula* subsp. *coriacea*. Both reach 55 cm (22 in) and have light pink flowers up to 10 cm (4 in) wide.

EUROPE

Peonies have been valued in Europe for many centuries. In Ancient Greece and probably earlier they were appreciated for their medicinal qualities, and the beauty of different forms and colours was enjoyed in the earliest gardens. They have a wide range, thriving in extraordinarily diverse soils and climates. Although wild plants are now rare, forms of *P. officinalis* were once found in Portugal, France, Italy, Switzerland, around the Mediterranean and in eastern Europe including Hungary, Romania and Yugoslavia.

Paeonia broteroi is a close relative of *P. mascula* (see below) found only in Spain and Portugal. It has glossy green leaves and rose-pink flowers about 10 cm (4 in) wide. It grows to about 36 cm (15 in).

Paeonia cambessedesii is a beautiful peony growing only in the Balearic Islands, especially Majorca, on precipitous cliffs. Jacques Cambessedes collected it, reputedly using a shotgun to detach his specimens from the rocky cliffs. It is extremely rare and is difficult to grow in the garden, needing a mild climate (Zone 7 or above) and very well-drained conditions. It grows to 45 cm (18 in) with purple-veined leaves on reddish stems and large, deep rose-red flowers.

Paeonia mascula subsp. **arietina** see above under 'Turkey and Asia Minor'. It is also found in Italy, Greece, Crete, Armenia and Yugoslavia.

Paeonia mascula subsp. **mascula** see above under 'Turkey and Asia Minor'. It is also found in southern Italy, Sicily and Greece in beech, oak and pine forests and on rocky hillsides. It has been found in Italy in former monastery gardens.

Paeonia mascula subsp. **russii** is nothing to do with Russia but was named in

Paeonia cambessedesii at Docwra's Manor, Cambridgeshire
with other low-growing plants including
dark-leaved sempervivums and *Festuca glauca*.

Paeonia officinalis subsp. *officinalis*.
Pl. 2 from *Paeonia*,1821 by Clara Maria Pope (1768-1838).

Paeonia officinalis 'Rubra Plena', the double form of the wild European peony.
Pl. 46 from the *Nassau Florilegium* by Johann Jakob *c*.1600-1679.

1816 after Joachimi Russo, abbot of the monastery at Monte Casino in Italy. This peony is very like *P. cambessedesii*. It grows in mountain scrub and subalpine meadows, mainly in Sicily but also in southern Italy and Greece. Purplish stems and leaves grow to about 45 cm (18 in). The pink flowers are 10 cm (4 in) across.

Paeonia mascula **subsp.** *triternata* see under 'Turkey and Asia Minor'. It is also found in south-east Europe.

Paeonia officinalis **subsp.** *officinalis* is the robust species from which Europe's earliest garden peonies derived, double red and white forms being described in 1636. The flowers of the species are single, up to 13 cm (5 in) across and usually pink, although red and, more rarely, white forms do occur in the wild. The plants vary in size between 35 and 60 cm (14 and 24 in).

Paeonia officinalis **subsp.** *banatica* was first discovered in the Banat region of Romania and is also native to parts of Hungary and Serbia. There is a minor difference in the leaves of this and subsp. *officinalis*.

Paeonia officinalis **subsp.** *humilis* (formerly *P. humilis* or *P. officinalis* subsp. *macrocarpa*). This pretty miniature form is found in Spain and southern France. The stems are 40 cm (16 in) long. Magenta flowers up to 13 cm (5 in) bloom in late spring and early summer.

Paeonia officinalis **subsp.** *villosa* is almost the same as subsp. *humilis* but is native to southern France and central Italy.

Paeonia tenuifolia see under 'The Caucasus' above. Also found in Hungary, Romania and Ukraine.

GREECE

A number of fine species grow in Greece, and some only there. Most are not reliably hardy in British gardens. They start into growth early in the year and the young shoots are vulnerable to frost.

HERBACEOUS PEONIES

Paeonia clusii is found only on the island of Crete. It was named in honour of the sixteenth-century botanist Clusius by the English botanist, gardener and peony expert Sir Frederick Stern and Dr William Stearn, author of *Wild Flowers of Greece* (1968). It has pinkish-purple stems 17-30 cm (8-12 in) long, pretty blue-green

Paeonia peregrina in the National Trust's Hidcote Garden, Gloucestershire.

dissected leaves and scented white flowers 8 to 12 cm (3 to 4 in) in diameter in mid-spring. As you might expect from a Cretan plant, it is not hardy enough to grow outdoors in British gardens.

Paeonia mascula* subsp. *hellenica was identified in 1978 by the Greek botanist D M Tzanoudakis who identified this and *P. parnassica* subsp. *hellenica*. It grows to 30 to 60 cm (12 to 24 in) and has numerous grey-green leaflets and, from mid to late spring, white flowers up to 12 cm (5 in) across.

paeonia mascula* subsp. *mascula see above under 'Turkey and Asia Minor'.

Paeonia mascula* subsp. *russii see above under 'Europe'.

Paeonia parnassica was identified as a separate species by Tzanoudakis. It grows in the mountains of south-central Greece, reaching 65 cm (26 in) high. The young leaves are purplish maturing to grey-green. The flowers, appearing in late spring, are deep maroon red and up to 12 cm (5 in) wide.

Paeonia peregrina This Greek peony, also found in Albania, Bulgaria, Romania, Serbia and Turkey, was one of the first to be cultivated in Europe. Introduced from Istanbul via Austria in 1583, in England it was called the Red Peony of Constantinople. The cup-shaped flowers, up to 12 cm (5 in) wide, are an intense, pure red. They are borne from mid to late spring above glossy, dark green leaves which turn yellow and red in autumn. Given a sheltered, semi-shaded position, it is a lovely garden plant.

Several of the species described above are worthwhile garden plants and are included in the alphabetical charts in Part III. Others have been and are important breeding material for the magnificent garden peonies available today. It is interesting to seek out these ancestors in botanical collections, and the sighting of a peony species growing in the wild is an unforgettable experience for any traveller.

CHAPTER 2

AN IMPERIAL FLOWER
THE PASSION FOR PEONIES
IN CHINA AND JAPAN

In front of the Emperor's audience hall many thousand-
petalled tree peonies were planted… When the flowers first
opened the fragrance of their perfume was perceived by
everyone… Every time His Majesty gazed on the sweet-
scented luxuriance he would sigh and say 'Surely there has
never before been such a flower among mortals.'

NINTH-CENTURY CHINESE WRITER.

IN CHINA 'PEONY' NEARLY ALWAYS REFERS to the tree peony or *Mudan* (Moutan in English, sometimes spelt *Mou Tan*) China's national flower. There are two schools of thought about the meaning of Mou Tan: it either means 'male scarlet flower' or is derived from Mutang, the Emperor of Flowers in Chinese mythology. In the past, tree peonies have also been called *Hua Wang* which means 'the King of Flowers'. Herbaceous peonies, not held in quite such high esteem, were called *Hua Liang*, 'the king's ministers'. Yet another name for the tree peony is *Fu Gui*, meaning 'wealthy and honourable', and for the herbaceous peony, *Shaoyao* which means 'medicinal herb plant' but can also mean both 'wealthy and honourable' and 'charming and beautiful'. Nowadays the general term *Mudan* is used in China for both tree and herbaceous peonies, although in the West, a Moutan is always a tree peony.

Tree peonies are known to have been valued and grown as ornamental plants during the Sui Dynasty (AD 581-618). Even earlier, a painting by Gu Kaizhi who lived from AD 345 to 406 shows a garden scene with tree peonies growing in the

Peonies, butterfly and bee. Painting on silk by Yu Feian, 1888-1959, China.

A courtly lady, one of a pair of paintings on glass,
Eighteenth century (Qing Dynasty 1644-1912).

background, so it seems that they were already established as garden plants.

It is possible that the garden history of peonies goes back even further. The Chinese have the oldest continuous tradition of garden making in the world: in the second millenium BC the princes of China set aside parks for hunting and other recreation and through the centuries they embellished their parks with lakes and terraces. By the fourth century BC gardens were already sophisticated, to judge by a poet's description of scarlet balconies, latticed pavilions, and winding waterways in a royal garden. By 221 BC, Qin Shi Huang, the first ruler to unite the Chinese states, was receiving rare plants and animals as tributes from different parts of his empire, and the rulers of the Han Dynasty (206 BC to AD 220) continued the collection. It seems likely that peonies were appreciated and formed part of such collections, but lacking firm evidence, we can only speculate.

The date of the earliest use of peonies as ornamental plants is uncertain. It is likely that they were first valued as medicinal and magical plants. An anonymous poem of about 600 BC translates roughly like this:

> Beyond the River Wei
>> The land is open and pleasant.
> A knight and a lady
>> Sport and play.
> Then she gives him a peony.

The word used is *Shaoyao*, a herbaceous peony. The lady's gift to the knight may have been a peony flower, but it may also have been the root, offered as a kind of love potion.

A reference to the medicinal properties of peony root has been found in a tomb dating from the first century AD. It is written on one of the bamboo panels that were used before paper was invented in AD 105, and recommends using the skin of a tree peony's root to prevent blood clotting. Herbaceous peonies grew wild throughout northern and central China and their roots were used for medicine and in some areas as food. In AD 536 the writer Hung King describes two kinds of peony, the red and the white. The Moutan, or male red peony grew, he wrote, in the eastern part of Sichuan province and the adjoining part of Shaanxi. This was the tree peony. The root of the herbaceous peony is still used today in Traditional Chinese Medicine (TCM). Confusingly, the herbaceous peony (as opposed to the tree peony) is also known as the white peony (*Paeonia lactiflora* meaning milk-flowered). Its flowers are not necessarily white, but can also be pink or red. Here is a description of its properties and uses, translated from a modern medical treatise.

WHITE PEONY ROOT (BAISHAO)

PHARMACEUTICAL NAME: *Radix paeoniae alba.*

BOTANICAL NAME: *Paeonia lactiflora.*

COMMON NAME: White peony root.

SOURCE OF EARLIEST RECORD: Shen Nong Ben Cao Jing.

PHARMACEUTICAL PREPARATION:
dig the roots in summer, clean the fibrous roots and peel
off the bark. Soak in hot boiled water and dry in the sun.
Soak again before cutting into slices.

PROPERTIES AND TASTE: bitter, sour and slightly cold.

MERIDIANS: liver and spleen.

FUNCTIONS:
1. to nourish the blood and consolidate the yin.
2. to pacify the liver and stop pain.

I have seen white peony root advertised elsewhere as one of the ingredients in a (perhaps not entirely reliable) pill to solve male problems and to 'increase sex drive'.

Alice Harding, the American peony expert, mentioned herbaceous peony roots being used as food in AD 536, 'surely', she wrote, '...the prototype of some of our modern breakfast foods.' In the cause of thorough research I have cooked and eaten a small nugget of peony root. It was fibrous and starchy and had a smell and flavour reminiscent of turnips soaked in wallpaper paste mixed with turpentine. I would prefer not have it for breakfast every day.

Girl seated on a rustic rock chair. Woodcut 1873, (Qing Dynasty 1644-1912)
China. The peony with pink and white flowers on the same bush is
probably 'Er Qiao' dating from the Yuanfeng era (1078-1086) of the
Northern Song Dynasty. It is named after two beautiful sisters who lived in
the Wu Kingdom between AD 220 and AD 280.

Beds of peonies surround a pavilion in the garden of
White Horse Temple, Luoyang, China.

During the Tang Dynasty (AD 618-AD 907) tree peonies became fashionable at court, and remained so until the end of the Song Dynasty (AD 960-1279). The Tang emperors' capital was at Changan in Shaanxi Province where suffruticosa peonies grew wild. They were brought into the imperial gardens from the hills around, and as the passion for peonies grew, enthusiasts experimented by raising plants from seed and grafting cuttings from the best specimens onto wild stocks. Later, herbaceous peony roots were used as stocks for grafting tree peonies.

An early *doyenne* of peony fanciers was the only woman to become empress of China in her own right, rather than merely the consort of an emperor. It is difficult to know whether to approve or disapprove of Empress Wu Zetian. She is rather a heroine among feminists who describe her as a zealous reformer. She put a stop to the practise of selling influential positions in the government to wealthy citizens and revised the system of stiff civil service exams, making knowledge of and proficiency in poetry one of the requirements for official promotion. She helped the peasants by lowering their taxes and took measures to increase agricultural production so that during her reign they enjoyed comparative prosperity. And she managed to reduce the size and influence of the army whilst at the same time fighting successful wars against Turkey and Tibet to consolidate China's boundaries.

Wu Zetian's methods of obtaining power and keeping it were particularly devious and cruel in an age when deviousness and cruelty were the norm. She started her life of intrigue at the age of thirteen in the court of the Emperor Tai Tsung. Her beauty, wit and accomplishments led to her becoming the Emperor's favourite concubine. After the Emperor's death, she transferred her allegiance to his son, Emperor Kao Tsung. Kao Tsung's consort, Empress Wang barred Wu's route to the throne, so Wu hit on an extraordinary way to remove her: Wu arranged the murder of her own baby daughter and accused Wang of the crime. Wu then became Kao Tsung's empress and ruled unofficially from the year AD 660 when the Emperor had a stroke until he died in AD 683. She then conspired against her own eldest son to place his younger brother Jui Tsung on the throne. Jui Tsung seems to have been a 'mummy's boy', content to let her govern for him and then to abdicate in her favour. In AD 690 she became 'Holy and Divine Emperor'. Her lovers are said to have included a monk who traded in aphrodisiacs and, when she was in her seventies, two brothers less than half her age.

During Wu Zetian's reign a flowering of the arts reflected political and economic stability. At that time the women of wealthy families were comparatively independent. They did not bind their feet and were taught to play music and to read and write poetry. When the Empress moved her court to Luoyang she assembled the most talented artists and craftsmen to build her new palace, then filled it with musicians, writers and painters. It was in this context that the peony, the Empress' favourite flower, became the height of fashion. It remained a favourite decorative motif for centuries, carved in wood or stone as architectural embellishment, painted on ceramic bowls, jugs and vases, and embroidered or woven into silk robes.

Wu Zetian arranged for the planting of thousands of tree peonies and it became virtually compulsory to emulate her passion. A later writer (Li Chao in AD 860) described the scene on a spring evening during the peony season:

> At the time of its flowering the whole city went berserk… Horses and carriages were coming and going in a frenzy and anyone who didn't go to see the peonies felt ashamed of themselves.

Courtiers and would-be courtiers vied with each other to produce the rarest and most beautiful blooms. The price of plants soared, resulting in paeoniamania similar to the tulipomania of seventeenth-century Holland. A specimen of the variety Pe Leang Kin was sold for a hundred ounces of gold.

A great poet put the mania in context:

> For the fine flower, a hundred pieces of damask;
> For the cheap flower, five bits of silk …
>
> … an old farm labourer
>
> … came by chance that way.
> He bowed his head and sighed a deep sigh;
> But this sigh nobody understood.
> He was thinking, 'a cluster of deep-red flowers
> Would pay the taxes on ten poor houses.'
>
> BAI JUYI AD 810.

'Wu Long Peng Sheng' (black dragon holds a splendid flower), a fancifully named but robust and easily-grown Chinese tree peony.

The peonies on the municipal litter bins in Luoyang get a fresh coat of paint
every spring at Festival time.

Today Chinese cities are still *en fête* when the peonies bloom and Empress Wu's capital, Luoyang, is still China's great centre of tree peony cultivation.

In the eleventh century in Luoyang, during the Song Dynasty, Ouyang Xiu (1007-1072) wrote the first known treatise on the tree peony. Moutan, he said, prefer cold to warmth and dryness to moisture, and are best suited by a situation half in sun and half in shade. With the right care by expert gardeners, plants could produce flowers with several hundred petals, measuring 30 cm (12 in) across; and marvellous new forms and colours sometimes occurred 'by spontaneous transformation'. Ouyang Xiu recorded more than ninety varieties, and some of those he would have known are still grown in and outside China. The flowers of 'Mei Yao Chen', described as inward-facing white clouds with purple spots and a centre the colour of the setting sun, was probably a fine form of *Paeonia rockii*, the romantic and beautiful tree peony that was to capture the imagination of British and American plant explorers nearly 900 years later. Also in cultivation in the time of Ouyang Xiu were 'Dou Lu' ('Pea Green') with very double flowers that are green when they open, turning white as they mature and 'Yao Huang' ('Yao's Yellow') with deliciously scented double flowers 20 cm (8 in) wide, the petals forming a central dome.

Ouyang Xiu left, as well as cultural advice and a list of varieties, instructions on the arrangement of the plants in the garden. His advice is addressed to 'Asist and Hsieh planting flowers at the Secluded Valley':

> The light and the dark, the red and the white, should be spaced apart;
> The early and the late should likewise be planted in due order.
> My desire is, throughout the four seasons, to bring wine along,
> And to let not a single day pass without some flower opening.

The Mongol invasion brought a period of artistic and cultural decline lasting for most of the fourteenth century, but then followed four centuries of relative stability and unparalleled artistic creativity under the Ming (1368-1644) and Qing (1644-1911) Dynasties. Hundreds of acres were planted with peonies to provide roots for medicinal use, plants for decorating gardens and flowers to be forced for flowering at Chinese New Year and other public and private anniversaries and festivals. During that period, 'Zi Yun Xian' ('Purple Cloud Fairy') tree peonies were planted in the garden of the Twin Pagoda Monastery at Taiyuan in Shanxi Province. Ten plants growing there today are said to be 300 years old. They are about 2 m (6 ft) tall and still flower profusely every year.

Wild Moutans were prolific in the hills of Shaanxi Province, and towards the end of the seventeenth century a Chinese writer noted that 'the whole hill appears tinged with red, and the air round about for a distance of ten *li* is filled with fragrance'. Ten *li* is just under one third of a mile, so even allowing for exaggeration, the carrying power of the peonies' scent must have been remarkable. When the English plant collector William Purdom visited the same site in 1912 there were no longer any peonies to be found. They are certainly very rare in the wild today, and in Purdom's day some species may already have been depleted almost to the point of extinction by local people gathering roots for medicine and cutting stems for firewood.

The demand for cultivated varieties continued as strong as ever, and travellers from Europe were entranced by them. Reginald Farrer wrote in 1914:

> The Moutan is par excellence the national flower of China… there is hardly a house or an abbey up the Border [with Tibet] without its bush or two of Tree Peony; while the Imperial Palaces revel in rows upon rows of them arranged in narrow shallow terraces, each just wide enough for a single line of plants and piled up one behind another till the effect of that towering long bank all ablaze with blossom must surpass the wildest imagination of the show bench.

In 1933 natural disaster overtook the peony growing industry: one of the worst ever floods on the Yellow River occurred at Heze, washing away more than half the stock of tree peonies. Many of the rest were dug up so that food crops could be planted to prevent the people starving, and by 1949 there were fewer than a hundred varieties left. Determined efforts to rebuild the peony industry were again halted by the Cultural Revolution (1966-1967). During that time the cultivation of flowers was forbidden. Peonies could only be grown as a medicinal crop.

Conversely, in the 1980s and 1990s, encouragement and funding by both national and local governments has revitalized the historic tradition of peony culture. Over 600 named varieties of tree peony are grown by nurseries in Heze and

The tree peony terraces described by Reginald Farrer in 1914
are still blooming today at the Summer Palace in Beijing.

Luoyang, supplying plants and cut flowers to customers in China and abroad. In Luoyang there are five tree peony gardens including one in Wang Cheng Park with 19,800 plants of 320 different varieties and since 1983 Luoyang has been the centre of one of China's two major annual peony festivals, held from 14 to 25 April. The other is the Heze International Tree Peony Fair and is celebrated from 20 to 28 April.

In these two cities, Luoyang and Heze, the peony industry is important to the local economy. At Heze in south-west Shandong Province, peonies have been grown since the fifteenth century, during the Ming Dynasty. Today Heze has more than 1,000 hectares planted with peonies and the area is expected to increase to 4,000 by the year 2000. Carried on the Beijing-Kowloon railway, peonies can be in Hong Kong in twenty hours, and they are exported much further afield, to Europe and the USA as plants and cut flowers. The city's authorities claim that in 1996 peony exports were worth US$ 33.7 million.

Besides plants and flowers for indoor and garden decoration, the roots of peonies are sold for medicine and the flowers are used in the popular 'County Flower Wine'. In Sichuan Province many fields are given over to the cultivation of the lovely, fragrant 'Feng Dan Bai' ('Phoenix White') and 'Feng Dan Fen' ('Phoenix Pink'), forms of the tree peony *P. ostii*, with semi-double flowers 15 cm (6 in) across. They are grown for the bark of their roots (*dan-pi*), an anti-spasmodic exported throughout Asia. At Tongling in Anhui Province ninety acres of 'Phoenix White' produce more than 300 tons of *dan-pi* each year. Besides *dan-pi's* anti-spasmodic qualities, scientific research has shown it to be effective in reducing the swelling of arthritic joints. It is an analgesic, a sedative and a cure for dysentery.

It was as a medicinal plant that the tree peony travelled to Japan from China in the eighth century, reputedly introduced by Koubou Taishi, a seafaring monk. He was one of a group of missionaries known as *kentoshi*, who travelled between China and Japan trading in goods, religion, philosophy and scientific knowledge.

Known as *Botan* in Japan, tree peonies soon came to be appreciated as much for the beauty of their flowers as the curative properties of their roots, and an almost universal passion for peonies ruled every year from mid to late spring, particularly after their reintroduction as a connoisseur's flower in the seventeenth century. Peony breeding took a different route in Japan from that taken in China. Although old Chinese varieties are still grown and valued in Japan, the preference is for single or

'Feng Dan Bai' (phoenix white), a tree peony farmed extensively in Sichuan and
Anhui Provinces for medicinal use.

The tree peony 'Hana Kisoi' reached Europe and the USA from Japan in 1926.

'Globe of Light', introduced by Kelway in 1928, is a classic example of the Japanese peony form, also known as 'imperial' or 'anemone-flowered'. The outer, guard petals are broad and rounded. At the centre the petals are ribbon or thread-like and are known as petaloids or staminoids.

An early, hand-coloured photograph shows ladies 'peony-gazing' in Tokyo.
Many of the flowers exhibited show the tousled, ragged petals of a
'Jishi' or 'lion's mane' bloom.

semi-double forms rather than the very double kinds appreciated so much in China. Michael Haworth-Booth gives a useful tip in his book *The Mountan or Tree Peony*; he points out that Japanese peonies with *Jisi* or *Jishi* in their name will have double flowers with muddled petals. The name means 'lion' and indicates an unkempt, · tousled mane, to be avoided if that is not your style.

It was said that the best Botan plants grew in the Nara area in Yomato Province but plants produced better flowers of stronger colouring in Tokyo and Yokohama where the climate is colder. Itoh Ifui, a Japanese gardener of about 1700, wrote in some detail about the growing of tree peonies, giving instructions for propagating by cuttings and by grafting. Japanese gardeners, then as now, were perfectionists and Itoh Ifui also recommended rubbing the stems with camellia oil to clear them of lichen or moss.

More recently, Japan has made two major contributions to peony culture. 'Japanese' peonies, also sometimes referred to as 'imperial', are a separate class of herbaceous peony, in addition to single, semi-double and double. They consist of one or two rows of large outer, or guard petals, surrounding a more or less showy central display of densely packed, narrow petaloids or staminoides. They are sometimes the same colour as the guard petals, sometimes a contrasting colour. When the petaloids almost completely fill the flower, it's form is sometimes described as 'anemone-flowered'. Throughout the book I have included anemone-flowered peonies in the Japanese category.

The second contribution is the achievement of a hybrid between tree and herbaceous peonies, which has come to be known as an 'Intersectional hybrid', something breeders have been striving after for a very long time. In the 1960s Toichi Itoh crossed the low-growing tree peony 'Alice Harding', a hybrid of *P. lutea* with the lactiflora 'Kakoden'. Sadly he did not live to see the seedlings flower. Four of them, 'Yellow Emperor', 'Yellow Crown', 'Yellow Dream' and 'Yellow Heaven' have since been produced commercially and caused great excitement. Yugen Higuchi has carried on the work in Japan, and the American Peony Society has now declared the new category valid under the name 'Itoh hybrids'. Today the peony industry in Japan is thriving and expanding, boosted by ravishing displays in Botan parks and gardens in the flowering season from late April to the middle of May.

A fine display of tree peonies in the garden of Toksu Palace, Seoul, Korea.

CHAPTER 3

THE PEONY, THE PHOENIX AND THE PEACOCK:
PEONIES IN ORIENTAL ART AND MYTHOLOGY

Peony stands out with special cultural message… Its fullness in bloom emits a sense of elegance, happiness, fortune and prosperity, the feelings of which are cherished in Oriental culture… Together with peacocks, butterflies, pigeons, dragons and phoenix, peony symbolizes enduring love and loyalty. Bring home wood carving and hang it around anywhere in your living room, guest room, bedroom and kitchen. Or let's just say, about anywhere in your home.

MAIL ORDER CATALOGUE, USA 1997.

IN WESTERN CULTURE it is possible to debate whether garden making should be considered an art or a craft. In classical China it would not have been worth asking the question: garden making was accepted as an art on the same level with painting, calligraphy, poetry and music. More than that, a scholar's or gentleman's garden was the setting which, by providing the raw material of contemplation, inspired creativity in the other arts. Guests visiting a garden were expected to contribute a few lines of poetry elegantly inscribed on a wall built for that purpose. At the very least they would show their appreciation with carefully phrased oral epigrams.

The main idea in a Chinese garden was to create an idealization of the natural landscape, using water, rocks, and plants. The plants were mostly trees and shrubs, the more gnarled and characterful the better. But this does not mean that the Chinese despised flowers. On the contrary, flowers played an important part in daily life and in religious and mystic symbolism. Flowers were not an important part of

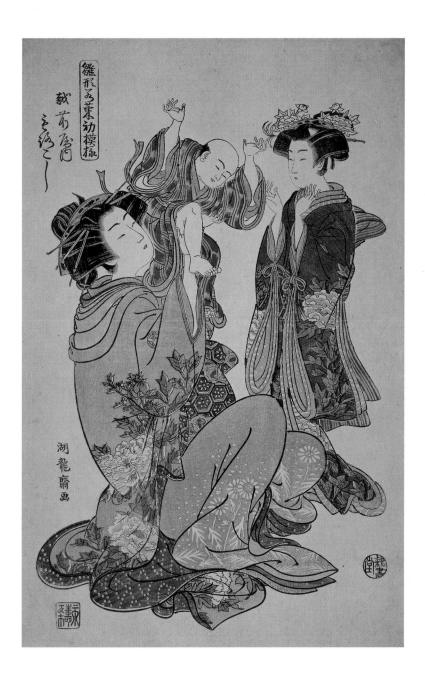

Peonies symbolized, among other things, feminine beauty. They were often worn embroidered on the robes of courtesans and as ornaments in their hair. *The Courtesan Morokoshi of Echizan with Child and Attendant*, Isoda Koryusai, *c.*1776, Japan.

One of a series of eighteenth-century paintings on glass, *Courtly Ladies*
(the other is on page 46). Qinq Dynasty 1644-1912.

the garden, but gardens were not necessarily attached to the dwelling house. Families or individuals would leave their house to go out and tend or contemplate their garden landscape, whilst at home, in the intimate environs of the house, in courtyards enclosed by the buildings and inside the house itself, flowers were lovingly cherished for the beauty of their shape and colour, for their fragrance and for their symbolic significance.

Each month is represented by a flower, and the month of the Moutan, or tree peony, is the fourth month of the Chinese calendar. In art the Moutan also represents spring; the lotus being summer, the chrysanthemum, autumn and plum blossom, winter. Scholars of the Ming Dynasty attributed special qualities to birds, animals and plants: peonies represented vitality, opulence, and the active male principle in the universe. Many-seeded pomegranates symbolized fertility; the lotus, purity. The pliant willow represented sexuality but the chrysanthemum, which endured the frost, stood for fidelity. Taoists believed that the Queen Mother of the Western Heaven lived in an orchard of peach trees, and the peach became an emblem of immortality. Necklaces of carved peach stones were worn to ward off evil spirits.

The gift of a Moutan symbolized an offer of friendship, and this became a politically significant gesture as well as a personal one. In the Sui Dynasty (AD 581-AD 618) the Emperor Yang received a tribute of twenty cases of tree peonies, named varieties in red and yellow. Much later during the Ming Dynasty, when the Emperor Yong Lo moved the Court to Peking at the end of the fourteenth century, he instigated an annual presentation of tree peonies from How Kow Ang to the Emperor every spring, and the ceremonial custom was continued for several hundred years. Recently, just such a diplomatic gift was made on 1 July 1997, when Jiangxi Provincial Government made a presentation to the Hong Kong SAR of a porcelain picture featuring peonies in full blossom, 'symbolizing the joy at Hong Kong's return to China.'

The short flowering season of tree peonies only served to increase their desirability. One would-be connoisseur described the difficulty of catching the plants in full bloom. In the eleventh century Ouyang Xiu wrote:

During my time in Luoyang, I lived through four springs. I first came to

Luoyang in 1031, but as my arrival was late I saw only the late-blooming varieties. In the following year, together with a friend we travelled to several sites, but returned to the city too late to see any Moutan in bloom. Then the year after, I suffered a bereavement in my family and had no time to look at the flowers. Finally in my last year in office, I had to leave for the Capital; thus I could only see the early flowering varieties. So I have never really seen the flowers at the height of their season. All I can say is that those I did cast my eye upon seemed to me absolutely unsurpassable in loveliness.

Since the tree peony was called 'the King of Flowers' and was also an emblem of prosperity, it was natural that it should become the Flower of Kings. Emperors surrounded themselves with Moutans. The Summer Palace of Emperor Ming Huang was planted with 10,000. The Emperor's Moutans achieved legendary status, rumours about them being reported in that bastion of British horticultural respectability *The Gardener's Chronicle* (4 June, 1864): 'It used to be said that these Chinese had a yellow variety, also one with black flowers and a double blue one, which, however, was only to be met with in the Emperor's garden. The latter produced blooms of extraordinary size, each having from 100 to 1,000 petals.' The Emperor's Palace in the Forbidden City in Beijing and other former royal palaces can still provide a magnificent display of Moutans every spring.

During the Tang Dynasty (AD 618-AD 907) the Flower of Kings was also seen as the Flower of Poets. The creative arts flourished and the Moutan was celebrated in poetry, song and paintings. Chinese poetry loses a great deal in translation, but here are two examples:

'THE RED PEONY'.
Voluptuous green so leisurely and tranquil
and robe of red now light, now dark
heart of the flower sadness about to break
but how could we know this from such spring colours

WANG WEI, AD 699-AD 731, TRANSLATED BY D LATTIMORE.

There is an enduring myth that blue peonies exist if you know where to look for them. Reports of enormous blue peonies in the Emperor of China's garden reached Europe in the 1860s. *Blue Peonies* by Zhang Daqian, 1899-1983, China.

An idealized landscape, rather like the spring scene in Beautifully Brocaded Valley
described by the Tang Dynasty poet Bai Juyi. *Peonies, Magnolia and Peach Blossom* by
Chiang T'ing Hsi, 1669-1732, China, is painted on a hanging silk scroll.

A Waley translated the same poem:

> The deep green foliage is quiet and reposeful,
> The petals are clad in various shades of red;
> The pistil droops with melancholy –
> Wondering if spring knows her intimate thoughts.

About 200 years later, another poet writes:

> My lover is like the tree peony of Luoyang.
> I, like the common willow.
> Both love the spring wind.
> When shall we hold each other's hands again?
> Incessant the buzzing of insects beyond the orchid curtain.
> The moon flings slanting shadows from the pepper-tree across the courtyard.
> Pity the girl
> Who does not equal the blossoms
> Of Luoyang.
>
> TING LIU NIANG, AD 891.

The great poet of the Tang Dynasty, Bai Juyi spent two years from AD 817 living in a simple wattle and daub cottage, Lu Shan Cao Tang which translates as 'Thatched Cottage on Mount Lu'. He wrote in praise of the garden there with its square carp pond planted with white lotus, its springs and waterfalls and rocky precipice, its ancient pine trees and rustling bamboos. Each season has its special inspiration: the clouds of Stone Gate Ravine in summer, the moonlight over Tiger Creek in autumn and the snow on Censer Peak in winter. For spring the poet singled out the peonies of Beautifully Brocaded Valley for praise.

In Chinese poetry the beauty of flowers was interchangeable with the beauty of women. Most of the written characters in the language which describe beauty are exclusively feminine, applying only to women, flowers and fruit. This gave rise to opportunities for puns and *doubles entendres*, and a traditional perception of flowers as erotic symbols. In the work of a poet of the Tang Dynasty, a favourite imperial concubine is compared to a peony, giving the King of Flowers a new role as a symbol of feminine beauty as well as love and affection. A poem written to accompany the seventeenth-century painter Yun Shouping's work *Tree Peonies* describes the cut flower he holds in his hand as a lovely woman dancing in his palm, a reference to a favourite concubine.

The Phoenix, king of birds and bringer of inspiration to poets and scholars, is shown with the Moutan, the King of Flowers and emblem of prosperity, on the embroidered robes of imperial princesses. Throughout the Ming (1368-1644) and Kang Hsi periods (1662-1796) tree peonies blossomed as motifs on embroidered and painted silks, on scrolls and screens, and on porcelain. There are various traditional combinations of motif. Swallows are shown with willow trees, storks with pine trees and quail with millet. Peonies are favourite companions in Chinese art to the phoenix, the peacock, the pheasant, the cock and the lion.

A peony in full flower symbolizes happiness, good fortune and material prosperity. It also represents enduring love and friendship, as do the phoenix, the peacock, dragons, pigeons, and butterflies. Peony flowers appear again and again in combination with these symbolic creatures or with other flowers such as the lotus or lily. Herbaceous peonies as well as tree peonies were given as friendship presents. Their Chinese name *Shaoyao* means 'most beautiful', providing a punning opportunity in an old Chinese song:

> If anyone will give his friend a present
> He hands a gift 'most beautiful' of all.

If the possession of a fine healthy peony in full bloom brings good luck and riches, the opposite, sad to say, also applies. If your peony's leaves should wilt and dry up or the flowers suddenly fade, you can expect disaster to strike your family or, at the very least, poverty to creep through your door. For lasting good fortune, a peony embroidered in fine silks is safer than a living plant.

To find beautiful examples of peonies decorating ceramics and textiles, look for work of the Song (AD 960-1279), Ming (1368-1644) and Kang Hsi (1662-1796) periods. With the development of the Silk Road for trade between China and the rest

Peonies painted on silk with peacocks and pine trees bring as much luck as living flowers and are more enduring. *Peacocks and Pines*, watercolour on silk, China, eighteenth to nineteenth century.

A dish carved with an overall pattern of peonies in lacquer on wood, a fine example
of the work of Xuande, 1426-1436.

A landscape with pheasants and peonies on an enamel dish masquerading as porcelain. Peonies also appear in the formal pattern of the border. Cantonese of the Kang Hsi period, late eighteenth century.

Today you can still buy embroidered 'Good Luck' panels. This twentieth- century variation of the peony, phoenix and pine tree theme is hand-embroidered in China.

of the world, the peony flower as an ornamental subject was also exported abroad. In fifteenth-century Persia, stylized peonies were woven into carpets, along with lotus blossoms and chrysanthemums, dragons and phoenixes. In paintings from Tabriz, the centre of Turkman rule, 'outsize peony blossoms and palmettes seem to expand on the page' (*A King's Book of Kings: The sha-ameh of Shah Tahmasp*, by S C Welch, 1972). Today it is still considered lucky to have images of peonies in your house, and in the USA as well as China one can buy prints of peonies by the popular artist Qing Bo with such titles as *Success in Spring Breeze*, *Black Jade of Spring* and simply *Prosperity and Good Luck*.

In the past a picture was a poor substitute for a living plant, but it was difficult to satisfy the demand for peonies blooming in spring in Canton and other southern cities where the climate is too hot to grow peonies successfully. In the 1840s the English plant explorer Robert Fortune observed that the problem was solved by shipping tree peonies by river from the mountains where they were cultivated. They came in baskets, without soil, just as the flower buds were forming. At the end of the journey they were potted up and sold and, after flowering, thrown away, because they would not thrive and flower another season without a cold winter dormancy.

Peonies are particularly obliging in that their flowering can be held back in cold storage, or forced prematurely by the application of heat. But such interference with natural timing is sometimes regarded with suspicion. It is the theme of a story from *Flowers in the Mirror*, a classical novel by Li Ruzhen of Hubei (1763-1830):

The Fairy of a Hundred Flowers has flown from her Cave of Beauty on the island of Penglai to carry a present of hundred-flower nectar to the Queen Mother of the Western World on her birthday. The Lady of the Moon asks her to celebrate the birthday by making all the flowers bloom at once. The Fairy refuses. 'The Fragrant Jade Maiden,' she says, 'has to plan in advance the number of petals and their exact shade. She is a genius and thinks of endlessly varied designs. They are ordered to bloom on earth at different times, in gardens where they can have care, nourishment and clean water, so that poets may sing their praises and people may enjoy them.' Any flower which did not flower at the proper time was punished by the Fairy who was also the magistrate.

Aunt Wind pointed out that flowers were sometimes forced to flower out of season by artificial means, but the Fairy of a Hundred Flowers still refused to make all the flowers bloom at once. But she said that if any mortal ruler was able to do it, she would not prevent it. The Empress Wu in Chang'an [Xian today] took up the challenge and succeeded with all the flowers except the peony. So the peony was banished from Chang'an to Luoyang, and there it has flourished ever since.

During the Qing Dynasty the Dowager Empress Ci Xi (1835-1908) declared the tree peony the national flower of China, and at the time of the Japanese invasion of China 'the Garden of Peonies' was a symbol for China itself in a popular song in which the Japanese invasion is referred to as a 'gruesome storm':

> There is a gruesome storm in the Garden of the Peonies,
> And the raindrops are like stones, and the wind like a broom.
> Yet though the petals fall like lovers' tears,
> The flowers will blossom to the end of time.

In 1994 a vote was taken throughout China to choose a new national flower. The tree peony came out top.

The design of classical Chinese gardens has never been concerned primarily with flowering plants. This approach is even more pronounced in Japan, where beautiful gardens are made by arranging rocks, water and plants chosen for their shape and foliage, according to traditional rules. Nevertheless, as early as the ninth century, flowers were loved and admired, and their appreciation was considered an art in itself. It was considered so important to be seen as a connoisseur of plants that the ladies of the court would plan the colours of their kimonos to suit the flowers or foliage they were going to see and be seen with.

The eleventh-century *Tale of Genji* describes how Prince Genji plants appropriate flowers outside the apartments of each of his ladies in Kyoto. For Lady Murasaki there was a spring garden of plum and cherry blossom, wisteria, kerria and azaleas. Lady Akikonomu's garden was planted for autumn colour and Lady Akishi's winter

A robe worn by the Dowager Empress Ci Xi, 1835-1908, who declared the tree peony the National Flower of China. The robe is embroidered with a phoenix (*feng huang*), a mythical guardian of the Celestial Empire, and peonies in the centre and around the borders.

White jade vessels elaborately carved with peonies, shown at the Great Exhibition,
London, 1851 by M Digby Wyatt.

garden combined snow-laden pine trees with chrysanthemums. We find 'the giant peony' in the summer garden of the Lady from the Village of Falling Flowers, along with white deutzias, orange trees 'whose scent reawakens forgotten love' and sweet-briar roses.

Tree peonies were traditionally grown in separate beds close to the ladies' apartments or in pots for display in courtyards or in the house. Today, however, *Botan* (tree peony) and *shyakuyaku* (herbaceous peony) parks and gardens are planted around temples and crowds make the pilgrimage to see them in flower every spring. In at least one garden, at Tsukuba, you can celebrate the peony season by eating Botan cakes and *mochi*, a rice-based dessert flavoured with Botan.

In Japan three flowers traditionally have royal rank: the peony, the cherry and the lotus. The tree peony was called 'the Flower of Prosperity' and 'the Flower of Twenty Days', an optimistic assessment of the length of flowering time.

The peony appears frequently in Japanese art and architecture, often with peafowl, which are the classic companions of the Botan, just as nightingales are of plum blossom, sparrows of bamboo and deer of maple trees. Peonies also feature in the ritual of the Shinto religious festival of Bommatsuri, a ceremony held at night to pay respect to the spirits of ancestors, when the processional route is lit by peony lanterns made from paper or silk, each lantern being carried at the end of a pole.

CHAPTER 4

THE PEONY TRAVELS WEST

PLANT EXPLORERS AND THEIR PATRONS

To ride in the mountains of North China when the tree
peonies are in bloom is to taste of paradise

E H WILSON, *A Naturalist in China*, 1913.

THE FIRST TREE PEONIES to arrive in Europe were preceded by rumours giving them almost mythical status. In 1656 a delegate from the Dutch East India Company described seeing, whilst on a mission from Canton to Peking, amazing flowers resembling roses but twice the size and without thorns, with petals of yellow or red or white with a touch of purple.

More than a century later, Sir Joseph Banks became interested in obtaining one of these spectacular plants for the Royal Botanical Gardens at Kew in Britain. Banks (1743-1820) was a distinguished naturalist, President of the Royal Society and scientific adviser to King George III, a post which put him in charge of the gardens at Kew and enabled him to send out plant explorers to every continent. Several plants bear his name, notably the lovely Chinese *Rosa banksiae*, named after his wife.

Banks commissioned Alexander Duncan, a surgeon with the British East India Company, to find and bring back a tree peony from China and in 1789 Sir Joseph was able to preside over the planting of the first specimen at Kew. Forty years later it was described as 2.5 m (8 ft) tall and 3 m (10 ft) wide with very double magenta flowers. In 1794 and 1797 two more varieties reached Kew, one of them having semi-double deep pink flowers. Once they had grown to a fair size and were flowering profusely, these early introductions caused great excitement. One plant was described in 1826 by the botanist Joseph Sabine as being 2 m (7 ft) high and 40 ft wide in its twenty-fifth year, bearing no less than 660 flowers. One can't help

The fashion for chinoiserie brought images of peonies into the houses of the
British aristocracy in the late-eighteenth-century wallpaper in the King's Rooms at the
Duke of Rutland's house, Belvoir Castle, Leicestershire.

Whitley, a nurseryman in Fulham, London, introduced one of the first *P. lactiflora* varieties to reach Europe in 1808. 'Whitleyi Major' is still in commerce today.

wondering whether there is an element of exaggeration in the description. Why are plants of such stature never seen today? On his return from China, Duncan grew tree peonies in his own garden at Arbroath on the east coast of Scotland, above the Firth of Tay. The descendent of one of his peonies has been moved from Arbroath to the Royal Botanic Garden at Edinburgh where it can be seen in flower in mid-May.

Herbaceous peonies were also finding their way from China to Europe. The single white *P. lactiflora* 'Whitleyi' was being offered in Fulham, London by a nurseryman of that name in 1808, although we don't know how Mr Whitley first obtained it. 'Whitleyi Major' is still available today, and is still among the very finest single white peonies. Another early herbaceous peony was 'Pottsii', collected by John Potts in 1821 in China for the Horticultural Society, later to become the Royal Horticultural Society.

The introduction of new plants from the east to Europe was often the work of keen and knowledgable amateurs. John Reeves (1774-1856) was born at West Ham in London and educated at Christ's Hospital. After a spell working for a firm of tea-brokers in London he became inspector of tea for the East India Company. From 1812 to 1831 he lived in China, dividing his time between Macau where he had an important garden, and Canton where he spent the tea season each year. He made himself responsible for shipping Chinese garden forms of peony, chrysanthemum, camellia and azalea back to England for the Horticultural Society. Reeves made sure that his plants arrived in good health after the long voyage by establishing them well in suitable pots which were then packed with great care. He took the trouble to persuade the ships' captains to take special care of them.

John Reeves commissioned drawings of plants from Chinese artists on behalf of the Society, some of which can still be seen in the British Museum and the Royal Horticultural Society's Lindley Library. The leaves and stems as well as the flowers are drawn with meticulous accuracy. Some of the peonies shown are single, some semi-double, some double, and one or two have the imperial or Japanese form (see page 63). One is unmistakably *P. rockii*, others have the dark wine-purple colouring that so excited Western plant collectors, and there is an excellent double yellow.

The earliest introductions seem not to have survived in English gardens. Perhaps their cultivation was abandoned because they had the problem sometimes found in highly-bred Chinese varieties of carrying flowers too heavy for their stems. Or perhaps the plants were grafted on to over-vigorous suckering rootstocks, and the rootstocks ousted the weaker grafts. Nowadays tree peonies are usually grafted on roots of the wild herbaceous peony, a satisfactory arrangement.

When he returned from China, Reeves was influential, through his fellowship of the Horticultural Society, in sending the Scottish gardener and plant collector Robert Fortune (1812-1880) to China to add to the Society's collection. Fortune began his career at the Royal Botanic Garden in Edinburgh before taking a post in charge of the hot-houses at the Horticultural Society's garden at Chiswick just outside London. At the age of thirty, having never been overseas, he was despatched to Hong Kong with instructions to make his way to the mainland of China in search of such mythical plants as a peach tree bearing fruits which weighed two pounds each (to be found in the Emperor's garden), camellias with yellow flowers and a blue-flowered peony. Although none of these objectives was achieved, Fortune turned out to be a very successful and discriminating collector.

The Opium War had ended in 1842 and under the Treaty of Nanking some of the restrictions on the movement of foreigners within China were lifted. Nevertheless it was dangerous to venture far from the centres of the main towns, as Robert Fortune found to his cost. On several occasions he was set upon by gangs of ruffians, once was attacked by pirates, and in general had some exciting adventures. He described them entertainingly in vivid, straight-forward prose in his first book *Wanderings in China*, published in 1847.

Fortune went about his work with great gusto, took the trouble to learn the local language and sometimes disguised himself as a Chinaman, complete with 'tail'. When not in disguise, in his own words he '… often found the benefit of having a joke with the natives'. He shipped home nearly 190 different plant species, buying from nurseries and gardens near Shanghai and the other treaty ports, and travelling inland whenever he was able to dodge the Chinese authorities. Here is his description of his first success in the quest for tree peonies:

A flower painter in Chusan had informed me that several very valuable varieties of the Moutan or Tree Paeony, were to be found in gardens near Shanghae… it was always asserted, although not believed, that in some part of China purple, blue and yellow varieties were produced, although

Two of the drawings made by Chinese artists during the 1820's
for John Reeves of the British East India Company.

The first plant of *Paeonia rockii* to reach Europe was probably brought from China
by Captain James Prendergast on his ship *Hope* in 1802.
Photographed at Highdown, Sussex.

these were never brought to Canton for sale. It was for these that I made the most particular inquiries, and this painter not only affirmed he had seen them, but also offered, for a small sum, to make me drawings from memory of all the different kinds. I employed him at once, and when he had finished the drawings, I took them with me to Shanghae. A nurseryman, who had a flower-shop in the town, to whom I showed these drawings, promised at once to procure living plants for me, but said they would be very expensive, as he would have to send to Soo-chow, a distance of nearly one hundred miles, for they were not to be procured in the vicinity of Shanghae, and a man would be absent at least eight days. I was, of course, glad to get them upon any terms, and gave the man the price he asked, which, after all, was not much out of the way, if they were to be brought a hundred miles. At the specified time the Moutans arrived, and proved most valuable kinds which, in England, would have brought a very high sum. Amongst them there were *lilacs* and *purples*; some nearly *black*; and one which the Chinese called 'the yellow', which, however, was only white with a slight tinge of yellow near the centre of the petals. Altogether the collection was a valuable one, and I was highly satisfied with my bargain. Great was my surprise when I afterwards found that these plants were brought a distance not more than six miles from the walls of Shanghae, and that the celebrated town of Soo-chow was, in fact, supplied with 'Moutans' from the very same place.

Fortune's success as a collector was partly due to the invention in the 1830s by Nathaniel Bagshaw Ward of the 'Wardian Case', a sealed glass box in which living plants could safely be transported. Robert Fortune was able to bring to Britain a number of the best varieties of tree peony then available in China. In Europe during the second half of the nineteenth century they became fashionable components of the naturalistic shrubberies then in vogue. Varieties of that era that have stood the test of time include 'Reine Elizabeth', still one of the best double rose-pink varieties; 'Jeanne d'Arc' with pretty, double, soft pink flowers; blush white 'Bijou de Chusan'; and 'Reine des Violettes' and 'Souvenir de Ducher', both with rare and sought-after violet colouring.

Meanwhile the search was on for the wild parents of them all. As early as 1802 a promising candidate appeared when Captain James Prendergast brought from China on his ship *Hope* a semi-double peony thought to be a wild species, white with purple blotches at the base of the petals. Its description is very like the plant we now know as *P. rockii*. It was planted in Sir Abraham Hume's garden at Wormleybury in Hertfordshire and by 1835 was reported as being 14 ft wide with 320 flowers. Sir Abraham (1749-1838) and his wife Amelia (1751-1809) and their gardener James Mean were keen collectors of Chinese plants. 'Hume's Blush', a tea-scented Chinese ancestor of the tea roses, was named after him. But his peony's status as a species was not confirmed until more than a century later when Reginald Farrer and William Purdom were exploring and collecting plants on the border between Gansu Province and Tibet.

Reginald Farrer (1880-1920) of Ingleborough in Yorkshire had a passion for rock plants and wrote the two-volume classic *The English Rock Garden*. Early expeditions to the European Alps were followed by the expedition with Purdom and, after the First World War, one with E H M Cox on the border between Burma and China where he died aged forty. Farrer describes his first sight in 1914 of the sought-after peony in his book *On the Eaves of the World*. His account puts the occasion in a class with the greatest events in plant-finding history, conveying the suppressed excitement, wild surmise and exultation of the occasion:

> After a very long stage we reached our haven at the Street of Happy Sons – Fu-erh-Gai – a tiny place, as pretty as are all these little valley-villages, and with a promise of nobler rugged ridges rising behind, while in front, across the beck, rose a long high hillside all copsed and weeded and blurred with promise, illuminated here and there with the tender pink of Pyrus or Dipelta. In the quiet evening we crossed the stream and ascended the woodland by different paths. My own object was a specially rosy tree of Pyrus, to which I at last attained toilsomely through the jungle, delayed only by one other new beauty, a wild-rose just beginning to break out in arching sprays of golden-yellow blossom. A lady-slipper was peering up, indeed, amid the brushwood, but it was as yet too undeveloped to be made out; it had, though, several buds to the stem, and thus differed from

LEFT
Reginald Farrer

RIGHT
Grigori Potanin, who discovered *Peonia potaninii* in China.

Clara Maria Pope, painted by her husband Francis Wheatley RA. She was herself an
accomplished botanical artist and a volume of her watercolours of peonies, *Paeonia*,
was published in 1821.

all those with which I came in contact later on. So I sat at last and rested, gazing down the steep loess tracks to the little village at my feet, so comfortable and pleasant-looking in its grove of poplars, till my eye was caught by certain white objects farther along the hillside, that were clearly too big by far to be flowers, yet must certainly be investigated if only to find out what clots of white wool, or yet whiter paper, surely could be doing in the wild coppice, perched up here and there above the small-fry of little barberries and so forth. Probably they had some religious meaning. I would see.

Through the foaming shallows of the copse I plunged, and soon was holding my breath with growing excitement as I neared my goal, and it became more and more certain that I was setting eyes on *Paeonia Moutan* as a wild plant. The event itself justified enthusiasm, but all considerations of botanical geography vanish from one's mind in the first contemplation of that amazing flower, the most overpoweringly superb of hardy shrubs. Here in the brushwood it grew up tall and slender and straight, in two or three unbranching shoots, each one of which carried at the top, elegantly balancing, that single enormous blossom, waved and crimped into the boldest grace of line, of absolute pure white, with featherings of deepest maroon radiating at the base of the petals from the boss of golden fluff at the flower's heart. Above the sere and thorny scrub the snowy beauties poise and hover, and the breath of them went out upon the twilight as sweet as any rose. For a long time I remained in worship, and returned downwards at last in the dusk in high contentment, to find that Purdom's only other record from his higher ascent was spiteful and hunchy *Ilex pernyi* abundant in the upper coppice of these comparatively dry regions.

Farrer's description matches that of Hume's plant at Wormleybury. The plant is also shown in a drawing by Clara Maria Pope dated 1822. It would be seen again in China by Joseph Rock in the monastery garden in south-west Gansu.

Farrer's companion, William Purdom, was the same age as Farrer and the two became good friends on their 1914-1916 expedition. Purdom was a relatively experienced China hand, having travelled in northern China from 1909 to 1911 for the British Veitch Nurseries and the Arnold Arboretum in the USA. Purdom could console himself for missing out on Farrer's visionary encounter with *Paeonia rockii* by recalling that on his earlier journey he had found the smaller species *P. jishanensis* in Shanxi Province in 1910. From 1915 until his death in Beijing he worked for the Chinese Government Forestry Commission.

Two other Chinese species have been very influential in the breeding of tree peonies: *Paeonia lutea* and *P. delavayi*. Both were sent to Paris in about 1888 by Père Jean Marie Delavay and were to become parents of some of the loveliest hybrids. Père Delavay (1834-1895) was born in Abondance, Haute-Savoie. He was sent as a missionary to Guangdong Province when he was thirty-three, and went on to spend most of the rest of his life in north-west Yunnan. His enthusiasm and energy were extraordinary; he collected over 1,500 new species, sending most of them to France as seeds or dried specimens. Besides peonies, he introduced the lovely scented evergreen shrub, *Osmanthus delavayi*; *Thalictrum delavayi*, one of the prettiest of all herbaceous plants, several rhododendrons and the elegant *Sorbus vilmorinii*.

For Russia, Grigori Potanin who was born in 1835 in Yanisheva, Siberia and died in Tomsk in 1920, made four expeditions between 1876 and 1894. He and his wife Alexandra explored and collected zoological specimens as well as plants in Mongolia, Gansu, Shanxi and Sichuan. They discovered many new species and sent their finds to St. Petersburg Botanical Gardens. Among them the tree peony from west Sichuan, *Paeonia potanini* which has the useful characteristic of spreading by underground stolons.

Tree peonies reached Europe from Japan as well as from China. Philipp von Siebold was responsible for the introduction of a number of fine trees and shrubs and was joint author of *Flora japonica*, the definitive book on Japanese plants. He worked for the Dutch East India Company and lived in Japan for some years. In 1844 he sent forty varieties of tree peony back to Holland. They came from the Imperial gardens in Tokyo and Kyoto. Later, in 1891, Professor Charles Sargent visited Japan for the Arnold Arboretum and brought back a dozen *Botan* varieties and from that time Japanese nurserymen began to export plants direct to their American and European counterparts.

Professor Sargent was the Arnold Arboretum's founder and first director. Situated at Jamaica Plain, Massachusetts, the Arboretum is part of Harvard University and has

William Purdom

'Lord Kitchener', a 1907 Kelway introduction, growing at Spetchley Park in Worcestershire. Miss Ellen Willmott, who sponsored seed-collecting expeditions to China, planted peony seedlings at Spetchley, where there is still a fine collection.

been immensely important in the discovery of plants. Among expeditions sent by the Arboretum under Sargent were those in China by E H Wilson, William Purdom and Joseph Rock.

Dr Joseph Rock (1884-1962), an American of Austrian birth, lived in Hawaii from the age of twenty-four to thirty-five and became an expert on the plants of the islands, but most of his working life was spent in China and south-east Tibet. He was at the Zhoni lamasery, a Buddhist monastery in Gansu Province for the winter of 1925-1926, and saw the wonderful peony growing in the lamasery garden. He photographed the plant and collected its seeds, later distributing them to botanical gardens on both sides of the Atlantic.

Arboreta and Botanic Gardens were the main sources of finance for plant-hunting expeditions, but valuable contributions were also made by private individuals. One such amateur enthusiast was Miss Ellen Willmott (1838-1934). A rich woman and a knowledgable and talented gardener, she inherited a historic garden at Warley Place in Essex. Her involvement with the gardens at Spetchley Park in Worcestershire was due to her sister's marriage to Robert Berkeley, the owner. Miss Willmott subscribed to E H ('Chinese') Wilson's expeditions and among the plants she successfully raised from seeds brought back by Wilson was *Paeonia obovata* var. *willmottiae*, a fine, strong form from Sichuan. The stems and leaf undersides are suffused with purple and the flowers are at least 2.5 cm (1 in) larger than the species. The descendants of these first seedlings still grow at Spetchley Park, where there is also a specimen of 'Souvenir de Maxime Cornu' brought there from Warley Place and a plant of *P. suffruticosa* said to have come from the gardens of the Imperial Palace in Beijing.

Sir Frederick Stern's exploration of peonies was carried out, not in the hills of Gansu or on the slopes of the Caucasus, but in botanic and private gardens, in libraries, at his desk, in conversation with other distinguished botanists and horticulturalists, and most of all in the remarkable chalk garden he made at Highdown in Sussex. The resulting *Study of Genus Paeonia*, published in 1946 with accurate, sensitive and beautiful illustrations by Lilian Snelling was the first to make sense of this complex subject. Sadly it is out of print. The garden at Highdown is now owned by Worthing Borough Council. Peonies that have survived there have done so because they are at home on the chalky slopes. A fine specimen of *P. rockii* grown from Joseph Rock's original seed is still there, so is the lovely 'Argosy'.

'Argosy', an early hybrid of *P. lutea* introduced by Saunders in 1928, not in commerce today. Photographed at Highdown, Sussex.

Peonies are great survivors; *P. delavayi* and *P. lutea* have hybridized and seeded themselves around, as have several herbaceous peonies.

Confusingly, another distinguished botanist who has helped unravel the tangle of *Paeonia* taxonomy is also called Stearn, albeit differently spelled. Dr William Stearn and Peter Davis jointly produced *Peonies of Greece* for the Goulandris Natural History Museum in 1984. In Greece as in China, there is still plenty to learn about wild peonies. The romance of plant discovery will only end when there are no wild places left to explore.

CHAPTER 5

EMBARRAS DE RICHESSE

THE PEONY IN EUROPE

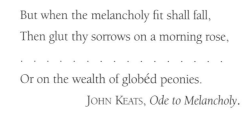

But when the melancholy fit shall fall,

Then glut thy sorrows on a morning rose,

. . . .

Or on the wealth of globéd peonies.

JOHN KEATS, *Ode to Melancholy*.

ERBACEOUS PEONIES were familiar in European gardens centuries before French and British explorers brought them from the Orient. They are among the earliest plants recorded as being grown in monastic and other gardens, for medicinal purposes and for their ornamental flowers. In the Middle Ages and earlier they would have been forms of *Paeonia officinalis*, the only peony native to Europe.

In Britain, Alexander Neckham, who was born in 1157 and became prior of the Augustinians at Cirencester, listed in his *De Naturis Rerum* the essential plants for a 'noble garden' including roses and lilies, turnsole (sunflowers), violets, and mandrake, fennel, coriander, and peonies. The inclusion of peonies next to fennel and coriander probably means they were valued for their seeds. 'Piones' appeared again in the company of flavouring spices, in Langland's *Vision of Piers Plowman* (1375) in the 'purs' of a poor woman: 'I have peper and piones' quod she, 'and a pounde garlike, a ferthyngworth of fenel seed, for fastyng dayes.'

It was again the seeds of the peony that interested John Gerard, the physician who looked after Lord Burleigh's gardens. He wrote:

The black graines (the seeds) to the number of fifteen taken in wine or

102

An early, very accurate drawing of *Paeonia officinalis*, showing the seed capsules
well developed and the pollen-dusted petals about to fall.
Pfingstrosen by Albrecht Dürer, 1471-1528.

Paeonia flore pleno incarnato (Paeonia officinalis 'Rubra Plena')
by Basil Besler, 1561-1629, showing the plant's tuberous roots
as well as its flower and leaves.

mead... is a special remedy for those that are troubled in the night with the disease known as Ephialtes or night mare which is as though a heavy burthen were laid upon them, and they oppressed therewith, as if they were overcome by their enemies or overprest with some great weight; and they are also good against melancholic dreams.

Gerard's *Herball* (1597) was a comprehensive herbal that remained the standard plant reference book for many decades. He gave a vivid, accurate description of *Paeonia mas*, the 'male' peony: its stems, the leaves 'not much unlike the leaves of the Wall-nut tree both in fashion and greatnesse', the flowers 'very like roses' and the seeds in their 'cods or husks'. He described all the sorts except the double white as growing in London gardens and wrote:

The male Peionie groweth wild upon a conny berry in Betsome, being in the parish of South-fleet in Kent, two miles from Gravesend, and in the ground sometimes belonging to a farmer there called John Bradley.

This is the only reference anywhere to a wild peony in Britain. Thomas Johnson who prepared a new edition for publication in 1633, cautioned 'I have been told thayt our Author himself planted that Peionie there, and afterwards seemed to finde it there by accident.'

Gerard also described the mythology of the peony, gathered from Theophrastus, the Greek naturalist writing in the second century BC and the Roman author Pliny. The peony was a dangerous plant; even to touch a growing plant was to court death. To pick it safely 'a string must be fastned to it in the night, and a hungry dog tied therto, who being allured by the smell of roasted flesh set towards him, may plucke it up by the roots.' The warning that the plant must be gathered only at night was repeated by Gerard 'for if any man shall pluck off the fruit in the day time, being seene of the Wood-pecker, he is in danger to lose his eies.' Having described these superstitions with relish, Gerard dismissed them as vain and frivolous.

Peonies also appear in John Rea's book of 1665, *Flora, Ceres and Pomona... or a complete Florilege, furnished with all requisites belonging to a florist.* There is also a first-hand account in the garden diary of Sir Thomas Hanmer, who, along with other

The double white 'Peionie' shown in Gerard's *Herball*, 1597

Piuoine Incarnat double.

Pauot violet double.

Peony and Double Poppy by Nicolas Robert, 1614-1685,
shows a stylized image of *Paeonia officinalis* 'Rosea Plena'.

titled patrons gets a mention in Rea's dedication. Sir Thomas described 'Peonyes' as having 'Glandulous rootes consist[ing] of severall glandules or lumpes, being joyn'd together at the top, and hanging in bunches, some of which are as bigg as the end of ones finger.'

Sir Thomas's ancestors were princes of Wales, and in 1646 he retired to Bettisfield in Flintshire to cultivate his garden until his death in 1678. His *Garden Book* was completed in 1659 but not published in his lifetime, or indeed for nearly 300 years. It finally appeared in 1933. He was a knowledgable and experienced gardener, sharing his enthusiasms with other distinguished horticulturalists of his day including John Evelyn and King Charles II's gardener John Rose. Hanmer's great passion was the tulip, but he also writes with affection:

OF THE PEONY

There are serverall **SINGLE** and **DOWBLE** flower'd **PEONYES**.

The **SINGLE** are the **RED** or **CRIMSON MALE**, the **RED FEMALE**, the **FLESH** colour'd **FEMALE**, the White **FEMALE**, and the Deepe **RED** of **CONSTANTINOPLE**, which hath large flowers consisting of eight leaves, the other single kinds not having above five or six, and the Deepe Murrey or **BLACKE**, as it is called, this is very rare.

Of **DOWBLE** Peonyes wee have the **COMMON CRIMSON**, the **BLUSH** Colour (this turnes not white), the **DEEPER CRIMSON**, or the **PURPLE**, as it is usually called, whose greene leafe is smaller & lighter & not soe deepe cutt as the former, the **CARNATION**, or light pinke colour, which is yet somewhat rare. The flower of this kind withers on the stalke, and shedds not its leaves as the other sorts doe.

They all flower in **MAY**.

And all prosper well abroad all the yeare in our gardens, and may bee remov'd at any tyme, but best in Autumne, and are easily encreast from their rootes and seed.

The peonies described by Gerard and Hanmer are all variations on *Paeonia officinalis*. The species and its subspecies grow wild in Portugal, southern France, Switzerland, northern Italy, Hungary, Croatia, Romania, and Albania. *Officinalis* in the Latin name can be directly translated as 'of the shop' ('Office' originally meant 'shop' and later

A mixed group of *Paeonia officianalis* by Antoine Berjon, 1754-1843.

came to refer to any place of business). The shop referrred to in plant names is that of the herbalist, so *officinalis* means medicinal or culinary or both.

The peony's medicinal credentials go back to the mythology of Ancient Greece. Aesculapius, son of Apollo the god of healing, was the first earthly physician. His pupil Paeon was given a peony by Apollo's mother Leto, and used it to heal a wound received by Hades, god of the underworld, from Hercules in the Trojan war:

> Sick at heart and in excruciating pain, Hades found his way to
> high Olympus and the Palace of Zeus. The arrow had driven into
> his shoulder muscle and was draining his strength. But Paeon the
> healer spread soothing ointments on the wound and cured him.
>
> Homer, *The Iliad,* Book V.

Not much later in the battle, Ares the god of war was in trouble, and Zeus asked Paeon to get his ointment out again. 'He made the fierce war-god well in no more time than fig-juice takes to thicken milk.' But Aesculapius, who had taught Paeon everything he knew, was jealous of his success and brought about his death. Ares, in gratitude to Paeon, gave him immortality of a kind by turning him into a flowering plant – a peony. And this is how the paeony (*Paeonia* in botanical Latin) got its name. Slightly confusingly, 'paean' as in 'paean of praise' comes from the same Greek root. It was originally a hymn of thanksgiving to Apollo after a battle victory, and later became more generally used to mean a song of praise.

Down the centuries peony roots have continued to be valued as medicine, in the West as in the Far East. Here is a medicinal recipe from *The Complete Confectioner* by Hannah Glasse, published in 1782:

COMPOUND PEONY WATER

Take eighteen piony roots fresh gathered, six ounces of bitter almonds, the leaves of rosemary, rue, wild thyme, and flowers of lavender dried, of each three ounces; of cinnamon, cubebs [a spice resembling pepper corns], seeds of angelica, coriander seed, caraway and anniseeds, each half an ounce, one gallon of rectified spirit of wine, with five gallons of soft water, and draw of three gallons by distillation. This is good in all nervous disorders.

THE USE OF THIS WATER: It is strong and powerful that it cannot be taken without the asistance of some other thing; but when dropt on crumbs of bread and sugar, you must take it the first thing in the morning, at four in the afternoon, and the last thing at night; you must not eat for an hour either before or after you take it; it is exceeding efficacious in all swoonings, weakness of heart, decayed spirits, palsies, appoplexies, and both to help and prevent a fit, it will also destroy all heaviness and coldness in the liver, restores lost appetite, and fortifies and surprisingly strengthens the stomach.

Hannah Glasse would have gathered her roots from the same single or double varieties of *P. officinalis* described and used by John Gerard and Sir Thomas Hanmer. Robust plants with beautiful flowers, they have been tenacious survivors on monastic sites and in cottage gardens, and today they continue to be excellent garden plants.

Towards the end of the eighteenth century, peonies from China were beginning to cause a stir. In France the Empress Josephine Bonaparte, always in the vanguard of plant collecting, added peonies to her collection at Malmaison. In his book *Description des plantes rares cultivées à Malmaison et à Navarre*, which describes and illustrates the collection, Aimé Bonpland showed a plant which he called *P. albiflora flore pleno* (*P. albiflora* is known today as *P. lactiflora*) with a double white flower. It was, he said, brought in 1784 to England where several varieties were grown. By 1811 both single and double peonies were being grown at Malmaison. There were at least three double forms, one pure snow white, one with yellow shading and one white mixed with pink. Bonpland also showed a plant he described simply as *Paeonia Moutan*, with very double, muddled mauve-pink flowers and purple-red leaf stems. It came, he wrote, from Mount Honan in Imperial China via London where Joseph Banks had acquired it in 1794 'after repeated requests'. It came to Malmaison in 1803.

Peonies from other sources besides China were arriving in France via England. *P. daurica*, sent to England from Siberia by John Bell in 1790, found its way to Malmaison in 1810. It is a compact plant with greyish leaves and bright magenta flowers now known as *P. mascula* subsp. *triternata*. But the Chinese plants, specially

Paeonia suffruticosa by Pierre-Joseph Redoute, 1758-1840. A tree peony probably painted at Malmaison.

Empress Josephine, 1763-1814, shown wearing a costume of silk peony petals in a portrait by Jean Baptiste Isabey, 1767-1855.

Pl. 3 from *Paeonia* 1821 by Clara Maria Pope, 1768-1838.

the Moutan peonies, caused the greatest excitement. Monsieur Bonpland made a trip to London in 1814 to see a collection of drawings of peonies in the library of the East India Company and was impressed by their richness. Perhaps they were the first batch of drawings by Chinese artists commissioned by John Reeves. In due course peony species and garden forms imported from China, specially *P. lactiflora* and its varieties, caused a revolution in peony breeding in Europe. Opulent, richly coloured and often deliciously fragrant, no wonder peonies became fashionable as garden plants and as cut flowers.

A set of drawings of the relatively few peonies already in cultivation in Britain was made in 1822 by Clara Maria Pope. Her *Species and Varieties of the Genus Paeonia* shows a dozen varieties with both the flowers and the leaves beautifully drawn and accurately coloured. The plants are not named but some are easy to identify. The recognizable ones include *P. rockii* and *P. mascula*. Three appear to be crimson, dark red and pink double forms of *P. officinalis* and one has a quite modern look to it, somewhere between a Japanese form and a double bombe, with large pale pink guard petals surrounding a centre of narrow, muddled pale yellow petaloids. A peony that sounds very like it called 'Reine des Français' was described by Alice Harding, the American peony expert, as being among the plants introduced to France by Modeste Guérin in 1842.

The demand for new varieties was soon insatiable. In France one of the first growers to recognise the demand was Nicolas Lemon at Porte St Denis just outside Paris. It is only too easy to confuse Lemon with Lemoine *père et fils* (Victor and Emile) who come on the scene thirty years or so later. Lemon was born in 1787 and still under forty when his reputation was assured by the introduction of 'Edulis Superba' (1824), a remarkable double pink lactiflora still popular today, especially as a cut flower. Lemon is also remembered for some good varieties of *P. officinalis*.

Also in Paris, Modeste Guérin worked with peonies from China and Japan to produce more than forty new herbaceous peonies between 1835 and 1866. They included the double pink 'Modeste Guérin' in 1845, 'Duchesse d'Orléans' the following year (also pink), the pale blush 'Madame de Vatry' in 1853, and 'Alexandre Dumas' in 1862. These are all fragrant and free flowering and available today. 'Festiva Maxima' 1851 and 'Madame Calot' 1856 are great classic peonies from this period, bred by Miellez.

Monsieur Guérin's collection was dispersed when the site his nursery occupied was sold in 1866 as building land. Many of his peonies were bought by Etienne Mechin, an amateur enthusiast who had been collecting under the guidance of the distinguished horticulturalist Bretonneau since 1840. Mechin and his grandson Auguste Dessert worked together to build up a remarkable collection. Besides the Guérin peonies, they took on part of a collection formed by Victor Verdier and his son Eugene. The Verdier peonies were inherited from Victor's uncle M Jacques, gardener to King Louis Philippe at Neuilly between 1830 and 1848. The Verdiers continued to breed from this Royal collection, producing some exceptional varieties including the much-loved, sweet scented 'Marie Jacquin'.

The shared passion of grandfather Mechin and grandson Dessert resulted in a collection of immense importance and in the introduction of some beautiful new peonies from the family nursery at Chenonceaux: 'Adolphe Rousseau' in 1890; 'M Martin Cahuzac' in 1899, 'Germaine Bigot' in 1902 and, in the prolific year of 1913, 'Dr H Barnsby', 'Laura Dessert', 'Souvenir de Louis Bigot' and 'Torpilleur'.

As so often happens in the horticultural world, interest and expertise passed from generation to generation. Two other great peony dynasties thrived in France: the Lemoines and the Rivières. In 1898 Victor Lemoine bought the nursery and collection of Félix Crousse at Nancy. Crousse, an extraordinarily talented and discriminating breeder, had acquired a remarkable collection of peonies from another great expert, Jacques Calot of Douai. Calot introduced more than twenty new peonies, Crousse over seventy-five. Many are still available. Some are less than robust, but of interest to collectors nevertheless. A remarkable number have stood the test of time and are plants of refinement that can hold up their heads (literally) among the best recent introductions. Calot's classics include, in date order, 'Duchesse de Nemours' 1856, 'Reine Hortense' 1857, 'l'Eclatante' 1860, 'Philoméle' 1861, 'Louis van Houtte' 1867, and 'Couronne d'Or' 1873. Félix Crousse contributed, besides his own namesake, 'Albert Crousse' 1893, 'Avalanche' 1886, 'Asa Gray' 1886, 'Monsieur Jules Elie' 1888, 'La Perle' 1886 and 'Mme de Verneville' 1885 to name but a few.

From Victor Lemoine and his son Emile came a cornucopia of ravishing flowers: lactifloras 'La France'and 'La Lorraine' in 1901, 'Sarah Bernhardt' 1906, 'Solange', 'Le Cygne' and anemone-flowered 'Primevère' in 1907 and, the result of crossing

'Madame Calot', an early French introduction showing the classic qualities of the best lactiflora peonies including sweet scent and a free-flowering habit. Photographed in the garden of Green Cottage, Lydney.

'Souvenir de Maxime Cornu', a *P.* x *lemoinei* hybrid tree peony bred by Professor Louis
Henry in 1919 was as greatly sought after then as it is today.

P. lactiflora with *P. wittmanniana*, 'Le Printemps' and 'Mai Fleuri' in 1905 and 'Avant Garde' in 1907.

As if all this were not enough, the Lemoines had something of a *coup* with their tree peonies. Père Delavay brought *Paeonia delavayi* and *P. lutea* to France from China in the 1880s. The Lemoines succeeded in crossing a Chinese suffruticosa peony with *P. lutea*, creating a completely new category known as *P.* x *lemoinei* with much sought-after yellow colouring. By 1909 they were exhibiting the lovely 'L'Espérance', a single yellow peony with petals flushed red at the base. It is almost if not completely identical to the Japanese variety 'Kintei', presented rather later than 'L'Espérance' by Mr K Wada. The Lemoines followed up with 'Chromatella' and in the 1930s and 1940s 'Alice Harding', 'l'Aurore', 'Flambeau', 'Sang Lorraine' and 'Mine d'Or'.

The Rivière family have been growing peonies since 1849, and have contributed major new herbaceous and tree peony forms including the herbaceous 'Philippe Rivoire' 1911, 'Madame Antoine Rivière' 1935, and 'Madame Henry Fuchs' 1955. They have given us the tree peonies 'Amateur Forest' 1935, 'Madame André Devillers' 1955, 'Isabelle Rivière' 1975, 'Monsieur Antoine Rivière' 1985 and brought us almost to the end of the twentieth century with 'Sylphide' in 1992. Under Jean-Luc Rivière, the sixth generation continues to grow and breed peonies and to support other breeders, among them Sir Peter Smithers whose tree peonies bred from *P. rockii* are distinctive and very beautiful. Look for his 'Ambrose Congreve' and 'Lydia Foote'.

As the nineteenth century gave way to the twentieth, across the Channel another dynastic nursery business was developing an interest in peonies. Kelway and Son of Langport, Somerset was the biggest nursery in Britain. James Kelway, founder of the firm, began breeding peonies in the 1860s. His grandson James the second (1871-1952) took a special interest in the peonies and greatly expanded the breeding programme. He kept meticulous records, making hand-written descriptions of his peonies in large, bound ledgers with columns for the name, description and quality from X to 5X, for example:

JAMES KELWAY (Kelway 1900) D.6. M Vfr 42" ac blush white changing to milk white with yellow glow at base. Perfect form often with large crown. semi-rose type. very sweet. vigorous rather tall. unequalled for quality of petal, except floriferous. remains half open for a long time. beautiful. 5X

JAMES W M KELWAY (Kelway 1926) SD.4. EL tall bright rose silvered. enormous flower of good shape. stout stems. vigorous. very fine. (compare with Dragon). 4X

He also wrote a short book *Garden Paeonies* describing them and extolling their virtues with happy enthusiasm. The only sour note creeps in when he feels obliged to mention the achievements of French nurserymen: '… a certain Monsieur Lemoine raised a freak which he called *prolifera tricolor*, in 1825'.

The peonies bred in France and England at the turn of the century shared qualities with fashionable women of the time: elaborate, heavy blooms on slender stems, reminiscent of big hairstyles and slender necks; perhaps this contributed to the success of peonies as cut flowers as well as in the garden. During their Edwardian heyday Kelways' peonies enjoyed enormous popularity. 'Few hardy plants have become so fashionable' (*Country Life Illustrated* 1905). The worlds of fashion and horticulture mingled in 'Peony Valley' at Langport in early summer when the peonies were in bloom, and special arrangements were made for trains to stop at a temporary station by the nursery, Peony Halt:

> Have you ever walked in the Valley of Paeonies and watched the different shades of blooms in the sun? Some like sea anemones… some like water lilies, some like flat saucers full of golden glory… As you go down the hill road to the valley the fragrance of the Paeonies comes floating up to you… very sweet and fresh and keen. When once you have been there you come out different… that valley makes you love Paeonies.
>
> BROADCAST BY MARION CRAN 1928

Kelways nurseries are no longer owned by the family and have been through some difficult times. But in the 1990s they are enjoying a renaissance. The best of Kelways' peonies are again on the market and Peony Valley is being replanted.

NAME	STOCK NUMBER	COLOUR AND FULL DESCRIPTION	QUALITY X XX XXX	SYNONYM, OR NEAREST VARIETY	QUANTITY AT H.B. HIGHER BARRYMOOR. L.B. LOWER BARRYMOOR. H.F. HUISH FIELD. N. NURSERY AND DATE.	
					STOCK OR SHOW PIECE	SALE PIECE
KELWAY'S GLORIOUS (Kelway 1908)	D.7. ML Vf V for 40"	white perfect. extremely fragrant the form of the flower is wonderfully lovely. 6-7 inches across. strong scent of roses creamy suffusion in depths. crimson streaks on outside of guard petals. medium height. strong stems dark green foliage. immense flower with deep funnel-like centre & wide spreading surrounding petals very free-flying and lasting & holds itself up well. the best double paeony.	5x		N/25 W 6/22 E 4/45	A/990 A/40 B/80
K's GORGEOUS (Kelway	S.4. EM Vf	pure deep rose with salmon pink flecked with silver. extremely strong. a fine strong clear colour	5x		NG 39/16 N/25	A/140 B/165
K's HUMORIST (Kelway 1918)	S.5. E tall	bright salmon rose or cherry pink. distinct colour. not much substance	3x	use for: D. of Portland	E 4/5	
		out				
K's LOVELY (Kelway 1905)	D.4. L E & M H 42"	bright violet rosy lavender, showing white & cream petaloids in the centre. massive flower extremely handsome flowers on tall.	4-5x	use: Alexander Dumas Langport Triumph	N/25 W 6/35 E 4/50	A/1,300 B/15 B/950

A page from the ledger in which James Kelway recorded all his peonies.

121

The toughness and longevity of peonies has ensured that they have never quite been lost from country house gardens where they were lined out in cutting beds or planted in bold clumps in herbaceous borders. In large gardens herbaceous peonies were sometimes given a border all to themselves. Photographs from *Country Life* magazine in 1898 show such a border in Lady Algernon Gordon-Lennox's garden at Broughton Castle. The peony border at Hazelbeach Hall in Northamptonshire was photographed the following year. Although it was quite narrow, it stretched for 140 yards.

Peonies were exported to other parts of Europe with other elements of English gardens. Ellen Willmott, the distinguished English gardener and author of *The Genus Rosa* made a garden at the Château de Tresserve near Aix-les-Bains in Savoy in 1890. She made a collection of peonies and irises and would visit the château just twice a year, once in spring when they were in flower, and again in autumn. She was also responsible for getting her sister off to a fine start with a collection of peonies at Spetchley Park in England.

When the French Riviera became the favoured location for holiday villas, architects and garden designers chose fashionable plants for their fashion-conscious clients. The architect Harold Peto would take on the design of the entire property, house, interior and garden, integrating the house and garden into the rocky riviera landscape by informal plantings of shrubs and trees. Perhaps surprisingly, in such a warm climate, he used tree paeonies among magnolias at Villa Sylvia, the Italianate house he built on Cap Ferrat in 1902 for Mr and Mrs Ralph Curtis. At Villa Maryland, built for Mr and Mrs Arthur Wilson about six years later, Peto devised a gold and white planting scheme for a formal parterre. Orange trees were underplanted with a mixture of dwarf mimosas and azaleas, followed by white peonies with dicentras.

The Vicomte de Noailles' garden at Grasse, begun in 1947, was one of the most beautiful in southern France. His peony garden, one of a series of enclosures to be visited in sequence, was approached from an English lawn with mixed borders, and had as its focal point a stone column copied from one at the Villa Aldobrandini at Frascati in Italy. The peony collection has just two plants of each variety. Charles de Noailles collaborated in collecting tree peonies with Mme Champin whose famous garden la Chèvre d'Or is at nearby

Tree peonies coming into flower at the Villa Noailles, Grasse, France, with *Cercis siliquastrum* flowering in the background.

Tree peonies succeed in warm climates where herbaceous peonies would fail.
The garden at Villa Monda, Sorrento, Italy.

Biot. Seed is saved every year to propagate the best of the collection.

Just across the border separating the French Riviera from Italy is La Mortola, the magnificent garden made by the Hanbury family. Here too, tree peonies braved long, hot summers in a shaded secret garden shared by Madonna lilies, made during the 1920s by Dodo Hanbury, the stylish and strong-willed wife of Cecil Hanbury. In Italy as elsewhere, English garden makers combined a delight in exotic, tender plants with nostalgia for the plants of English gardens. Alec Hood, later the fifth Duke of Bronte, developed such a garden at Castello di Maniace in Sicily between 1876 and the 1930s. Beyond formal terraces and parterres, he made an English woodland garden of hawthorn, peonies, irises, primroses and violets. More recently English migrants have favoured the hills of Tuscany where it is easier to indulge a taste for peonies. The winters are uncompromising enough to ensure the dormant period required for healthy growth. Both tree peonies and herbaceous peonies bloom around Tuscan holiday villas and converted farmhouses.

Although tree peonies succeed in Italy and the South of France, herbaceous peonies struggle without a frosty winter. But in northern France, of course, they have been grown for centuries, in formal box-edged beds or spilling out of borders with irises, delphiniums and lilies.

Monet grew peonies at Giverny, delighting in their opulent shapes and vibrant colours. He was particularly fond of a group of Japanese tree peonies in his water garden, some of which had been given to him by Japanese friends, and others imported directly from Japan. During the cold winter of 1895 he wrote to his wife from Norway where he was travelling, to ask if she had covered up the Japanese peonies. 'It would amount to murder if you have not already done so,' he wrote. The tree peonies grew on the banks of the pool with irises, cytisus and Judas trees, their reflection in the water mingling with the water lilies.

Vase of Peonies painted by Albert Williams.

European artists found peonies irresistable subjects. The sweet-scented peony
'Duchesse de Nemours' is in the foreground of *Spring Flowers*, by Claude Monet,
1864. It closely resembles *P. albiflora flore pleno*, an introduction to Empress
Josephine's collection from China via England.

PART TWO

PEONIES FOR THE TWENTIETH CENTURY

CHAPTER 6

PEONIES IN THE NEW WORLD

THE AMERICAN PEONY, CANADA AND NEW ZEALAND

No class of flowers has recently attracted more attention in Europe than the peonies... Most of the varieties are extremely splendid and others possess striking peculiarities. Anticipating that a similar taste would be evinced in this country, the proprietor has, by a great exertion, obtained every variety possible from Europe and also a number from China.

WILLIAM PRINCE, *Catalog of Trees and Plants in the Botanic Garden,*
Flushing, Long Island, 1829.

So MANY AREAS OF THE USA have difficult climates for gardening that it is good to find a plant as adapted to problematic conditions as the peony. Herbaceous peonies thrive down to Zone 2 and in most areas the hardiness of the tree peony is never in doubt either. Mr John Wister, director of the Scott Arboretum, wrote that 'in the Philadelphia area, in the past thirty-four years, only once (in 1921) have the flower buds been injured by frost. That year an early spring overnight drop of temperature from eighty to fifteen degrees Fahrenheit destroyed practically all spring flowers and killed roses and privet hedges to the ground.'

The ability of peonies to survive the heat of southern states is even more surprising. In an American Peony Society bulletin of 1928 Mr Pope M Long of Gordova, Alabama wrote, 'Paeonies certainly grow nicely as far south as Atlanta, Ga., Birmingham, Ala. and possibly as far as Montgomery, Ala.' He thought 'Kelway's Glorious' and other Kelway varieties did well in the south, as did 'Lady Alexandra Duff'.

'America', introduced by Rudolph in 1976, is one of the finest herbaceous peonies
bred in the USA.

'Bunker Hill', an early (1906) American classic bred by George Hollis of
Massachusetts USA.

The first peonies to be grown in American gardens were forms of *P. officinalis* originating in Europe. Thomas Jefferson grew them at Monticello, and in 1807 a few forms were listed in the catalogue of nurseryman John Bartram of Philadelphia. Twenty-two years later William Prince of Flushing, Long Island, was alerted to a burgeoning demand for new varieties. He mentioned in his catalogue the vogue for peonies in Europe and was well prepared to cater to a similar taste in the USA, offering forty kinds from Europe and China at prices between fifty cents and twenty dollars.

By the 1850s the arrival at Prince's and other nurseries of numerous forms of *P. lactiflora* (still known at that time as *P. albiflora*), encouraged peony pioneers to embark on a programme of cross pollination. The Chinese peonies brought the coveted attribute of fragrance and made possible a wide range of shapes and colours. Among the earliest American-bred peonies to have survived are the deep crimson double 'Grover Cleveland' introduced by H A Terry of Crescent, Iowa in 1904. The rose-pink double 'Walter Faxon' was bred by John Richardson in his own small garden at Dorchester, Massachusetts. Mr George Hollis of South Weymouth and T C Thurlow of West Newbury were two other Massachusetts breeders of peonies. Hollis' legacy includes the classic cherry-red scented 'Bunker Hill' (1906) and among Thurlow's stars were 'Cherry Hill' (1915) a very early, fragrant, free-flowering crimson semi-double and the mauve-pink double 'President Wilson' (1918) which is also scented.

In the early days most commercial peony growers were producing blooms for the cut-flower market. They farmed acre upon acre of popular, scented, huge-headed double varieties starting with stock from Lemoine in France or Kelway in England. Gardeners too were importing peonies. In July 1890 *The Garden and Forest*, a New York magazine, printed a description of a Peony Exhibition held by the Royal Horticultural Society and praised Kelway's flowers for their size, colour and fragrance. James Kelway found it worth while to take his peonies across the Atlantic and to donate prizes at American horticultural shows. Mr Thurlow won the Kelway bronze medal for a collection of eighteen named albiflora (lactiflora) blooms at Boston in 1897, beaten into second place by Kenneth Finlayson. The following year he was again pipped at the post, this time by Dr C G Weld. Only one of the Doctor's peonies mentioned in *The American Florist*'s report of the show is still available:

'François Ortegal' a double red introduced in France by Parmentier in 1850. On the other hand much of Mr Thurlow's exhibit could be assembled today and could probably still win prizes: 'Baroness Schröeder' was Kelway's own; 'Bridesmaid' ('Marie Jacquin'), 'Festiva Maxima', 'Jeanne d'Arc', 'Modeste Guérin' and 'Edouard André' were all of French breeding.

In due course American bred peonies ousted the Europeans in popularity. Oliver Brand (1844-1921) had opened his nursery in Faribault Minnesota in 1867 at the age of just twenty-three, growing apple trees and peonies. The peony trade thrived and in the early years of the twentieth century he introduced some of the best American varieties including 'Longfellow', 'David Harum' 'Martha Bulloch' and 'Frances Willard' in 1907, 'Richard Carvel' and 'Chestine Gowdy' in 1913. Archie Brand, born in 1871, joined his father in the business. Allan Rogers tells in *Peonies* how in 1913 Archie exhibited his peonies for the first time. He and a friend took eight boxes of peony buds by train, streetcar and, for the last half mile, on foot to a show at St Paul, Minnesota. They had great success on that occasion and still greater in Chicago in 1920 when, at the American Peony Society's Show they sold a great number of roots for fifty dollars apiece and some for a hundred dollars each – princely sums in those days.

The 1920s were golden years. Producing a new peony variety is a slow business. Each seedling takes several years to flower and each young plant takes several more years to prove its health and vigour. Perhaps one seedling in a thousand is a success. But in the 1920s the patient work of American peony devotees came to fruition in wonderful ways. The Brands introduced the highly scented 'Myrtle Gentry' and gold medal winner 'Hansina Brand' (1925) and 'Krinkled White' (1928). Sadly, the Brand enterprise was badly hit by the Great Depression and Archie had to plough up all his seedlings. In due course he revived his business selling peony roots, but hadn't the heart to reinstate his breeding programme. He died in 1953 leaving thirty-two acres of peony roots to Miss Myrtle Gentry, the school teacher who had come to help out in the office in 1918 and stayed on as a partner.

The Wilds of Missouri were another family of nurserymen whose story has an almost legendary quality. Their patriarch, Herman Wild, arrived at his fertile corner of south-west Missouri in a waggon train in 1868. He saw the promised land, staked his claim and started the Wild Nursery. It thrived in the care of four generations of

TOP 'Festiva Maxima', a French introduction,
won the Kelway bronze medal for Mr T C Thurlow at Boston in 1897.

ABOVE 'Chestine Gowdy', bred by Oliver Brand in Minnesota,
is one of the earliest (1913) American-bred peonies to have stood the test of time.

TOP 'Krinkled White' (1928), one of Archie Brand's great successes.

ABOVE 'Flame' (1939) one of Lyman Glasscock's most successful crosses: *P. lactiflora* x *P. peregrina*.

Wilds until 1991 when it was sold as a going concern. It was Herman's grandson Gilbert who developed a passion for peonies. When Gilbert was eight years old he begged his father James to buy him some peony roots. James spent forty-five dollars, Gilbert planted the roots and the business was up and running. Gilbert and his son Allen began hybridizing peonies in the 1920s and introduced some forty new forms. They also excelled at recognizing quality in other breeders' plants and introduced plants for, among others, Edward Auten Jr, a Harvard-educated banker in Princeville, Illinois. Auten was responsible for the early dark red singles 'Chocolate Soldier' and 'Early Scout'.

People have come to peonies from a wide range of places and occupations: William Bockstoce ('Carol', 'Diana Parks', 'Henry Bockstoce') of Pittsburgh, Pennsylvania and Lyman Glasscock ('Salmon Glow', 'Red Charm') of Elmwood, Illinois were building contractors. Glasscock's outstanding achievement was to devise a way of delaying the flowering of *P. officinalis*, which allowed him to cross it with *P. lactiflora*. Orville Fay was a taste and colour expert for a candy company and developed his own taste for peonies at the Mission gardens in Techny, Illinois. His introductions included the lovely 'Prairie Moon' and 'Paula Fay'. Arthur Murawska was a locomotive engineer in Chicago. He had loved peonies from his childhood and when he retired he set his heart on producing peony plants with overall good habits. 'Moonstone' and 'Princess Margaret' are his notable successes. Kent, the founder of New Peony Farm at Faribault, Minnesota in 1980, also practises as a physician.

Lack of space prevents me mentioning others with equally fine achievements to their credit. For a more detailed account I recommend Allan Rogers' book *Peonies*. But he is too modest to describe his own achievements. What began as a hobby pursued with great zeal by all the family, became a family business. The Rogers' collection of herbaceous peonies at Caprice Farm near Portland, Oregon, began with the purchase of Walter Marx's stock when his nursery closed. Marx's main objective had been to produce peonies with improved fragrance; 'Chinook', a strong, double white, 'Mt St Helens', double red, the Japanese 'Louise Marx' and the single white 'Walter Marx' all bear witness to his success. The Rogers family's holding of Marx's stock was augmented with carefully chosen cultivars from other growers and an important part of the Saunders collection when it was split up.

Professor A P Saunders (1869-1953) made immensely important contributions to the world of peonies. He was professor of chemistry at Hamilton College in Clinton, New York and in 1905 was already raising seedlings of *P. lactiflora*. By 1915 he was collecting peony species from around the world in order to make crosses between them. He also fell for the French-bred tree peony hybrids bred by Lemoine at Nancy from *Paeonia delavayi* and *P. lutea*, and experimented with breeding from these using pollen from single-flowered Japanese varieties. Some of the results were spectacular, completely new and very recognizable shades of apricot, amber, buff and yellow, sometimes shot through with crimson and scarlet. When exhibited at the American Peony Society's shows they caused a sensation. The first was 'Argosy'(1928). Most were introduced between 1948 and 1952 and are available today in Japan as well as in the West. A Japanese authority warns that 'Regent', 'Renown', 'Thunderbolt' and 'Vesuvian' have weak stems. This does not mean one should not grow them, for the individual flowers are very beautiful, but one should be aware of the problem. The yellow APS Gold Medal winning 'Age of Gold' and 'High Noon' are sturdier and 'Chinese Dragon' is a fine red.

Another of Professor Saunders' great achievements was that of crossing forms of *P. lactiflora* with *P. peregrina*. Among the forty good plants produced were 'Cytherea', 'Ellen Cowley' and 'Lovely Rose'. Saunders was also a key figure in the American Peony Society. John C Wister has written a detailed account of all aspects of his work in *The Peonies* (1962).

One more peony dynasty must be mentioned: its founding father, John Klehm was a German immigrant who started a nursery near Chicago in 1852. His son Charles C Klehm (1867-1957) was closely involved in setting up the American Peony Society and began a hybridizing programme which was further developed by his son Carl G Klehm (1916-1973). Carl coined the name 'Estate Series' for the Klehm introductions, characterized by strong stems and reliable performance as garden plants. 'Charlie's White', 'Mister Ed' and 'Pillow Talk' are fine examples of the Klehm style. Roy Klehm, ran the nursery for the fourth generation of his family. He launched, among others, peonies in the 'Cheddar' group and in 1993 he published *The Peony*.

Roy Klehm's book was an edited and updated version of Alice Harding's *The Book of the Peony* (1917) and *Peonies in the Little Garden* (1923). Alice Harding (Mrs

TOP 'Chinese Dragon' (Saunders 1948). A tree peony with
very large flowers and slightly dusky leaves.

ABOVE 'High Noon' (Saunders 1952): one of the best yellow tree peonies,
winner of the American Peony Society's Gold Medal in 1989.

'Cheddar Gold', one of several scented herbaceous peonies in the 'Cheddar' series introduced by Carl and Roy Klehm.

'Alice Harding' (Lemoine 1922), one of three peonies named in honour of
Mrs Edward Harding, the New Jersey peony connoisseur
and writer of *The Book of the Peony*.

Edward Harding) lived in New York City but gardened on her estate in New Jersey. She was immensely knowledgeable and enthusiastic about all manner of plants, but especially peonies. She encouraged breeders by donating cash prizes for the best new herbaceous peony seedlings and was three times rewarded by the fragile immortality that having a plant named after you bestows. E J Shaylor's 'Mrs Edward Harding' (1918) and Lemoine's double blush lactiflora 'Alice Harding' (1922) are still in commerce. Her third namesake was a yellow tree peony from Lemoine, 'Alice Harding' (1935) also known as 'Kinko.' Her book *The Peony* is full of fascinating information about the history and mythology of peonies as well as down-to-earth practical advice. In *Peonies in the Little Garden* she wrote 'Owners of small gardens are often fearful of having insufficient room for this stately subject. I think that they do not realize how much pleasure comes from the possession of even half a dozen plants, or three, or two – or just one.' A persuasive philosophy.

Dr Walter Upjohn, founder of the Upjohn Corporation of Kalamazoo Michigan, was another amateur benefactor of the peony. An avid collector of peonies, he donated plants to start the Peony Garden at Nichols Arboretum, Ann Arbor. The garden was laid out in 1927 by Professor Aubrey Tealdi, Chairman of the University of Michigan's Landscape Architecture Department and the Arboretums's first director. After a period of neglect the collection was restored in the 1980s and now boasts over 700 plants in more than 260 varieties, most of them from between 1907 and 1925. The Nicholls Arboretum is just one of a series of collections of herbaceous peonies. All of them attract vast numbers of visitors when the plants are in full flower.

Tree peonies have a smaller but no less enthusiastic fan club. Old Chinese and Japanese varieties are well established and continue to be imported and grown in the USA. Since the Second World War, America has been the undisputed leader in developing new hybrids. The baton of Professor A P Saunders was taken up by his erstwhile colleague William Gratwick. Gratwick introduced two tree peonies of truly exceptional beauty and refinement, 'Companion of Serenity' and 'Guardian of the Monastery', before going into partnership with Nassos Daphnis. After William Gratwick's death Nassos continued the work. They share with Saunders the achievement of introducing a ravishing group of tree peonies with their own very distinctive style.

The Chinese tree peony 'Purple of Sung Dynasty'
at Cricket Hill Garden, Thomaston USA.

The Chinese tree peony 'Gong Yang Zhuang' (palace dress)
at Cricket Hill Garden, Thomaston USA.

The story of Toichi Domoto is a little sad. He started a tree peony nursery in Hayward, California, using stock originally imported from Japan by his father and built up a fine reputation. On one occasion Mrs du Pont, the distinguished chatelaine of Longwood Gardens visited the equally distinguished Toichi Domoto when his tree peonies were at their peak. A call came for her from a dinner where she was due to speak. 'Well that can wait,' she said, 'only once in a lifetime will I get a chance like this to see so many tree peonies in bloom.'

The sad part of the story is that, along with others of Japanese descent, he was interned during the Second World War and lost his five acres of peony seedlings. After the war he built up a successful bonsai nursery but never quite recovered his interest in peonies.

The most recent and exciting developments with tree peonies are the result of the relaxation of restrictions on visitors to China. It has at last become possible for growers such as David and Kasha Furman at Cricket Hill Nurseries to exchange information and plants with their Chinese colleagues, and the result is a fresh and long overdue appreciation of Chinese tree peonies, some of them with a history of more than a thousand years.

The apparently impossible dream of peony hybridizers was, for a long time, the crossing of a tree peony with a herbaceous peony. The impossible was achieved in 1948 by Mr Toichi Itoh of Tokyo. His cross of the tree peony 'Alice Harding' with the herbaceous peony 'Kakoden' produced viable seed. Sadly Mr Itoh died before his seedlings flowered. Under the care of Mr Shigao-Oshida, his assistant, they flowered in 1963. Some half dozen excelled, with double yellow flowers on low, herbaceous plants, an effect peony growers had been striving after for generations. Referred to as Intersectional hybrids or Itoh hybrids, they are a very significant development coming at a time when you would have thought every possible permutation of herbaceous peonies had been tried. I am a little uneasy with the great size of the flowers proportionate to the whole plant, but the flowers are beautiful and they have a bright future.

Louis Smirnow brought Intersectional hybrids to America from Japan. Pinks, whites, peachy-copper tones and reds have been added to the original yellows by specialist breeder Roger Anderson of Wisconsin. Don Hollingsworth's Gold Medal 'Garden Treasure' is generally considered the best of the yellow hybrids.

PEONIES IN CANADA

Letters received by James Kelway at his nursery in Somerset, England at about the same time as this article appeared in *Canadian Home and Gardens*, confirm that peonies were indeed well suited to the harsh climate. 'I have been growing paeonies in Manitoba for twenty-five years,' wrote Mr A Wilson of Portage La Prairie, 'and have never lost a plant on account of the cold. I never cover them.'

A little further west in Saskatoon, Saskatchewan Mr J Neilson had never known a plant to be killed by frost or noticed any deterioration in bloom in a summer following an unusually cold winter. 'We have a short summer, a long cold winter and little spring or autumn. Early in May we jump suddenly into summer, and in October back again into winter... the paeony... can laugh at fifty degrees below zero... Unfortunately many of the finest perennials do not succeed here, but in the paeony we have one which can defy our winter's frost, and which it would almost seem comes back reinvigorated after our severest winters'.

The Kelways had been sending peonies to customers in Canada since 1895, and by 1927 they were considered the most suitable flower to commemorate a royal visit. To mark a tour of Canada by the Prince of Wales, a gift of Canadian grown peony plants was made to every city, town and village in the Dominion, distributed through the branches of the Bank of Montreal. 'The Prince has been assured that paeonies flourish unprotected in any part of the country' (*The Times* from Toronto Sept 7 1927). Two years later a customer of Kelways wrote from Kitchener, Ontario to tell him, 'In our neighbouring city of Galt there is a large bed exculsively of Kelway's, and in season it makes a glorious showing worth going miles to see.' At about the same time the President of the American Peony Society recommended 'Kelway's Glorious' and 'Lady Alexandra Duff' for Canadian gardens together with two French-bred peonies, 'Le Cygne' and 'Thérèse'.

The American Peony Society has always embraced Canada as well as the USA, holding shows in Ontario and including Canadian exhibitors in their other shows. Among the seedlings shown at Guelph in 1948, 'Ann Cousins' attracted the most attention. This very large white double flower was introduced by Lyman Cousins (1889-1973) of Ontario. He was an artist and lithographer who fell in love first with irises, then with peonies. The results of his experiments with colour became known as 'Innerglow hybrids' and included the glowing peach shading of 'Etched Salmon'

The lactiflora variety 'Lady Alexandra Duff' with *Geranium endressii* in the foreground.
It was recommended for Canadian gardens in the 1920s and still is today.
Photographed at Green Cottage, Lydney.

'Etched Salmon', truly a peony of the New World, bred in Canada by Lyman Cousins, introduced in the USA by Roy Klehm and grown at the Peony Gardens at Lake Hayes, New Zealand, by Dorothy and Bruce Hamilton.

and 'Coral'n'Gold' introduced by Roy Klehm who took over Cousins' stock.

In the USA, American-bred peonies have to a great extent ousted those from England and France, but in Canada, although American varieties are appreciated the Europeans are still widely grown. Perhaps they do better in the harsh winters because they have had longer to acclimatize.

PEONIES IN NEW ZEALAND

New Zealanders have been growing peonies in their gardens for about as long as Canadians and almost as long as Americans. Some of the early settlers arriving in both Australia and New Zealand in the nineteenth century brought with them a few roots or seeds of *P. officinalis*, that traditional cottage garden favourite at 'home'. They may have valued peonies for their medicinal properties (see Hannah Glass's recipe on page 110), but I think it more likely that they carried them, together with seeds of larkspurs, pinks, sweet williams and wallflowers, with the intention of making a garden to assuage their homesickness. Perhaps those who were not able to bring their peonies with them, wrote home, once they had established a garden, asking relations or friends to send out seeds or dormant plants. From the 1840s onwards live plants could successfully be transported on long sea voyages in glass Wardian cases, the invention of Nathaniel Bagshaw Ward (1791-1868) a doctor practising medicine in London's docklands.

Peonies are great survivors, and in old gardens, as well as the different forms of *P. officinalis*, the early lactiflora varieties 'Edulis Superba', 'Festiva Maxima', 'Félix Crousse' and 'Sarah Bernhardt' have survived. They were mostly imported directly from Kelways of Somerset, England or from Klehm, Smirnow or Wild in the USA, by small commercial nurseries or by private gardeners who would then pass roots on to their friends and neighbours.

Peonies were found to thrive on the South Island where the winters are colder, but they also succeeded well enough on the North Island for a nursery in Masterton near Wellington to import a batch from Kelway's in 1925. In his catalogue for that year James Kelway quoted the nurseryman's letter of 8 October: 'I am very pleased to be able to state that everything is coming on splendidly, especially the Paeonies and Gladioli. Hoping to have the pleasure of again dealing off you in the near future.' Harrison's, another North Island peony-growing nursery was trading at Taranaki in the 1940s. Mr Harrison's son now runs it under the name 'Fiesta', supplying garden centres throughout New Zealand.

Before the Second World War, a few Chinese and Japanese tree and herbaceous peonies were brought home from China and Japan by New Zealanders working in Asia. As so often happens, they were not labelled or if they were the labels were lost and it was only after the formation of the New Zealand Paeony (*sic*) Society in 1990 that some of them have been identified. The Society has been the catalyst in a surge of enthusiasm for peonies. It was formed as a trade association by ten growers of peonies for the cut flower market. Growers in New Zealand have the great advantage of being able to supply the USA, Japan and other northern hemisphere countries with flowers out of season. The enterprise has been a great success; there are now 140 commercial growers. One important function of the Society is to provide field inspections by scientists to ensure that stock remains healthy. As well as sharing a commercial interest, society members naturally share a passion for peonies, and inevitably some have embarked on breeding programmes. Interesting results are emerging. So far just one New Zealand variety has been registered by the American Peony Society, the official registration body. 'Glad McArthur' is named after Mrs Gladys McArthur, who grew peonies in Central Otago, the prime peony-growing district of the South Island and preached the peony gospel to anyone who would listen.

Other Central Otago growers include Tony and Judy Banks who started twelve years ago in order to diversify on their fruit farm. Now they export 100,000 peony blooms during the six-week cutting season. In South Canterbury another husband and wife team have been in business for about the same period; Julie and John Allan run Marsal Peonies, selling roots to other growers, to garden centres and to private gardeners. They are specially interested in Itoh Hybrids and have bred some promising varieties which await registration. There are other young enterprises beginning to thrive in New Zealand, producing peonies as cut flowers, as dried flowers, and as plants for the garden and the landscape - proof, if any were needed, that wherever in the world the climate is right, sooner of later peony enthusiasts will emerge.

'Coral Charm' (Wissing 1964), with its modern colouring and robust growth, is
proving a success in New Zealand as a cut flower and a garden plant.

CHAPTER 7

GARDENING WITH
PEONIES

PEONIES FOR PAST, PRESENT
AND FUTURE GARDENS

I have learnt much from the little cottage gardens that help to make our English waysides the prettiest in the world. One can hardly go into the smallest cottage garden without learning or observing something new.

GERTRUDE JEKYLL, *Wood and Garden*, 1899.

THE WORDS 'GERTRUDE JEKYLL' are shorthand for a certain kind of garden, quintessentially British, and typified by broad, rather grand herbaceous borders planted to a carefully planned colour scheme. Miss Jekyll was certainly the most influential British gardener in the twentieth century. Rather surprisingly her style, which suited large country house gardens so well, was firmly rooted in the modest village gardens of her Surrey childhood. She had a great fondness for traditional plants and peonies were no exception.

Peonies have a long history in cottage gardens. Thomas Tusser mentioned them in a list of flowers for windows and pots in his book *A Hundred Good Points of Husbandry*. It was published in 1557 and became an early bestseller. Written in verse and addressed to the farmer, or husbandman, it also offered advice to his wife who was in charge of the garden. Tusser's plant list builds a picture of a cottage garden style to which many gardeners still aspire. As well as peonies, there are roses, hollyhocks, lilies, marigolds, snapdragons, sweet williams and nigella, all plants which we regard as typical of cottage gardens, and imbued with comforting nostaglia.

Peonies played an essential part in the idealized cottage gardens portrayed
by English painters at the end of the nineteenth century.
A Devon Cottage by Claude Strachan, 1865-*c*.1935.

'The great peonies… are one mass of crimson or white.' *Cottage Gardening* (1896)
by A Gentleman of Great Practical Experience. *The Hotel Belvedere, Lacerla*
by Ernest Arthur Rowe, 1862-1922, shows the cottage gardening style
in a grand setting far from England.

Miss Jekyll was not the first writer to admire such gardens, with their familiar flowers arranged in an unpretentious style to suit well-crafted cottage architecture. In *Our Village* Miss Mitford, writing between 1824 and 1832, described the gardens in Three Mile Cross in Hampshire. Nearly 300 years after Thomas Tusser, her list of plants is not very different from his and again includes peonies. By the end of the century cottage gardens had become something of a cult among the well-to-do. An anonymous writer describing himself as 'A Gentleman of Great Practical Experience' described June flowers in *Cottage Gardening* (1896):

> Along the lines of the walk parallel to the cottage, as well as the centre walk leading from the highway to the cottage door, are numbers of sweet flowers standing alone, each a clump in itself, so well grown are they… The great peonies, the giants of the border, are one mass of crimson or white. The double scarlet lychnis sends up a forest of spikes... nestling on the ground are campanulas in blue and white.

This is just the kind of effect that Miss Jekyll refined and distilled to make her magnificent country house borders. Early cottage garden peonies would have been the double red, pink and white forms of the European *P. officinalis*, supplemented here and there with a root or two of the more exotic lactiflora varieties grown in the cut-flower beds at the 'Big House'.

Herbaceous peonies flower at just the right time to get a border off to a good start in early summer. They can be planted at regular intervals along the border, singly or in groups of three of a kind, depending on how much space is available. In a border of generous width, place them halfway between the back and front of the border, leaving space for taller plants behind and shorter in front. The minimum width for a satisfactory herbaceous border is really 2.5 m (8 ft), but a narrow border is better than none. A width of 90 cm (3 ft) gives just enough space for a mature peony plant.

It is worth choosing companions for your peonies with care. In spring, months before they flower, the emergent peony shoots have their own charm. The 'dear rosy snouts' (Gertrude Jekyll's phrase) unfurl into sprays of glossy young leaves of intense ruby red, gradually becoming green as they open out. It is rare to find red colouring of such depth in early spring, and it makes a fine contrast to the yellows, creams,

Paeonia mlokosewitschii: Gertrude Jekyll's 'dear rosy snouts' unfurling among the glaucous young leaves of *eryngium variifolium*.

TOP *Paeonia mlokosewitschii* in full flower.

ABOVE *P. mlokosewitschii* seed pods

violets and blues of small bulbs. Plan your planting so that the peony shoots push up through a carpet woven from early bulbs. The Planting Plan opposite shows a spring scheme for underplanting part of the peony walk described in Chapter 8.

The scheme starts with early-flowering crocuses, more delicate in form than the Dutch kinds that come later: violet *Crocus tommasinianus*, pale, milky 'Blue Pearl', white 'Snow Bunting' and 'Cream Beauty'. The last three are all scented. Add groups of the violet-purple *Iris reticulata* or one or more of its named forms such as 'Cantab' with pale, not quite Cambridge blue flowers, and a few clumps of *Erythronium dens-canis*, the dog's-tooth violet.

To overlap with these very early flowers and follow them, there is a wide choice of miniature daffodils (*narcissus*). Usually I don't like to see daffodils in beds and borders; I prefer them naturalized in grass where they look at home and where, after flowering, their untidy leaves can be ignored. But the small kinds planted in drifts of each variety, interlocking with groups of other bulbs, have great appeal, and the fading leaves will be hidden by the developing peony leaves. The windswept upturned flowers of various forms of *Narcissus cyclamineus* and *N. triandrus* have a special charm. *N. cyclamineus* 'Jumblie', 'Little Witch' and 'Tête à Tête' are yellow, *N. triandrus* 'Albus' and 'April Tears' are white. None are more than 22 cm (90 in) tall, and they do well in sun or light shade.

If you have enough open space it makes sense to relegate daffodils to grassy parts of the garden where they will be perfectly happy, and to use the peony bed to grow bulbs which cannot cope with the competition of grasses. Early-flowering tulips are prime candidates. *Tulipa kaufmanniana* (the water-lily tulip), *T. greigii* and their hybrids are short stemmed and sturdy. Those with *T. greigii* parentage have broad spreading leaves of greyish green, striped and mottled with purple red. The flowers too are often bi-coloured. Their creamy-yellow petals are streaked with pinkish red or vice versa. Simpler and more artless in form but startling in colour is scarlet *Tulipa praestans* 'Fusilier'. Almost all the tulip species are desirable and most are easy to please. If you plant clumps of taller, later flowering tulips among the early ones, you can achieve a non-stop display until the peonies take over. For the sake of a horticultural pun, plant 'peony-flowered' tulips to flower with the earliest genuine peonies. Peony-flowered tulips have double, peony-like flowers and include the apple-blossom-pink 'Angelique', scented rose-coloured 'Eros' and white 'Mount

PLANTING PLAN FOR SPRING FLOWERS IN THE PEONY BORDER

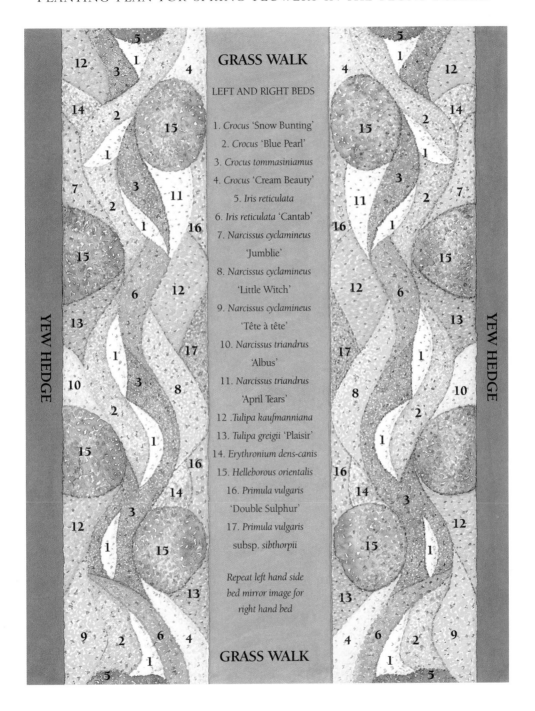

GRASS WALK

LEFT AND RIGHT BEDS

1. *Crocus* 'Snow Bunting'
2. *Crocus* 'Blue Pearl'
3. *Crocus tommasiniamus*
4. *Crocus* 'Cream Beauty'
5. *Iris reticulata*
6. *Iris reticulata* 'Cantab'
7. *Narcissus cyclamineus* 'Jumblie'
8. *Narcissus cyclamineus* 'Little Witch'
9. *Narcissus cyclamineus* 'Tête à tête'
10. *Narcissus triandrus* 'Albus'
11. *Narcissus triandrus* 'April Tears'
12. *Tulipa kaufmanniana*
13. *Tulipa greigii* 'Plaisir'
14. *Erythronium dens-canis*
15. *Helleborous orientalis*
16. *Primula vulgaris* 'Double Sulphur'
17. *Primula vulgaris* subsp. *sibthorpii*

Repeat left hand side bed mirror image for right hand bed

GRASS WALK

YEW HEDGE

YEW HEDGE

Tacoma'. The staying power of tulips is unpredictable. In some gardens they disappear after two or three years, so it is a good idea to keep the supply topped up by planting more each year.

Peonies in full flower look best set off by contrasting shapes and colours. Irises are their classic partners and offer the widest possible range of colours. But, as a complete contrast to the rounded form of peony flowers and of the peony plant, I would choose flowers held on tall spikes and spires. Lupins flower at just the right time and will provide the bonus of a second flowering in late summer if you cut down the spent stems. At 1.2 m (4 ft) they are tall enough to rise above most peonies. The yellow lupin 'Chandelier' contrasts well with vibrant pink or red peonies, and the deep violet flowers of 'Thundercloud' add opulence. The ivory-white 'Noble Maiden' flatters all shades of pink.

Other suitable spire-bearing plants include *Campanula persicifolia* with long-lasting white or soft blue flowers, and foxgloves. Try *Digitalis purpurea* 'Apricot' with white peonies, or the soft yellow-flowered perennial *D. grandiflora* among mid to late-flowering peonies in strong pinks and reds. *D grandiflora* is not as tall as other foxgloves, so group it to drift forwards beside and in front of the peonies. Delphiniums, the other great stars of the midsummer border, coincide with late-flowering peonies.

Once the peonies have finished flowering, other plants take over. Gertrude Jekyll used to drop pots of hydrangeas or lilies into her borders to fill the gaps left when midsummer flowers faded; a trick worth copying. In China and Japan, tree peonies have a long history as pot plants for both indoors and out. If you grow your peonies in pots, it is a matter of swapping one pot for another, removing the peonies after flowering and bringing in the lilies or hydrangeas to replace them. The pots should have a minimum width and depth of 30 cm (12in) and you should make sure the containers have efficient drainage holes. Plunge the pots in an out-of-the-way corner of the garden when the plants are not in flower.

Miss Jekyll's influence crossed the English Channel, contributing to the idea of *le jardin Anglais*, an informal style designed with an eye for the plants rather than the architecture of the garden. She had a hand in several gardens in France, including Les Moutiers at Varengville near Dieppe. The English architect Lutyens built the house and laid out the gardens for Guillaume Mallet. Jekyll advised on the planting

PREVIOUS PAGES Peony-flowered tulips with forget-me-nots and violas. *The Herbaceous Border* by Patrick William Adam, 1854-1930

THIS PAGE Lupin 'Chandelier' with the Japanese peony 'Kelways Majestic'.

163

Pink and white peonies with the promise of lilies and roses to follow. The sunken
garden at Manor House, Upton Grey, a restored Jekyll-designed garden in Hampshire.

The tree peony 'L'Espérance' in a formal setting at the National Trust's Hidcote
Gardens, Gloucestershire.

schemes. Monsieur and Madame Mallet, their daughter-in-law Mary and her son Robert have kept faith with the Lutyens-Jekyll style. Just one small event among many delightful effects is a group of the lovely tree peony *P. rockii* drawing the eye in a mixed border.

Tree peonies play a role in the garden not unlike that of rhododendrons. They flower at about the same time of year, their flowers are equally dramatic, and the colour range is similar. But tree peonies have the edge over rhododendrons in several important respects: for rhododenrons to succeed they must be grown in acid soil in sheltered, woodland conditions. Tree peonies, on the other hand, will tolerate most soils provided they are not waterlogged. It is worth noting that they are also happy in industrially polluted atmospheres. In their flowering time they fill a useful gap between such spring-flowering shrubs as Chaenomeles and Viburnums, and the roses. Since they tolerate draughty positions, Michael Haworth-Booth suggests a cool, airy position against a north-facing house wall; not usually an easy spot to fill, but ideal for tree peonies. In this position they could be preceded in flower by camellias and followed by hydrangeas.

I also like to see tree peonies well away from the house in very informal situations, among other shrubs or grouped alone at the edge of a wood or orchard where the quiet effect of their foliage can be enjoyed when their burst of flower is over. Opportunities to use them in this way only occur in gardens of a certain size, but even in a small garden there is room for one or two in a mixed border, or perhaps just one in the angle of a wall or boundary fence. Shelter from the wind is the one essential; the necks of the heavy flowers can so easily be snapped, or the fragile petals torn.

Herbaceous peonies also have a place in the wild garden. William Robinson, Gertrude Jekyll's contemporary, suggested growing the herbaceous kinds in a meadow, the ultimate in informality. He was a passionate advocate of the kind of naturalistic planting that is fashionable again today, having anticipated the 'new' style of herbaceous planting in his book *The Wild Garden* by 120 years. Here is one of his suggestions:

> … one of the most beautiful effects obtained in his wild garden by an acquaintance of mine… succeeded well in a not very favourable site.

A tree peony sharing wall space with *Wisteria sinensis*
at Trotton Old Rectory, Hampshire.

Formal, box-edged peony beds at Sun House, Long Melford, Suffolk
with 'Sarah Bernhardt' in the foreground.

Herbaceous Paeonies were amongst those that succeeded best. The effect was very beautiful, either close at hand or seen at a considerable distance off… The effect of the blooms amongst the long grass is finer than any they present in borders, and when out of flower they are not in the way.

and another:

I saw a group of the double scarlet kind… in an unmown glade, quite away from the garden proper; and yet, seen from the lawn and garden, the effect was most brilliant. To be able to produce such effects in the early summer is a gain from a landscape point of view, apart from the beauty of the flowers when seen close at hand.

I have planted *P. officinalis* 'Rubra Plena' in this kind of situation and it has worked very well. Cow-parsley arrived, as it tends to all over my garden, and looked pretty flowering with the peonies. I intend to add *Aconitum anglicum* and *Campanula persicifolia* to the group and then resist the temptation to do more.

The most uncontrived effects in the wild garden are achieved by using wild peonies. The species from around the world are just as ornamental as garden varieties of complex breeding, but they also have a simplicity and naturalness which makes them very appropriate in rough grass or on stony banks. Most of them flower in late spring, a little earlier than the garden kinds. *P. obovata, P. mascula* and its subs. *arietina* and *triternata* should do well without cosseting, provided you take the trouble to give them a good start. The lovely, fragrant white *P. emodi* is a Himalayan plant with fresh green leaves which make a good contribution in the landscape long after the flowers have faded. It associates well with *Paeonia anomala*'s large red flowers and dark green, much-divided foliage. *P. Peregrina* and *P. veitchii* also have finely-cut leaves that are glossy and of a fresh bright green that sets off the brilliant scarlet-red flowers of *P. peregrina* and the soft magenta-pink flowers of *P. veitchii*.with their pale cream anthers.

The finest leaves of all are those of *P. tenuifolia*, the fern-leaved peony. They are feathery and soft to the touch when young, and the flowers sit close above them.

Although it is fairly robust, it is safer to grow it in a bed were you can provide ideal conditions. It shares with P. peregrina and P. veitchii its relatively small stature, usually no taller than 50 cm (20 in) and so it occupies quite a small space at the front of a border or in a rock garden. And of course no gardener would dream of allowing the incomparable P. mlokosewitschii to take its chance in the wild garden. Give it a cherished position where you can drool over it during its ten days in flower. It has to be said that none of the species last long in flower. However, many of them show attractive autumn colour in their leaves and have interesting seed pods if you take the trouble to look. They all need well-drained soil and are happiest in semi-shade with the exception of P. anomala, P. mascula, P. mlokosewitschii which thrive in a sunny position.

The unique British system of opening your garden to visitors a few times each year, when it is at its seasonal best, provides plenty of opportunities to enjoy peonies grown in different situations and expressing different gardening styles. At Toddington Manor in Bedfordshire, lactiflora peonies such as 'Shirley Temple' and 'Laura Dessert' are the star feature of a large, informal mixed border. The peonies are planted in bold groups of nine of a kind against a dusky bronze background of Cryptomeria japonica 'Elegans' and Cotinus coggyria 'Royal Purple'. Unusual foxgloves and tall grasses provide a vertical line, dianthus and alchemilla make the foreground and lilies follow on after the peonies have flowered.

A traditional English arrangement of luxuriant, informal planting within a formal framework is followed at Cruckfield House near Shrewsbury. Here a long walk enclosed by clipped hornbeam hedges forms a vista from the house. The walk passes under arches planted with white solanum, wisteria and honeysuckle. The borders are planted with peonies and old-fashioned and shrub roses. The flowering season opens with Chinese tree peonies interplanted with Darwin, parrot and lily-flowered tulips. As they give way to pink, cream and white herbaceous peonies, planted in groups of three, bearded irises and alliums come into flower and finally the peonies bow out and roses take over.

There are more delightful plant associations at Portesham House in Dorset, where pink lily-flowered tulips flower under the pink-flowered tree peony 'Lord Selborne' and the double white 'Mrs William Kelway' is accompanied by a very tall white iris. In this garden the owners have had the inspired idea of clothing the rather gaunt,

Large-flowered varieties of clematis bloom at the same time as herbaceous peonies
and provide a pleasing colour contrast. Spetchley Park, Worcestershire.

171

'Barbara' growing through lavender at Penshurst Place, Kent.

bare stems of the tree peonies with *Lathyrus sativus*, an annual pea which scrambles to just the right height, or with exotic-looking *Rhodochiton atrosanguinem*. After the tree peonies, herbaceous peonies follow in company with delphiniums, tall campanulas and Veronica teucrium.

Anyone wanting to get to know the opulent Victorian and Edwardian peonies must not miss the garden at Green Cottage, Lydney where the National Collection of pre-1920 lactiflora peonies grows in a charming garden setting with carefully chosen companions, some familiar, others rare, but all in harmony with the peonies and each other.

Gardeners who feel they are in need of inspiration will find it in these and the other gardens listed in the Appendix. In fact there are very few British gardens where peonies cannot be found in flower in May and June.

CHAPTER 8

DESIGNING WITH PEONIES
A SCENTED WALK

Fragrance… ranges from mild to dense, from sweet through
woodsy to spicy. We have had visitors to our garden claim that
they haven't smelled anything like it since their childhood in
China and the scent is making them dizzy.

KASHA AND DAVID FURMAN, CRICKET HILL GARDEN, USA.

HERBACEOUS PEONIES ARE DELIGHTFUL COMPANIONS to other plants in borders
or grouped informally among shrubs, but if there is enough space to give
them a border to themselves the effect can be truly stunning. The peony
border at Penshurst Place, 120 m (130 yds) long, is the ultimate peony experience.
The border is backed by a hedge of *Berberis thunbergii atropurpurea* and edged with
lavender. The peonies are lactiflora varieties in every shade of pink from vibrant
magenta to palest blush, and when they are in full flower they assail the senses: the
scent and the sight of them is overwhelming and the urge to touch the frail petals
and cup the great blooms in your hands is almost irresistible.

I have planned a double peony walk on a smaller scale, with a path between two
borders, using only scented varieties. It is designed so that the simplicity of single
flowers contrasts with the lush opulence of fully double blooms, and there is every
possible gradation in between. The colours, baldly classified as red, white and pink,
encompass maroon, ruby, blood, cherry, crimson, scarlet, carmine, rose, salmon,
blush, pearl, cream and silver. During the flowering season each day brings changes
as buds open from tight green balls to mature into wide open bowls or great shaggy
mops. The colours may also change daily as some varieties fade gradually from
crimson to palest blush.

The effect is enhanced if the peonies can be shown against an appropriate

The peony border at Penshurst Place, Kent is 120 m (395 ft) long.

At Penshurst Place walls and hedges contain the scent of the peonies and a seat is
strategically placed for visitors to pause and enjoy it.

background on both sides of the walk. Enclosure also has the effect of concentrating the fragrance within the walk. Peonies do enjoy a fairly open situation, but a wall, fence, or belt of taller shrubs at least on one side will provide shelter from cold winds and driving rain. The ideal background is a hedge. The dark maroon of the berberis at Penshurst sets off the peony colours well, but I like the sobriety and matt texture of yew best of all.

The borders shown in my plan are 9.5 m (30 ft) long and 2.5 m (8 ft) wide. I could happily make them twice as long, but I have to recognize that most gardeners are likely to have less space available rather than more. In that case the planting scheme can be reduced by using one plant where I have shown two or three, or by using just half or two thirds of the plan.

If you are making your own planting plan, there is such a wide choice of peonies available in every colour and shape that you may find it difficult to narrow the field. If you choose from the 'specially recommended' varieties in the chart in Part III, you will not be disappointed. Some nursery catalogues are also frank about which are the most reliable plants, so if you are choosing from a catalogue, follow the nursery's recommendations or look for the phrase 'free flowering' and for varieties that remain in flower over a long period. Your choice will also be focused by the need to grade heights from tall at the back of the border to short at the front, and to achieve the longest possible flowering season by combining early, middle and late-flowering varieties.

In general, whether you are planning a complete garden or an area within a garden, it will have a more distinctive character if you work to a theme. The theme could be a particular colour scheme. The peony walk might be restricted to soft, pale colours, excluding reds and the stronger shades of pink. Or it could be planned for opulence, with dark reds, crimsons, and brilliant pinks backed up by the spires of violet and cobalt delphiniums. Or you might want to stick to varieties that perform particularly well as cut flowers.

The colour spectrum of peonies is already restricted to variations of white, pink and red, so where there is enough space I prefer not to limit my choice of colours. Instead I have chosen scent as my main theme. It comes as a wonderful surprise that some peonies are as fragrant as the sweetest rose and choosing only those varieties with a pronounced sweet scent brings the options within manageable limits.

PLANTING PLAN FOR A PEONY WALK

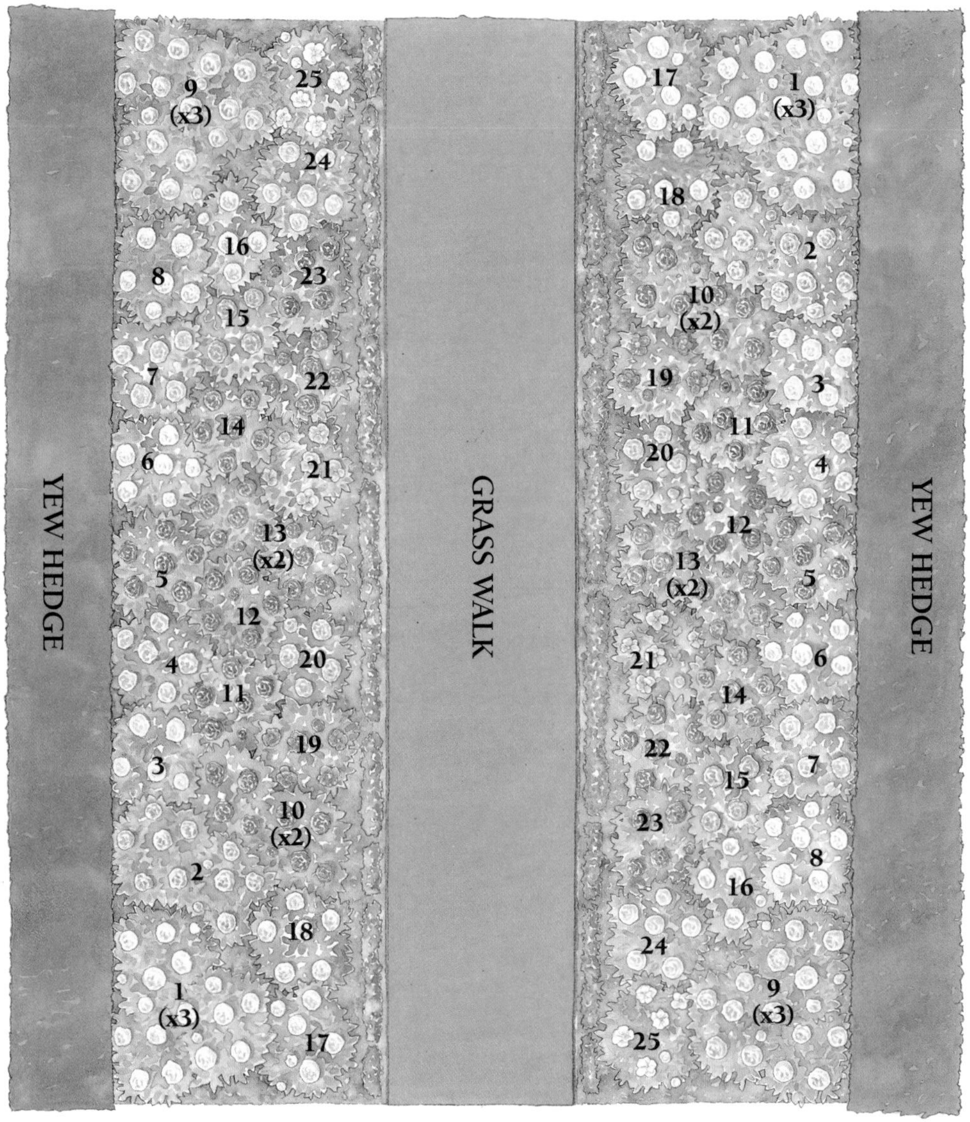

YEW HEDGE

9
(x3)

25

24

16

8

23

15

7

22

14

6

21

13
(x2)

5

12

4

11

20

3

19

10
(x2)

2

18

1
(x3)

17

GRASS WALK

YEW HEDGE

17

1
(x3)

18

2

10
(x2)

19

3

20

11

4

12

13
(x2)

5

21

6

14

22

7

15

23

8

16

24

9
(x3)

25

KEY TO THE PLANTING PLAN

KEY
NUMBER
NAME
flower form colour
height in cm season

1
CHARLIE'S WHITE
Double
cream/white
120 cm
early to mid

2
LADY ALEXANDRA
DUFF
Double
lavender pink
fading
90 cm
mid (long in flower)

3
LAURA DESSERT
Double
creamy yellow white
91cm
early to mid

4
MARIE JACQUIN
Semi-double
pale rose fading to
white
87 cm
mid to late

5
INSTITUTEUR
DORIAT
Japanese
carmine maroon
100 cm
mid

6
KELWAY'S
GLORIOUS
Double
white and cream
100 cm
mid to late

7
REINE HORTENSE
Double
soft pink
90 cm
mid to late

8
FESTIVA MAXIMA
Double
white
100 cm
mid

9
M JULES ELIE
Double
pink fading to white
110 cm
early to mid

10
FELIX CROUSSE
Double
magenta carmine
75 cm
mid to late

11
CHARM
Japanese
dark mahogany red
85 cm
late

12
POSTILION
Semi-double
scarlet red
90 cm
early

13
AUGUSTE DESSERT
Semi-double
deep pink, gold
centre
76 cm
mid to late

14
DIANA PARKS
(USA)
Double
carmine red, fading
85 cm
early to mid
or KNIGHTHOOD
(UK)
Double
deep maroon
crimson
75 cm
mid to late)

15
ASA GRAY
Double
rosy pink
85 cm
mid to late

16
MADAME CALOT
Double
pale pink fading
75 cm
late

17
DUCHESSE DE
NEMOURS
Double
white
80 cm
mid to late

18
MISTER ED
Double
blush fading to
white
70 cm
early

19
BURMA RUBY
Semi-double
bright red
70 cm
early

20
MRS FRANKLIN
D ROOSEVELT
Double
blush pink
70 cm
mid

21
NYMPHE
Semi-double
flesh pink
65cm
late

22
NICE GAL
Semi-double
deep cerise pink
55 cm
late

23
CHERRY HILL
Semi-double
crimson purple
85 cm
very early

24
TOP BRASS
Double
white, pink, yellow
tones
70 cm
mid to late

25
MISS AMERICA
Semi-double
white
90 cm
early

179

'Instituteur Doriat' no. 5 on the plan.

'Reine Hortense' no. 7 on the plan.

'Auguste Dessert' no. 13 on the plan.

TOP 'Duchesse de Nemours' no. 17 on the plan.
ABOVE 'Nymphe' no. 21 on the plan.

TOP 'Miss Eckhardt', a mid-season, free-flowering variety with a musk rose scent.
ABOVE 'Vogue', sweet scented, early and free flowering.

I have narrowed the choice further by only including plants that are good doers: strong, free-flowering varieties. In general it makes sense to stick with peonies that are tried and tested in your local climate although avid collectors may be unable to resist sending to the other side of the world for something rare and special. Even within these constraints, I still found I was spoilt for choice. The plants I finally chose are shown in the Key to the Planting Plan on the previous page. But there are others that I could hardly bear to leave out. So I have put them into a sort of *salon des refusés* under More Scented Varieties.

MORE SCENTED VARIETIES

Afterglow, Albert Crousse, Alice Harding, Baroness Schröeder, Bev, Big Ben, Blushing Princess, Bunker Hill, Butch, Camellia, Cheddar Cheese, Cheddar Supreme, Cheddar Surprise, Chiffon Parfait, Crimson Glory, Dr Alexander Fleming, Doris Cooper, Edulis Superba, Eugenie Verdier, Fairy's Petticoat, Festiva Supreme, Florence Ellis, Gardenia, Gleam of Light, Gloire de Charles Gombault, Honey Gold, Irwin Altman, James Kelway, June Rose, Kelway's Supreme, La France, La Perle, Louise Marx, Mme Auguste Dessert, Miss Eckhardt, Mme de Verneville, Mme Ducel, Montezuma, Myrtle Gentry, Paula Fay, Philippe Rivoire, Primevère, Princess Margaret, Red Charm, Requiem, Rose of Delight, Sea Shell, Shirley Temple, Vogue, Walter Marx, Whitleyi Major, Wiesbaden

In a well planned herbaceous border the peonies come on, do their act and then retire, letting the spotlight focus on later blooming performers. If an entire border is given over to peonies it has to be admitted that, however stunning the display, it lasts for weeks rather than months. The problem is solved by interplanting peonies with bulbs and herbaceous plants to extend the season in both directions: back into spring and forward towards autumn.

In the previous chapter I suggested spring bulbs for peony beds, and there are other spring-flowering plants well suited to underplant peonies. Wild primroses and their garden forms enjoy similar semi-shaded positions; for example a west-facing bed under a light tree canopy. The pale, soft yellow of the primroses contrasts prettily with the intensely blue flowers of *Omphalodes cappadocica*, or the blue bulbs *Scilla siberica*, chionodoxa or grape hyacinths. Pulmonarias make trouble-free ground cover with leaves that may be plain (*P. angustifolia*, *P. rubra*), white-spotted (as in *P. saccharata*, *P.* 'Sissinghurst White') or silvered (*P. vallarsae* 'Margery Fish'). Grouped to make a tapestry they will flower from late winter till late spring and still carry their decorative leaves after the peony stems have shrivelled and been cut down.

By midsummer the last peonies have flowered, and their leaves are tall and dense. Plants with courage and persistence are needed to push through the canopy and flower for the rest of the summer into autumn. There are a few bulbous and herbaceous perennials that can do it, but the peonies must be planted at least 90 cm (3 ft) apart to give them a chance. The bulbs of *Galtonia candicans*, sometimes called the summer hyacinth, can be planted in groups of three between the peonies. In late summer their white, bell-shaped flowers hang downwards from fleshy spikes up to 1.2 m (4 ft) tall.

The robust *Anemone* x *hybrida* (Japanese anemone) enjoys semi-shade and alkaline soil as do the peonies. If it is well suited it will spread and hold its own among them. Like Galtonia, most forms of *A.* x *hybrida* are tall enough to carry their flowers above the peony foliage and will flower for a long period from late summer into autumn. 'Honorine Jobert', 1.5 m (5 ft) tall with single white flowers is the best of all. 'Prince Henry' has deep pink flowers.

There is a gap to fill in the peony bed after the last peony has faded and before the galtonia and anemones begin to flower. In a sunny place, Eremurus (fox-tail lilies) may solve the problem. *E* 'Shelford Hybrids' carry 1.5 m (5 ft) spikes packed with tiny flowers giving an overall soft, furry impression. The colour range is from dusky and orangey pinks to buff. The flowers are followed by shiny green seeds. In very cold areas the roots should be protected from severe frost with dry bracken or conifer branches.

Some of the taller day lilies will also succeed interplanted with peonies. *Hemerocallis* 'Bonanza' is a strong and reliable plant with buff-orange flowers, each with a red star at the centre. 'Classic Simplicity' with chrome yellow flowers and 'Heirloom Lace' (soft peachy-yellow) both carry plenty of fragrant flowers over a long period. 'Pink Damask' is still the best of the pinks and 'Neyron Rose' is a deeper, duskier shade.

The peony border need not be restricted to herbaceous varieties. Tree peonies will be in flower several weeks earlier and can bring yellow and apricot shades to the

TOP Some scented tree peonies. 'Fen Pan Tao Qui' (laurel on a pink tray) has a light rose scent. Shown at Cricket Hill, Thomaston USA.

ABOVE 'Hua Hu Die' (multi-coloured butterfly) has a spicy scent. Photographed at Cricket Hill, Thomaston USA.

187

'Jin Zui Yang Fei' (tipsy imperial concubine) with petals in sweet disorder and a
delicate scent. Shown at Cricket Hill, Thomaston USA.

'Souvenir de Maxime Cornu' is lightly scented.

Zhuang Yuan Hong' (number one scholar's red) has a dense fragrance.
Photographed at Cricket Hill, Thomaston USA.

colour range. The taller kinds can be used to give extra height behind the herbaceous peonies. Tree peonies and Intersectional (Itoh) hybrids that are scented are listed below.

SCENTED TREE PEONIES
Chromatella (slightly), Comtesse de Tuder (sometimes), Da Ye Hu Die, Fei Yan Hong Zhuang, Fen Pan Tao Qui, Fragrans Maxima Plena, Fuji-no-mine, Gei Jin Zi, Guan Shi Mo Yu, Hei Hua Kui, Hephestos, Hesperus, High Noon, Hua Hu Die, Icarus, Jeanne d'Arc (slightly), Jin Zui Yang Fei, Leda, Mine d'Or, Nike, Princesse Amélie (slightly), Qing Long Wo Mo Chi, Rinpo, Sang Lorrain, Souvenir de Ducher, Souvenir de Maxime Cornu (slightly), Wu Long Peng Sheng, Ying Luo Bao Zhu, Zhao Fen, Zhu Sha Lei, Zhuang Yuan Hong

SCENTED INTERSECTIONAL HYBRIDS
Bartzella, Canary Brilliants, Yellow Dream, Yellow Emperor, Yellow Heaven.

CHAPTER 9

PEONIES INDOORS
THE FLOWER ARRANGER'S FLOWER

DRAWING ROOM AND BOUDOIR

In the selection of vases for these rooms, those of medium size should never be exceeded, unless the room is of unusual proportions. For general purposes glass vases will be found the best in every way… for the *Paeonias* with flowers of light shades of pink and rose, we would prefer a dark blue vase… . Rustic baskets look exceedingly pretty when not over-crowded.

JAMES HUDSON, 'DECORATIVE USE OF FLOWERS',
Cassell's Popular Gardening, 1867.

ERBACEOUS PEONIES have a long history as cut flowers. They were recommended, with lilies, sweet williams, carnations and nigella as flowers for pots and window-sills by Thomas Tusser in the sixteenth century. They frequently figured, with roses, larkspurs, columbines and striped and twisted tulips in the romantic, artistically dishevelled arrangements painted with such loving attention to detail by Dutch artists. Later on, at the beginning of this century, peonies were especially popular again. The introduction of new and beautiful varieties coincided with a general taste for the opulent in fashionable women's dresses and hairstyles, and in the decor of their houses. Peonies catered admirably to the prevailing taste. An 1899 issue of the magazine *Fashions and Fancies* noted that peonies were '… employed in the choicest room and table decorations, as bouquets for drawing rooms and smart weddings – in fact their presence is welcomed everywhere.' And in the same year *Country Life Illustrated* suggested that

Peonies were an essential component of early arrangements of cut flowers. *Large Bouquet of Flowers in a Wooden Tub* 1606-1607 by Jan Breughel the Elder, 1568-1625.

'Peonies are employed in the choicest room and table decorations'. *Fashions and Fancies* magazine, 1899. *Arranging the Peonies* by George F Carline, 1855-1920.

Harvesting peonies in Communist China: a New Year card entitled *Spring is Here*
by Shao Wen-chin and Chang Fu-lung.

The big blooms make noble decorations when gathered into large bowls and vases. A sweet perfume pervades a *Paeony*-adorned room – a perfume as delicious as the Rose, though more pronounced in some varieties than others.

Today peony farmers in China, America and New Zealand make a good living growing blooms to cut and send to market, not only meeting local needs, but in many cases sending peonies by air freight to supply florists on the other side of the world.

Tree peonies, too, are occasionally cut and displayed in vases. The huge flowers are carried on quite short stems, but if they are arranged so that they float among their own leaves in a wide, shallow bowl, the flowers can be enjoyed in close-up and will last in water for fourteen days or more. A bowl made of bronze or other dark metal gives the arrangement a suitably oriental air.

Herbaceous peonies are much in demand as cut flowers because they travel so well and can be held back in cold storage whilst still in bud and brought on to flower almost at will. There is an excellent account of techniques for growing peonies as cut flowers commercially in Allan Rogers' book *Peonies*. Those listed in the following table are recommended by professional growers.

HERBACEOUS PEONIES RECOMMENDED AS CUT FLOWERS

(KEY: * = scented)

RED	PINK	PALE PINK	WHITE, CREAM
DOUBLE			
Best Man	Claire Dubois	*Baroness Schröeder	Ann Cousins
*Big Ben	*Dr Alexander Fleming	*Chiffon Parfait	*Avalanche
*Bunker Hill	Doris Cooper	*Fairy's Petticoat	Bowl of Cream
Chippewa	Dinner Plate	Hermione	Bridal Gown
*Diana Parks	Duchesse D'Orleans	*James Kelway	Bridal Icing
*Félix Crousse	*Edulis Superba	*Lady Alexandra Duff	*Charlie's White
Felix Supreme	Madylone	*Mister Ed	*Cheddar Cheese
Henry St Clair	Minuet	Moon River	*Cheddar Surprise
Kansas	*Monsieur Jules Elie	Moonstone	*Duchess de Nemours

'Duchesse de Nemours' in *Still Life of White Peonies* 1870
by Ignace Henri Jean Fantin-Latour, 1836-1904.

RED	PINK	PALE PINK	WHITE, CREAM
Karl Rosenfield	*Mrs Franklin D Roosevelt	*Reine Hortense	Elsa Sass
Longfellow	Mrs Livingston Farrand	*Shirley Temple	*Festiva Maxima
Louis van Houtte	*My Pal Rudy		Florence Nicholls
Maestro	Pillow Talk		*Gardenia
Mt St Helens	*Princess Margaret		*Honey Gold
P. officinalis 'Rubra'	*Raspberry Sundae		*Kelways Glorious
Paul M Wild	Sarah Bernhardt		Lancaster Imp
Red Charm	Vivid Rose		*Top Brass
Shawnee Chief			
The Mighty Mo			
SEMI-DOUBLE			
	Coral Charm		*Miss America
	Cytherea		
	*Paula Fay		
	Rosedale		
JAPANESE			
	Cora Stubbs		Louise Marx
	Gay Paree (pink and white)		
SINGLE			
*Burma Ruby	Roselette		Krinkled White
Flame	*Sea Shell		Le Jour
*Mahogany			Le Printemps

On a domestic scale, If you just want to pick a few blooms from your garden plants, almost all peonies are suitable and will last well in water. They can be grown as part of a herbaceous border or in a traditional cutting bed. For serious flower arrangers much the same rules apply as for commercial growers. For example, the sort of flower that can be sold in a florist's shop has a long, straight stem and just one large flower to each stem. To achieve this, check your plants regularly and nip off any side buds as soon as they appear.

Peonies picked in bud and allowed to open indoors often retain their colour better than outdoors where warm sunshine tends to bleach out some varieties. The time to

At one time peonies would have been grown in cutting beds in the kitchen garden,
carefully staked to ensure long, straight stems, as shown here in the order beds at the
National Trust's Hidcote Garden, Gloucestershire.

Tree peonies are usually short stemmed and can be floated in a bowl or used,
like *P. rockii* here, in small, informal arrangements. *White Peonies in a Blue Jug*,
by Elizabeth Jane Lloyd, 1928-1995.

cut them is when colour is just beginning to show on the buds. On commercial peony farms the flowers are cut while the buds are still quite tight, early in the morning, and plunged directly into buckets of water. The stems are then stripped of their leaves and put in cold storage. At temperatures between 0°C (32°F) and 6°C (43°F) they can be kept for four weeks, a useful attribute if you are 'doing the flowers' for a special occasion and want to be sure of having enough good blooms unspoiled by bad weather. But if you want an instant full-blown effect, pick flowers that are fully open.

Cut your peonies first thing in the morning, as the professionals do. Resist the temptation to strip your plants of all their flowers, even if they are grown specially for cutting and you do not need the flowers for garden effect. It is impossible to take long flower stems without also removing quite a lot of leaves and the plant needs the leaves for nourishment, so leave at least two leaves to each stem and never cut more than half the blooms from each plant.

Once the flowers have been cut and arranged they have a long vase life of up to two full weeks. You can make sure of this by giving them an immediate drink in a bucket of water dosed with a florists' preservative. The same solution can be used in the vase when you arrange the flowers. As an alternative, Allan Rogers recommends a home-made mix of a quart of water, two tablespoons of fresh lemon or lime juice, a tablespoon of sugar and half a teaspoon of household bleach. The peonies will last even longer if you change the water every day and slightly shorten each stem with a sharp knife at the same time – a counsel of perfection rather than practical advice. Double, semi-double and single peonies are all wonderfully adaptable for flower arranging; they look just as right in artless, uncontrived arrangements of cottagey flowers as they do in big, formal set pieces for a wedding or a ball. Choose fragrant varieties if you can.

From late spring to mid-summer there is a wide choice of flowers to mix with peonies: the early peonies overlap with lily-flowered tulips, parrot tulips, lilacs, columbines and wallflowers. A little later, use the stately spikes of lupins, delphiniums, foxgloves and larkspurs to contrast with the rounded peony flowers. The soft, furry leaves of *Ballota pseudodictamnus* and the sharp, lime yellow-green flowers of euphorbias are good for cooling the strong reds and crimsons of early and mid-season peonies. Wear gloves when picking euphorbias, as many people are

A romantic outdoor arrangement. *Peonies in an Urn in a Garden*
by Louis Marie Lemaire.

allergic to their milky sap. To prevent the sap leaking and to prolong their vase life, the stems can be dipped in boiling water for twenty seconds.

Good background plants for peonies include the umbelliferous flowers and fine leaves of dill and fennel (the bronze form as well as the green) and hedgerow cow parsley (*Anthriscus sylvestris*). Sear the stems in boiling water to prevent the flowers and leaves wilting. Gypsophila, called 'Baby's Breath' by florists, and the lovely blue-mauve *Thalictrum delavayi* both flower just in time to overlap with later flowering peonies and are unrivalled companions.

The leaves of many tree and herbaceous peonies are invaluable flower arranging material from spring through autumn, and some have spectacular seed pods to use in autumn arrangements.

PEONIES AS DRIED FLOWERS
Peonies dry well for autumn and winter arrangements, the reds and darker pinks retaining their colour exceptionally well. By combining them with dried delphiniums, foxgloves, gypsophila, lavender and nigella, you can achieve beautiful effects light years away from the depressing, dusty beige arrangements of grasses, hydrangea heads and faded everlastings that used at one time to be all that was available. Peony petals can also be used to add colour and scent to pot-pourri mixtures.

HERBACEOUS PEONIES RECOMMENDED FOR DRYING
Ann Cousins, Auguste Dessert, Chippewa, David Harum, Félix Crousse,
Glad Tidings (NZ), Karl Rosenfield, Maestro, Richard Carvel, The Mighty Mo

The easiest way to dry peonies is to hang them upside down in a warm, dry, dark place for two weeks. An airing cupboard is ideal. Pick them when they are fully open, on a dry day, with stems up to 20 cm (8 in) long. Strip off the leaves and tie the stems loosely but firmly, not more than half a dozen in each bunch. The flowers can also be detached from the stems and speared on florists' wire before drying. An alternative method of drying is to cook the flowers in a microwave oven. Put them on several layers of kitchen paper and give them from two to three minutes on a medium setting. If, after three minutes, the paper is damp, replace it and repeat

Peonies occupy the place of honour on the dais behind the painters in this
Japanese print. *Painting and calligraphy party at the Manpachiro Tea House*
by Utagawa Kunisada, 1786-1864.

the process. Silica gel, used to dry small numbers of flowers at a time, is particularly good for preserving the brightness and clarity of petal colours.

POT-GROWN PEONIES

Drying techniques provide an opportunity to enjoy peonies all winter. You can also cheat the seasons and have herbaceous peonies in flower a couple of months early by planting them in large pots or tubs and bringing them into a cold greenhouse in winter, first allowing them a brief cold spell outdoors during their dormancy. James Kelway recommended bringing them inside in January or February.

In China and Japan there is a long tradition of using tree peonies growing in pots as indoor decorations. They were often more than mere decorations, being revered subjects for philosophers to study, for poets to praise and for artists to paint. In Japan the peony, as the queen of flowers, was always displayed alone indoors; a single plant in full flower would be placed on a dais in the most prominent recess of a room.

In the Far East today tree peonies growing in pots are still used to decorate rooms indoors and outdoor courtyards. In the West they are seldom used in this way, but they are ideal for patios and terraces, specially if an out-of-the-way corner can be found to plunge the pots when the plants are not in flower. If you grow them in this way, choose containers of a generous size with a good deep layer of pebbles at the base for drainage. Instructions for cultivating peonies in pots can be found in Chapter 10.

PART THREE

PEONY LISTS

HOW TO USE THE LISTS

T HE MAIN DESCRIPTIVE LISTS are designed to help you to choose peonies for planting in the garden or the wider landscape. They are my personal choice, and those described more briefly in the general lists are not necessarily inferior. The peonies should all be commercially available as they are listed in one or more nursery catalogue in each country mentioned. If the peonies you choose are difficult to obtain, the American Peony Society in the USA or *The Plant Finder* published by the Royal Horticultural Society in the UK are useful sources of information. If information such as breeders' names or dates of introduction has been omitted it is because it is not available.

In China today there are nine recognized flower shapes for peonies; they can be translated as single-petal, lotus, chrysanthemum, rose, sweet-scented osmanthus-holding, golden-ring, crown, silk-ball and pavilion. To avoid making the list too complicated, I have reduced the number of categories to the four recognized by the Royal Horticultural Society: single, semi-double, double and Japanese (also called imperial or anemone form). The Chinese have also developed a system of colour categorization, with nine colours: yellow, white, pink, red, purple, black, green, blue and multi-coloured. Colour names are always problematic; there is no such thing as a blue peony or a black peony, but blue-pink or crimson-black might be accurate descriptions. When interpreting my descriptions, please bear in mind that it is part of the charm of some peonies that their colours change and fade as the flowers mature.

Peonies occupy such a wide geographic and climatic range that the flowering season and the height of each plant may vary either side of the average given here.

TREE PEONIES

KEY:

PLANT NAME
IN **BOLD TYPE** = highly recommended.
* = American Peony Society Gold Medal
♉ = RHS Award of Garden Merit
Note unless otherwise described,
the tree peonies listed here belong to
the suffruticosa *group*.

*AGE OF GOLD

A leafy plant with golden-yellow flowers.
The lightly ruffled petals have red flares.
SAUNDERS, USA 1948
SEMI-DOUBLE YELLOW
EARLY MID
90-120 CM / 3-4 FT
AVAILABLE IN EUROPE NZ USA

P. X. *LEMOINEI* 'ALICE HARDING'
SYN. KINKO

A cross between *P. lutea* and 'Yaso Okina'
forming a low plant with large, lemon-
scented flowers with red flares, half hidden
by the leaves. A parent of the first Itoh
hybrids.
LEMOINE, FRANCE 1935
SEMI-DOUBLE YELLOW
FRAGRANT
EARLY MID
40-50 CM / 16-20 IN
AVAILABLE IN FRANCE NZ USA JAPAN

AMBROSE CONGREVE

One of Sir Peter Smithers' lovely *P. rockii*
cultivars. Palest pink ruffled petals are flared
and veined with deeper pink. Fresh green,
deeply-cut leaves on a strong plant.
SMITHERS, 1994
SINGLE PINK
MID
120CM / 4FT
AVAILABLE IN FRANCE

L'AURORE

Rosy-orange petals surround a big boss of
vivid yellow stamens. Red and yellow
veining gives a vibrant depth of colour.
Vigorous, free flowering.
LEMOINE, FRANCE 1935
SINGLE ORANGE-PINK
MID
120 CM / 4 FT
AVAILABLE IN FRANCE

BANQUET

Glowing strawberry-pink flowers, darkening
at the centre to display a ring of gold
stamens. Good deep-cut foliage.
SAUNDERS, USA 1941
SEMI-DOUBLE RED
EARLY MID
90 CM-120 CM / 3-4 FT
AVAILABLE IN FRANCE NZ USA JAPAN

BLACK DRAGON BROCADE *see*
KOKURYU-NISHIKI

BLACK PANTHER
Large, shaggy mahogany-red flowers and
deep-cut foliage. Increases by underground
stolons.
SAUNDERS, USA 1948
SEMI-DOUBLE RED
EARLY MID
90 CM-120 CM / 3-4 FT
AVAILABLE IN FRANCE USA NZ

BLACK PIRATE
Very dark red, shiny petals contrast with
yellow stamens. The large flowers are held
above the leaves but are sometimes too
heavy for the stems.
SAUNDERS, USA 1948
SINGLE OR SEMI-DOUBLE RED
EARLY MID
90-120 CM / 3-4 FT
AVAILABLE IN JAPAN NZ USA

BOREAS
Enormous wine-red flowers with ruffled and
slightly twisted petals.
DAPHNIS (D-311) USA
SEMI-DOUBLE RED
EARLY MID
90-120 CM / 3-4 FT
AVAILABLE IN FRANCE NZ USA

BROCADE OF THE SUN AND MOON *see*
KOKURYU-NISHIKI

CARDINAL VAUGHAN
A typical Kelway peony with enormous,
purple-red flowers. The purple petals
develop silvery margins when the flowers
are fully open.
KELWAYS, UK
SEMI-DOUBLE PURPLE-RED
MID
150 CM / 5 FT
AVAILABLE IN UK USA

CHARMING AGE *see* HOKI

*CHINESE DRAGON
Very large crimson petals with darker flares.
Dark green slightly bronzed leaves on stems
tinged with red.
SAUNDERS, USA 1948
SINGLE OR SEMI-DOUBLE RED
EARLY MID
90 CM / 3 FT
AVAILABLE IN FRANCE JAPAN NZ USA

P. X. *LEMOINEI* CHROMATELLA SYN.
KINSHI
Stunning very full flowers have yellow petals
edged with rose red, giving an overall effect
of soft, pale orange. Robust plants but the
heavy heads can droop sadly after rain.

Black Pirate

Duchess of Marlborough

Light lemony scent.
LEMOINE, FRANCE 1920
DOUBLE YELLOW
FRAGRANT
MID
90 CM / 3 FT
AVAILABLE IN FRANCE UK

CINNABAR RAMPARTS *see* ZHU SHA LEI

CINQ GRAND PAYS *see* GODAISHU

COMPANION OF SERENITY
Palest mauve-pink petals with deep pink
flares. Ruffled petals, pinked margins and
tissue texture give a beautiful air of fragility.
GRATWICK, USA 1959
SINGLE PINK
EARLY
120 CM / 4 FT
AVAILABLE IN NZ USA

COMTESSE DE TUDER
Vigorous, with deep-cut bronzed green leaves
and huge bomb-shaped flowers, pale rose
pink with blush shadows, very free flowering.
EUROPE PRE-1866
DOUBLE PINK
FRAGRANT
MID
90 CM / 3 FT
AVAILABLE IN FRANCE

CONG ZHONG XIAO (SMILING IN THE
THICKETS, ONE FLOWER SMILES)
Soft, mauvish-pink, rose-like petals with
darker flares open to form a shallow bowl.
The flowers are held on strong stems.
CHINA USA
SEMI-DOUBLE PINK
FRAGRANT
EARLY
250 CM / 8 FT
AVAILABLE IN CHINA USA

CORAL TERRACE *see* SHAN HU TAI

DUCHESS OF MARLBOROUGH
Lovely flowers with silky ruffled petals in
warm tones of flesh pink around a tidy boss
of short stamens.
KELWAY, UK
SEMI-DOUBLE PINK
MID
120 CM / 4 FT
AVAILABLE IN UK

DUCHESSE DE MORNY
A strong plant, often found in old,
neglected gardens. The large flowers form a
broad bowl of luminous mauveish petals,
darkening at the base. Prolific, excellent cut
flower.
FRANCE PRE-1955
DOUBLE PINK
MID

120 CM /4 FT

AVAILABLE IN FRANCE

ETERNAL CAMELLIAS *see* YACHIYO-
TSUBAKI

P. X. *LEMOINEI* L'ESPERANCE SYN. KINTEI
Wonderful colouring in flowers and foliage.
Primrose petals flared and edged with light,
clear red give an overall effect of soft peachy
orange. Leaves, edged with pinky red, have
a greyish bloom. Pink sepals, purple-pink
seed pods with bright crimson tips.
LEMOINE, FRANCE 1909
SINGLE TO SEMI-DOUBLE YELLOW
MID
120 CM /4 FT
AVAILABLE IN FRANCE JAPAN UK

FEN DAN BAI (PHOENIX WHITE, WHITE
PHOENIX)
Classical flowers of breath-taking purity
with lightly ruffled petals. Robust and
reliable, probably a cultivar of *P. ostii*.
CHINA
SINGLE WHITE
FRAGRANT
EARLY
UP TO 300 CM / 10 FT
AVAILABLE IN CANADA CHINA UK USA

FEN ZHONG GUAN (SUPREME PINK)
Easy to grow, with pale, delicate rose-pink,

outward-facing flowers, high crowned and
slightly ruffled with a light scent.
CHINA
DOUBLE PINK
FRAGRANT
MID
180 CM TO 250 CM / 6 FT TO 8 FT
AVAILABLE IN CHINA USA

FLIGHT OF CRANES *see* RENKAKU

FLORAL RIVALRY *see* HANA-KISOI

FUJI-NO-MINE (SNOW-CLAD FUJI)
Pure white petals with fringed edges and a
touch of pink in the stamens. Good, dense
foliage. Free flowering.
JAPAN
SEMI-DOUBLE WHITE
FRAGRANT
EARLY
100 CM /3 FT
AVAILABLE IN GERMANY JAPAN USA

GAUGIN
A spectacular hybrid of *P. lutea*. Large yellow
flowers suffused and veined with red, dark
red flares. Overall colouring like a blood
orange.
DAPHNIS (D-22) USA
SINGLE YELLOW/RED
MID
120 CM / 4 FT

AVAILABLE IN USA EUROPE NZ

GESSEKAI (TSUKISEKAI, KINGDOM OF THE MOON)

Very large, beautiful, pure white flowers with fringed, ruffled and twisted petals. Vigorous. One of the earliest to flower.

JAPAN

SEMI-DOUBLE WHITE

EARLY

120 CM / 4 FT

AVAILABLE IN NZ UK USA

GIANT GLOBE *see* GODAISHU

GODAISHU (GIANT GLOBE, CINQ GRANDS PAYS)

Very large, bowl-shaped flowers, carried well above the foliage. Pure white with a large boss of golden-yellow stamens.

JAPAN

SEMI-DOUBLE WHITE

EARLY

120 CM / 4 FT

AVAILABLE IN CANADA EUROPE JAPAN NZ UK USA

GOLD SOVEREIGN

One of the best yellow tree peonies. Strong stems carry large, flat, symmetrical flowers well above the leaves. Good in warm climates.

SAUNDERS, USA 1949

SEMI-DOUBLE YELLOW

EARLY MID

150 CM / 5 FT

AVAILABLE IN FRANCE USA

GOLDEN ERA

Another excellent yellow peony, quite pale with red-brown flares, the flowers held high on strong stems.

REATH, USA 1984

SEMI-DOUBLE YELLOW

LATE MID

100 CM / 3 FT 6 IN

AVAILABLE IN USA

GOLDEN HIND

Large flowers between double and semi-double, a soft, pretty shade between yellow and cream. Lightly ruffled petals with dark red flares. Sturdy, very dark leaves, strong stems.

SAUNDERS, USA 1948

DOUBLE YELLOW

MID

90 CM / 3 FT

AVAILABLE IN NZ USA

GOLDFINCH

Large pale yellow flowers. Vigorous plant.

SAUNDERS, USA 1998

SINGLE YELLOW

MID

90-120 CM / 3-4 FT

AVAILABLE IN GERMANY NZ USA

GREEN DRAGON LYING ON A CHINESE
INK STONE *see* QING LONG WO MO
CHI

GUARDIAN OF THE MONASTERY
Large lavender-pink flowers with black-
purple flares and purple-pink veins paling at
the margins. Yellow stamens. Vigorous,
resembling a pink *P. rockii*.
GRATWICK, USA 1959
SEMI-DOUBLE PINK
EARLY
150 CM / 5 FT
AVAILABLE IN NZ USA

HAKUOJISHI (KING OF WHITE LIONS,
WHITE-TAILED LION)
Pretty flowers, delicate in spite of their large
size. Pure white petals have faint, pale
purple smudges at their bases. Golden-
yellow stamens. Autumn colour. Strong, free
flowering.
JAPAN
SEMI-DOUBLE WHITE
MID
120 CM / 4 FT
AVAILABLE IN EUROPE JAPAN NZ UK USA

HANA-DAIJIN (MAGNIFICENT FLOWER,
MINISTER OF FLOWERS) *see also* 'SHIMA
DAIJIN'

Very large, lush flowers, nearly double, rich
red purple, almost violet. Very free
flowering.
JAPAN PRE-1910
SEMI-DOUBLE PURPLE
MID
120 CM / 4 FT
AVAILABLE IN CANADA EUROPE JAPAN UK USA

HANA-KISOI (FLORAL RIVALRY)
Considered one of the best of all tree
peonies, with large, clear rose-pink flowers
on strong stems. Cupped, lightly curled
petals vary from deep to pale pink, giving a
lively, light catching effect. Golden-yellow
stamens, bright green leaves. Vigorous.
JAPAN 1926
SEMI-DOUBLE PINK
FRAGRANT
MID TO LATE
120 CM / 4 FT
AVAILABLE IN CANADA EUROPE JAPAN NZ UK
USA

HEAVENLY DANCE *see* NIGATA
TEN'NYO-NOMAI

HELENE MARTIN
P. potaninii **var.** *trolliodes* x 'GESSEKAI'
Beautiful, very large flowers with fragile,
tissue-like petals, white with tawny red
flares at the centre, bleeding and fading into
faint orange-yellow veins. Plentiful, pretty

leaves, deeply cut and bright green.
JEAN CAYEUX, FRANCE 1980.

SINGLE WHITE

MID

120 CM / 4 FT

AVAILABLE IN FRANCE

HEPHESTOS

One of the best red *P. lutea* hybrids. Huge
flowers held well above glossy green leaves.
Slightly crinkled, velvety petals, rich wine
red.

DAPHNIS (D-240) USA

SEMI-DOUBLE RED

FRAGRANT

MID

93 CM /3 FT 1 IN

AVAILABLE IN GERMANY NZ USA

HESPERUS

Flowers held well above the leaves, with
ruffled petals in a subtle and beautiful
combination of old rose and soft yellow.
Sometimes flowers again in late summer.

SAUNDERS, USA 1948

SINGLE PINK, YELLOW

FRAGRANT

MID

120 CM / 4 FT

AVAILABLE IN EUROPE NZ USA

*HIGH NOON

Scented, cup-shaped flowers, sunshine

yellow with crimson flares, held upright
above the leaves. Sometimes flowers again
in late summer. Free flowering.

SAUNDERS, USA 1952

SEMI-DOUBLE YELLOW

FRAGRANT

MID

150 CM / 5 FT

AVAILABLE IN EUROPE JAPAN NZ UK USA

HOST OF THE CHERRY BLOSSOM
see YAE ZAKURA

HOKI (HOWKI, HOOKI, CHARMING AGE, SWEET SEVENTEEN)

Large, shapely flowers with petals slightly
curved inwards, bright, clear red with a tidy
tuft of creamy-yellow stamens. Strong, free
flowering.

JAPAN

SEMI-DOUBLE RED

MID

90 CM /3 FT

AVAILABLE IN EUROPE JAPAN NZ UK USA

ISABELLE RIVIERE

Glowing rose pink flowers with almost
black flares and petals edged and
occasionally striped with white. Very strong,
free flowering.

A RIVIÈRE, FRANCE 1975

SINGLE PINK

EARLY

120 CM / 4 FT

AVAILABLE IN FRANCE

JADE IN A BLUE FIELD *see* LAN TIAN YU

JEWELLED SCREEN *see* TAMA-SUDARE

JITSUGETSU-NISHIKI (SUN AND MOON
BROCADE).
Cup-shaped crimson-red flowers with
slightly ruffled petals, some narrowly edged
in white, well presented.
JAPAN PRE-1927
SEMI-DOUBLE RED
MID
120 CM / 4 FT
AVAILABLE IN EUROPE NZ JAPAN

JOSEPH ROCK *see* PAEONIA *ROCKII*

KAMADA BROCADE *see* KAMADA-NISHIKI

KAMADA-FUJI (WISTERIA AT KAMATA,
MONTROSE)
Very big lavender-pink flowers, valued for
their unusual colour.
JAPAN PRE-1893
SEMI-DOUBLE MAUVE
EARLY
UP TO 120 CM / UP TO 4 FT
AVAILABLE IN EUROPE JAPAN NZ USA

KAMADA-NISHIKI (KAMADA BROCADE).
Very large purplish-pink flowers with ruffled
petals, darker at the centre, paling at the
margins as the flower ages.
JAPAN PRE-1893
SEMI-DOUBLE PINK
EARLY
120 TO 150 CM / 4 TO 5 FT
AVAILABLE IN JAPAN EUROPE UK USA

KAO (KAOW, KING OF FLOWERS)
Dramatic (up to 25 cm / 10 in), almost
double flowers with bright red, lightly
ruffled petals fading to purple pink as they
age. Yellow stamens. Exceptionally free
flowering, strong stemmed.
JAPAN
SEMI-DOUBLE RED
MID
150 CM / 5 FT
AVAILABLE IN EUROPE JAPAN UK USA

KING OF FLOWERS *see* KAO

KING OF WHITE LIONS *see* HAKUOJISI

KINGDOM OF THE MOON *see* GESSEKAE

KINKAKU SYN. GOLDEN TEMPLE OF
NARA, *see* SOUVENIR DE MAXIME
CORNU

KINKO *see* ALICE HARDING

KINSHI *see* CHROMATELLA

KINTEI *see* L'ESPERANCE

KISHU CAPRICE
Pale mauve with purple flares, purple and
gold centre. Luxuriant foliage.
SASAKI, JAPAN 1988
SINGLE TO SEMI-DOUBLE MAUVE
MID
150 CM / 5 FT
AVAILABLE IN NZ USA

KOKURYÛ-NISHIKI (BROCART DE SOLEIL
ET DE LUNE IN / BLACK DRAGON
BROCADE)
Very dark purple with violet tones; the outer
petals have white veins and green-white
edges.
JAPAN PRE-1905
SINGLE OR SEMI-DOUBLE PURPLE
MID
120-150 CM / 4-5 FT
AVAILABLE IN FRANCE JAPAN UK

LAN TIAN YU (SKY BLUE JADE, JADE IN A
BLUE FIELD).
Bowl-shaped flowers with masses of soft
mauve-pink petals on a spreading but tidy
plant. Light scent.
CHINA
DOUBLE PINK
FRAGRANT

MID
UP TO 120 CM / UP TO 4 FT
AVAILABLE IN UK USA

LARGE GLOBE *see* GODAISHU

LEDA
Very beautiful large flowers with ruffled
mauve-pink petals, flared and shot through
with darker veins, giving depth of colour
and fragile-seeming texture. The flowers are
held well above shiny dark green leaves.
DAPHNIS (D-308) USA
SEMI-DOUBLE PINK
FRAGRANT
EARLY MID
90 CM / 3 FT
AVAILABLE IN EUROPE NZ USA

LUOYANG HONG (LUOYANG RED)
Large flowers up to 25 cm /10 in wide. Red
petals symmetrically arranged around a
yellow centre.
CHINA
DOUBLE RED
MID
UP TO 300 CM / UP TO 10 FT
AVAILABLE IN EUROPE USA

LYDIA FOOTE
A modern classic bred from *P. rockii*.
Perfectly formed rosettes of white petals
with flares at their bases like crimson brush

marks, carried well on a vigorous plant.
SIR PETER SMITHERS, SWITZERLAND 1978
SEMI-DOUBLE TO DOUBLE WHITE
MID
TO 150 CM / TO 5 FT
AVAILABLE IN FRANCE

MADAME ANDRE DE VILLERS

Wonderfully strong and free flowering.
Great big, long lasting, very double flowers
with rose-red, satin-textured petals.
A RIVIÈRE, FRANCE 1955
DOUBLE RED
EARLY
TO 120 CM / TO 4 FT
AVAILABLE IN FRANCE USA

MAGNIFICENT FLOWER *see* HANA-DAIJIN

MARCHIONESS

A very dramatic peony with rounded
apricot-yellow petals suffused with rose.
Dark red flares give shadowy depths at the
centre, around a large tuft of yellow
stamens. Vigorous, free flowering.
SAUNDERS, USA 1942
SINGLE APRICOT
EARLY MID
UP TO 120 CM / UP TO 4 FT
AVAILABLE IN FRANCE NZ USA

MINISTER OF FLOWERS *see* HANA DAIJIN

MONTROSE *see* KAMADA-FUJI

NANIWA BROCADE *see* NANIWA-NISHIKI

NANIWA-NISHIKI (NANIWA BROCADE)

One of the best. Bright rose red petals
enlivened with white rims and radiating
stripes. Golden stamens. Strong, very free
flowering.
JAPAN PRE-1929
SEMI-DOUBLE ROSE
EARLY
UP TO 120 CM / UP TO 4 FT
AVAILABLE IN EUROPE JAPAN UK USA

NIIGATA TEN'NYO-NOMAI (HEAVENLY DANCE)

Soft rose-pink petals, gradually paling
towards lightly ruffled margins. Darker
veining gives depth of colour and an
appearance of fragility. Well poised flowers,
leaves with a blueish bloom. Vigorous.
JAPAN
SEMI-DOUBLE PINK
LATE MID
90 CM /3 FT
AVAILABLE IN FRANCE JAPAN USA

NUMBER ONE SCHOLAR'S RED *see*
ZHUNAG YUAN HONG

❦ *PAEONIA LUTEA* VAR. *LUDLOWII*
(*P. DELAVAYI* VAR. LUDLOWII).

It is now thought likely that *P. lutea* and *ludlowii* are yellow-flowered varieties of the red *P. delavayi*. They are described with the other wild species in Chapter 1. *P. ludlowii* makes a fine shrub for large informal gardens. It flowers very well in New Zealand.

DISCOVERED BY LUDLOW AND SHERIFF, TIBET 1936

SINGLE YELLOW

EARLY

UP TO 250 CM / UP TO 8 FT

AVAILABLE IN EUROPE NZ UK USA

PAEONIA ROCKII (*P. SUFFRUTICOSA* SUBSP. *ROCKII*, 'JOSEPH ROCK', 'ROCK'S VARIETY')

Rare, beautiful and much sought after, this peony's story is told on page 99. A classic flower with two symmetrical rows of petals, sometimes with a faint blush on opening, but soon becoming pure white. At the base of each petal a flare of deepest, velvety black-purple is edged with delicate crimson rays.

DISCOVERED BY ROCK, CHINA 1926

SINGLE TO SEMI-DOUBLE WHITE

EARLY

UP TO 200 CM / UP TO 6 FT 6 IN

AVAILABLE IN EUROPE NZ USA

PHOENIX WHITE *see* FEN DAN BAI

QING LONG WO MO CHI (GREEN DRAGON LYING IN A POOL OF BLACK INK/ON A CHINESE INKSTONE)

Dark green bases to the petals and green carpels represent the dragon. Dark magenta-purple petals with even darker flares are the black ink.

CHINA

SEMI-DOUBLE PURPLE

FRAGRANT

MID

300 CM / 10 FT

AVAILABLE IN UK USA

RED FORTRESS *see* ZHU SHA LEI

REINE ELIZABETH

A great survivor, going strong after 150 years. Jean-Luc Rivière considers it the best pink tree peony. Very large flowers, vivid pink suffused with flame, well presented on a free-flowering, vigorous plant.

UNKNOWN ORIGIN PRE-1846

DOUBLE PINK

MID

200 CM / 6 FT 6 IN

AVAILABLE IN JAPAN FRANCE NZ

RENKAKU (FLIGHT OF CRANES)

One of the most reliable white tree peonies, and one of the loveliest. Flowering profusely on a shrub broader than it is tall.

JAPAN 1931

Paeonia rockii

SEMI-DOUBLE WHITE
EARLY
100 CM / 3 FT
AVAILABLE IN EUROPE NZ UK USA

RICH RED FIREPLACE *see* SHENG DAN
LU

RINPO (RIMPO, BIRD OF RINPO, SACRED
BIRD)
Rich mauve-magenta flowers, well formed
with the creamy-yellow centre clearly
visible, held on strong stems.
JAPAN PRE-1926
SEMI-DOUBLE TO DOUBLE PURPLE
FRAGRANT
EARLY
UP TO 120 CM / UP TO 4 FT
AVAILABLE IN EUROPE JAPAN USA

ROCK'S VARIETY *see*
P. ROCKII

ROMAN GOLD
Bright yellow petals with dark red flares.
Substantial shrubs in quite a short time.
Free flowering. Lemon scent.
SAUNDERS, USA 1941
SINGLE YELLOW
FRAGRANT
MID
110 CM / 3 FT 10 IN
AVAILABLE IN JAPAN NZ USA

SACRED BIRD *see* RINPO

SAVAGE SPLENDOUR
Strange, dramatic colouring: purple edging
and veins on an ivory ground with gold
overtones and very dark flares at the base of
each ruffled and twisted petal.
SAUNDERS, USA 1950
SINGLE CREAM, PURPLE
MID
120 CM / 4 FT
AVAILABLE IN NZ USA

SEVEN GODS OF FORTUNE *see*
SHICHIFUKUJIN

SHAN HU TAI (CORAL TERRACE)
Pinked and ruffled petals are cupped
around yellow stamens to form 20 cm / 8 in
upward-facing flowers of intense coral pink
at the heart, paling at the margins.
CHINA
SEMI-DOUBLE TO DOUBLE PINK
FRAGRANT
MID
180 CM TO 250 CM / 6 FT TO 8 FT
AVAILABLE IN CHINA USA

SHENG DAN LU (TAOIST STOVE FILLED
WITH THE PILLS OF IMMORTALITY, LE
NOEL VERT)
Very large (up to 25 cm / 10 in) crimson-
pink flowers with a dome of small petals

held in a bowl of larger petals of the same
colour. The leaves are also on a grand scale.
CHINA
DOUBLE CRIMSON
LATE
UP TO 300 CM / UP TO 10 FT
AVAILABLE IN CANADA FRANCE

SHICHI-FUKUJIN (SITIFUKUJIN, SEVEN GODS OF FORTUNE)

A reliable variety with very large, shapely
flowers, warm satin pink paling at the
margins.
JAPAN 1896
SEMI-DOUBLE PINK
MID
UP TO 120 CM / UP TO 4 FT
AVAILABLE IN FRANCE JAPAN UK

SHIMA-DAIJIN *see* HANA-DAIJIN

One of the hardiest. Plenty of well-formed
purple-red flowers.
JAPAN
SEMI-DOUBLE PURPLE
EARLY
120 CM / 4 FT
AVAILABLE IN JAPAN NZ USA

SMILING IN THE THICKETS *see* CONG ZHONG XIAO

SNOW-CLAD FUJI *see* FUJI-NO-MINE

P. X *LEMOINEI* SOUVENIR DE MAXIME CORNU SYN. KINKAKU

P. lutea x 'La Ville de Saint Denis'. Absolutely
stunning flowers, huge, very double with
ruffled and pinked petals delicately edged
with orangey-pink and shaded with buff:
soft, peachy overall effect. The heavy heads
tend to droop but you can't have
everything.
HENRY, FRANCE 1907
DOUBLE YELLOW
FRAGRANT
LATE
UP TO 120 CM / UP TO 4 FT
AVAILABLE IN FRANCE JAPAN NZ USA UK

SUN AND MOON BROCADE *see* JITSU GETSUNISHIKI

SUPREME PINK *see* FENG ZHONG GUAN

SWEET SEVENTEEN *see* HOKI

TAMA-SUDARE (JEWELLED SCREEN)

Very large white flowers with golden-yellow
centres. Strong plants with crimson-flushed
leaves. Free flowering.
JAPAN
SEMI-DOUBLE WHITE
FRAGRANT
EARLY
120 CM / 4 FT
AVAILABLE IN FRANCE UK USA JAPAN

P. x *lemoinei* 'Souvenir de Maxime Cornu'

TAOIST STOVE FILLED WITH THE PILLS
OF IMMORTALITY *see* SHENG DAN LU

THUNDERBOLT
Black-crimson glossy petals and pretty, fine-
cut foliage, but the stems can be too weak
for the flower heads. Free flowering.
SAUNDERS, USA 1948
SINGLE DARK RED
MID
110 CM / 3 FT 10 IN
AVAILABLE IN FRANCE JAPAN USA

TRIA
A star among the many good yellows. Large,
crinkled flowers are carried three to a stem
and open in succession. Their bright, pure
yellow fades and softens as the flowers age.
Attractive, delicate leaves. Longest flowering
season.
DAPHNIS (D-3) USA
SINGLE YELLOW
EARLY TO MID
90 CM / 3 FT
AVAILABLE IN EUROPE JAPAN NZ USA

TSUKISEKAI *see* GESSEKAI

VALSE DE VIENNE
Unusual and beautiful. Soft, clear pink
petals, ragged and crumpled like those of a
parrot tulip are cupped around golden
stamens. Free flowering and in flower for a

long time.
RIVIERE, FRANCE 1983
SINGLE PINK
MID
90 CM / 3 FT
AVAILABLE IN FRANCE

WHITE PHOENIX *see* FEN DAN BAI

WHITE-TAILED LION *see* HANUOSHISI

WISTERIA AT KAMADA *see* KAMADA-FUJI

YACHI-YO-TSUBAKI (ETERNAL CAMELLIA)
Generally agreed to be one of the best and
most reliable. Symmetrical flowers with
smooth, silky petals, clear pink with a touch
of coral, are set off by beautiful, fine-cut
leaves overlaid with smoky bronze. Free
flowering.
JAPAN PRE-1931
SEMI-DOUBLE PINK
EARLY
120 CM / 4 FT
AVAILABLE IN FRANCE JAPAN NZ UK USA

YAE ZAKURA (HOST OF THE CHERRY
BLOSSOM)
Shapely flowers, pure pink with a hint of
blue, are very large but not out of
proportion as they are born on a substantial
shrub.
JAPAN PRE-1931

Yachi Yo-Tsubaki

SEMI-DOUBLE PINK

EARLY

150 CM / 5 FT

AVAILABLE IN FRANCE JAPAN NZ UK USA

YAO HUANG (YAO'S YELLOW, YAO'S FAMILY YELLOW)

Said to be over a thousand years old and still worth growing. Tightly-packed clear lemon petals form a very large globe on a base of larger guard petals. The colour fades to cream.

CHINA PRE-1831

DOUBLE YELLOW

MID

UP TO 300 CM / UP TO 10 FT

AVAILABLE IN GERMANY JAPAN UK USA

ZHI HONG

Loosely double, scented flowers with light scarlet-red crinkled petals are held upright on a strong, fast-growing plant. Good in shade.

CHINA

DOUBLE RED

FRAGRANT

MID

180 CM TO 250 CM / 6 FT TO 8 FT

AVAILABLE IN CHINA USA

ZHU SHA LEI (CINNABAR RAMPARTS, RED FORTRESS)

Small, deep crimson-pink flowers with darker shading at the centre, on a dense, compact shrub.

CHINA

SEMI-DOUBLE PINK

FRAGRANT

EARLY

120 CM / 4 FT

AVAILABLE IN CANADA EUROPE JAPAN UK USA

ZHUANG YUAN HONG (ORIGINAL RED, NUMBER ONE SCHOLAR'S RED, 'LE MANOIR ROUGE')

Large scarlet-red petals symmetrically arranged. Big, leafy plants.

CHINA

DOUBLE RED

VERY FRAGRANT

MID

UP TO 250 CM / UP TO 8 FT

AVAILABLE IN CANADA FRANCE JAPAN

ZI LAN KUI

Huge lavender-pink globes of ruffled petals, upward facing on a strong, vigorous plant. Light scent.

CHINA

DOUBLE BLUE-PINK

FRAGRANT

MID

180 CM TO 250 CM / 6 FT TO 8 FT

AVAILABLE IN CANADA CHINA UK USA

INTERSECTIONAL OR ITOH HYBRIDS

BARTZELLA

Each plant has up to sixty large, open-faced flowers in a soft shade of yellow. Free flowering, long in flower.

ANDERSON, USA 1986

DOUBLE YELLOW

FRAGRANT

MID

UP TO 120 CM / UP TO 4 FT

AVAILABLE IN GERMANY HOLLAND NZ USA

CALLIE'S MEMORY

Light apricot and cream flowers with maroon flares.

ANDERSON, USA

SEMI-DOUBLE APRICOT

MID

90 CM / 3 FT

AVAILABLE IN GERMANY NZ USA

CANARY BRILLIANTS

Small to medium sized light to dark yellow flowers. Some scent.

DOUBLE YELLOW

SLIGHTLY FRAGRANT

MID

90 CM / 3 FT

AVAILABLE IN GERMANY HOLLAND NZ USA

CORA LOUISE

Palest lavender fading to white, dark lavender flares. Dark green leaves on a strong plant.

ANDERSON, USA 1986

DOUBLE SEMI-DOUBLE WHITE

MID TO LATE

90 CM / 3 FT

AVAILABLE IN NZ USA

COURT JESTER

Small, apricot-yellow single flowers with red flares.

Anderson, USA

single yellow

mid

90 cm / 3 ft

available in USA

FIRST ARRIVAL

Lavender-pink flowers fading as they age. Free flowering.

ANDERSON, USA 1986

DOUBLE TO SEMI-DOUBLE PINK

FRAGRANT

LATE MID

90 CM / 3 FT

AVAILABLE IN GERMANY HOLLAND NZ USA

*GARDEN TREASURE
'Alice Harding' x *P. lactiflora*. Large, bright
yellow flowers with small red flares.
Luxuriant foliage.
HOLLINGSWORTH, USA 1984
SEMI-DOUBLE YELLOW
MID TO LATE
75 CM / 2 FT 6 IN
AVAILABLE IN GERMANY USA

HILLARY
Medium-sized cream flowers which are
suffused with red.
DOUBLE RED/YELLOW
MID
90 CM / 3 FT
AVAILABLE IN GERMANY HOLLAND NZ USA

JULIA ROSE
Small, red-orange flowers fading to yellow.
ANDERSON, USA
SINGLE RED/YELLOW
MID
90 CM / 3 FT
AVAILABLE IN NZ USA

KOPPER KETTLE
Small, reddish-yellow and orange flowers.
SINGLE TO SEMI-DOUBLE RED
MID
250 CM / 8 FT
AVAILABLE IN USA

LEMON DREAM
Large, semi-double yellow flowers but
sometimes half lavender.
SEMI-DOUBLE YELLOW
MID
120 CM / 4 FT
AVAILABLE IN USA

LOLLIPOP
Large yellow flowers marked with a few red
stripes.
SEMI-DOUBLE TO DOUBLE RED/YELLOW
MID
90 CM / 3 FT
AVAILABLE IN HOLLAND USA

MORNING LILAC
Medium sized, fuchia-pink flowers.
SINGLE PINK
MID
90 CM / 3 FT
AVAILABLE IN GERMANY HOLLAND NZ USA

NORWEGIAN BLUSH
Large, white, single flowers flushed with
pink.
ANDERSON, USA
SINGLE WHITE/PINK
MID
90 CM / 3 FT
AVAILABLE IN GERMANY NORWAY USA

PASTEL SPLENDOR
Large, white single flowers, red flares
and white stamens.
SINGLE WHITE
MID
90 CM / 3 FT
AVAILABLE IN GERMANY NZ SWITZERLAND
USA

SCARLET HEAVEN
Small, red flowers.
SINGLE RED

MID
90 CM / 3 FT
AVAILABLE IN GERMANY HOLLAND NZ USA

SEQUESTERED SUNSHINE
Small, yellow, single flowers on a plant that
is slightly taller than average.
ANDERSON, USA
SINGLE YELLOW
MID
120 CM / 4 FT
AVAILABLE IN USA

Age of Gold

TREE PEONIES - GENERAL LIST

AKASHIGATA Japan semi-double magenta pink mid
120 to 150 cm/4 ft to 5 ft available in Japan UK Germany

ALHAMBRA Saunders USA 1948 semi-double yellow mid
120 cm/4 ft available in France Germany NZ USA

ALICE IN WONDERLAND Reath USA 1995 semi-double yellow
late 100 cm/3 ft 6 in, available in USA

ALICE PALMER Kelway UK semi-double mauve pink mid
120 cm/4 ft available in UK

AMATEUR FOREST Rivière France 1935 semi-double mauve-pink
mid 120 cm/4 ft available in France

AMBER MOON Saunders USA 1948 single yellow mid
120 cm/4 ft available in USA

ANGELET Saunders USA 1950 single yellow and pink mid
120 cm/4 ft available in Germany Japan USA

ANNA MARIE Seidl 1984 single lavender-pink late-mid
100 cm/3 ft 6 in, available in USA

APHRODITE Daphnis USA D-33 double white late-mid
50 cm/20 in, available in USA

ARASHI YAMA Japan double pink mid 120 cm / 4 ft available in
France

ARCADIA Saunders USA 1941 single yellow mid 100 cm/3 ft 6 in,
available in USA

ARGOSY Saunders USA 1928 single yellow mid 90 cm /3 ft
available in USA

ARIADNE Daphnis USA D-304 semi-double peach and rose mid
100 cm / 3 ft 6 in, available in USA

TOP Alice Palmer

ABOVE Argosy

ARTEMIS Daphnis USA D-14 S yellow mid 110 cm/3 ft 10 in,
available in Germany NZ USA

ASA (god of Japan) Japan double white early 110 cm/3 ft 10 in,
available in Japan USA

ASAHI-MINATO Japan semi-double red mid 150 cm/5 ft available
in Japan NZ

ASAHI NO-SORA (sky at sunrise) Japan 1896 semi-double pink
early 75 cm/2 ft 6 in, available in France Japan

AURORA Daphnis USA semi-double yellow mid 100 cm/3 ft 6 in,
available in USA

BAI YU (white jade) China double white scented mid up to
120 cm/4 ft available in Germany Japan UK USA

BARONNE D'ALES Gombault France double pink mid 90 cm/3 ft
available in France Germany

BEAUTE DE TWICKEL Europe double crimson 60 cm/2 ft available
in Switzerland Germany

BEAUTIFUL PURPLE SCARF *see* GE JIN SI

BELLE D'ORLEANS France double mauve-pink mid 120 cm/4 ft
available in France Germany

BEST BLACK JADE *see* GUAN SHI MO YU

BLACK DRAGON HOLDS A SPLENDID FLOWER *see* WU LONG
PENG SHENG

BLACK FLOWER KING *see* HE I HUA KUI

BLANCHE DE HIS *see* HISIANA ALBA

CANARY Saunders USA single yellow mid 120 cm/4 ft available
in USA

CARNEA PLENA France double pale pink mid 120 cm/4 ft available
in France

CHOJURAKU Japan semi-double pink mid 120 cm/4 ft available in
France Japan NZ

CHRYSANTHEMUM PEONY *see* KIKUBOTAN

COILED DRAGON IN THE MIST GRASPING A PURPLE PEARL
see YAN LONG ZI ZHU PAN

CORONAL Saunders USA 1948 semi-double yellow mid
100 cm/3 ft 4 in, available in NZ USA Germany

COUCHER DE SOLEIL *see* HIGURASHI

CROWN OF PURPLE JADE *see* GUAN SHI MO YU

DA JIN FEN (gold dusted pink) China semi-double pink scented
early up to 120 cm/4 ft

DAFFODIL Saunders USA 1948 semi-double yellow mid 90 cm/3 ft
available in Japan USA

DA YE HU DIE (great winged buttefly) China semi-double red and
white flowers on the same plant scented mid 120 cm/4 ft
available in USA

DEEPEST INK *see* SUMINOICHI

DOU LU (pea green) China double green turning white late
120 cm/4 ft available in Japan UK USA Germany

DUCHESS OF KENT Kelway UK semi-double pink mid
150 cm/5 ft free flowering

DUSK *see* HIGURE

EMPEROR'S CROWN *see* TEIKAN

ER QUIAO (two Qiaou sisters, twin beauties) China double half
pink half red scented mid 250 cm/8 ft available in Japan USA

EUGENE VERDIER Sénéclauze France double mauve-pink mid
120 cm/4 ft available in France

FALSE PURPLE SCARF *see* JIA GE JIN ZI

FAYTH Fay-Reath USA 1994 semi-double pink Early
90 cm/3 ft available in USA

FEI YAN HONG ZHUANG (flying swallow in red, geese in red sky)
China double red scented mid up to 120 cm/4 ft available in UK

FIRE THAT MAKES THE PILLS OF IMMORTALITY *see* HUO LIAN
JIN DAN

FLAMBEAU Lemoine France 1930 double orange-red mid
100 cm/3 ft available in France Germany Sweden

FLORA Japan single white mid 120 cm/4 ft France

FLYING SWALLOW IN RED *see* FEI YAN HONG ZHUANG

TOP Duchess of Kent

ABOVE Ge Jin Zi (purple kudzu scarf)

FUSO NO TSUKASA (god of Japan) Japan double white early
110 cm/3 ft 10 in, available in Japan USA

FRAGRANS MAXIMA PLENA France pre-1955 semi-double to
double pink scented 120 -150 cm/4 ft to 5 ft available in France
Germany USA

GATE OF OPULENCE *see* IMPUMON

GATEWAY TO SPRING *see* KENSHUMON

GEESE IN RED SKY *see* FEI YAN HONG ZHUANG

GE JIN SI (purple kudzu scarf, beautiful purple scarf) China double
purple-pink scented early 300 cm/10 ft available in China UK
USA Germany

GENGIORAKU Japan semi-double white mid 120 cm/4 ft available
in France

GEORGES PAUL Sénéclauze France pre-1886 double purple-red
120 cm to 150 cm/4 ft to 5 ft available in France

GLISTENING SILVER PINK *see* YIN FEN JIN LIN

GOD OF JAPAN *see* FUSO NO TSUKASA

GOLD DUSTED PINK *see* DA JIN FEN

GOLD IN FIRE *see* HUO LIAN JIN DAN

GOLDEN BOWL Saunders USA 1948 single yellow mid
110 cm/3 ft 10 in, available in NZ USA

GOLDEN ISLES Saunders USA 1948 semi-double yellow mid
90 cm/3 ft available in France Japan USA

GOLDEN MANDARIN Saunders USA 1952 double yellow mid
90 cm/3 ft available in NZ USA

GOLDEN VANITIE Saunders USA 1960 single yellow mid
100 cm/3 ft 6 in, available in Germany NZ USA

GOSHOZAKURA Japan semi-double pink mid 120 cm/4 ft available
in France Germany Japan

GREAT EMPEROR *see* TAIYO

GREAT WINGED BUTTERFLY *see* DA YE HU DIE

GUAN SHI MO YU (crown of purple jade, best black jade) China
double crimson-black scented late 120 cm to 250 cm/4 ft to 8 ft

available in UK USA Germany

GUNPODEN (temple adored with many flowers) Japan semi-double purple-pink early 120 cm/4 ft available in Japan USA Germany

HAKU-BAN-RYU (many white dragons, de nombreux dragons blancs) Japan semi-double white late 120 cm/4 ft available in France Japan NZ USA Germany

HAKUGAN Japan semi-double white early 120 cm/4 ft available in Japan UK

HAKUSHIN Japan semi-double white mid 120 cm/4 ft available in NZ Germany

HAKU-UNKAKU Japan single to semi-double palest pink almost white mid 120 cm/4 ft available in France Japan

HAPPY DAYS Saunders USA 1948 semi-double yellow and red mid 90 cm/3 ft available in France USA

HARUNO-AKEBONO (sunrise in spring) Japan semi-double very pale pink mid 120 cm/4 ft available in France Japan Germany

HARVEST Saunders USA 1948 semi-double yellow mid 90 cm/3 ft available in France USA

HATSUGARASU (1'ére couronne de l'année) Japan pre-1929 semi-double dark maroon mid 120 cm/4 ft available in Europe Japan

HEI HUA KUI (black flower king, rare black flower) China semi-double black-purple scented mid 120 cm/4 ft available in Germany UK

HIGURASHI (the cricket, coucher de soleil) Japan pre-1929 single red mid 120 cm/4 ft available in France Japan USA

HIGURE (dusk) Japan semi-double pink early 120 cm/4 ft available in NZ

HINODESEKAI (world of the rising sun) semi-double red early 60 cm/2 ft available in Japan NZ USA

HISIANA ALBA (Blanche de His) Mouchelet France semi-double white free flowering mid 120 cm/4 ft available in France Germany

HOADI Japan double pink mid 120 cm/4 ft available in Japan NZ

HORAKUMON (invitation to abundant pleasure) Japan semi-double

Hoadi

purple late 120 cm/4 ft available in Japan China

HU HONG (Hu's red) China semi-double to double red scented
mid 120 cm/4 ft available in USA UK

HUO LIAN JIN DAN (fire that makes the pills of immortality, gold
in fire) China semi-double red very early
180 cm to 250 cm/6 to 8 ft available in Japan UK USA

ICARUS Daphnis USA D-254 single scarlet scented mid
100 cm/3 ft available in USA

ICE STORM Smithers Switzerland 1989 single white mid
120 cm/4 ft France

IMITATION OF JIN'S PURPLE *see* JIA GE JIN ZI

IMMORTAL LION *see* YACHIYO JISHI

IMPUMON (gate of opulence) Japan semi-double red mid
60 cm/2 ft available in Japan

INFANTA Saunders USA 1948 single white mid 90 cm/3 ft available
in USA

INVITATION TO ABUNDANT PLEASURE *see* HORAKUMON

IPHIGENIA Daphnis USA D-303 single red mid 90 cm/3 ft available
in NZ USA Germany

IWATO-KAGAMI (sacred mirror) Japan semi-double pink early
120 cm/4 ft available in Japan USA

JEANNE D'ARC Sénéclauze France pre 1889 double pink scented
mid 120 cm/4 ft available in Europe

JEWELLED LOTUS *see* TAMA FUYO

JIA GEN JIN ZI (imitation of Jin's purple, false purple scarf) China
double magenta mid 90 cm/3 ft available in Japan UK

KENREIMON (gate of Kenrei) Japan semi-double purple-red mid
120 cm / 4 ft available in Japan

KENSHUNMON (gateway to spring, porte de printemps) Japan
semi-double white and purple mid 120 cm/4 ft available in
France Japan

KIKUBOTAN (chrysanthemum peony) Japan pre-1919 semi-double
pink mid 120 cm/4 ft available in France

Jia Gen Jin Zi (false purple kudzu scarf)

KING OF PEONIES *see* YO-YO-NO-HOMARE

KINPUKURIN (gold-encrusted, incrustation d'or) Japan single red mid 120 cm to 150 cm/4 ft to 5 ft available in France Japan

KOCK'S WEISS syn. 'Weiss' double white mid 120 cm to 150 cm/ 4 ft to 5 ft available in France Germany

KOKAMON Japan semi-double red mid 120 cm/4 ft available in Germany Japan NZ USA

KOSHINO-YUKI Japan semi-double white mid up to 120 cm/4 ft available in Germany Japan UK

KRONOS Daphnis USA D-23 semi-double red mid 90 cm/3 ft available in Germany NZ USA

LA LORRAINE Lemoine France 1913 double apricot yellow mid 120 cm to 150 cm /4 ft to 5 ft available in France Japan

LACTEA David or Guérin 1839 double white mid 90 cm/3 ft available in France Germany

LAMBERTIANA Makoy double mauve mid 120 cm/4 ft available in France

LOUISE MOUCHELET Mouchelet France 1860 double pink mid 120 cm to 150 cm/4 ft to 5 ft available in France

MADAME EMILE JOUBERT Rivière France 1990 double pink mid 120 cm/4 ft available in France

MADAME LOUIS HENRY Henry France 1907 single pink mid 150 cm/5 ft available in France

MADAME VICTOR GILLIER France 1899 double pink mid 120 cm to 150 cm/4 ft to 5 ft available in France

MAJOR HOWELL semi-double pale mauve pink mid 120 cm/4 ft available in France

MANY WHITE DRAGONS *see* HAKU BAN RYU

MARIE LAURENCIN Daphnis USA D-24 semi-double lavender mid 75 cm/2 ft 6 in, available in USA Germany

MINE D'OR Lemoine France 1943 single yellow scented mid 120 cm/4 ft available in France Germany Sweden

MIZUKAGE (silhouette reflected on water) Rivière from Japan 1902 single pink mid 120 cm/4 ft available in France

MONSIEUR ANTOINE RIVIERE Rivière France 1985 single mauve-pink mid 120 cm/4 ft available in France

MRS SHIRLEY FRY Kelway UK single or semi-double white mid 120 cm/4 ft available in UK

MRS WILLIAM KELWAY Kelway UK semi-double cream mid 120 cm/4 ft available in UK

MUREGARSHU Japan semi-double purple-red mid 70 cm/2 ft 4 in available in Switzerland Germany

MYSTERY Saunders USA 1948 single to semi-double lavender, crimson mid 90 cm/3 ft available in France USA Japan NZ

NEW HEAVEN AND EARTH *see* SHINTENCHI

NIKE Daphnis D-368 single peach, mid up to 150 cm/5 ft USA

NIHONK (rose of Japan) Japan semi-double pink mid 120 cm/4 ft available in France

OFUJINISHIKI *see* 'Shimane chojuraku'

ORION Saunders USA 1948 semi-double yellow early mid 90 cm/3 ft USA

✡ *PAEONIA DELAVAYI* China single red mid 180 cm/6 ft available in China Europe Japan USA

PAEONIA POTANINI VAR. *TROLLIOIDES* single yellow 18 cm/9 in China Japan USA

PALACE OF GEMS *see* SHUGYOKUDEN

PALACE OF PURPLE SHADOWS *see* SHIUNDEN

PEA GREEN *see* DOU LU

PERSEPHONE Daphnis USA D-26 semi-double cream mid 90 cm/3 ft USA Germany

PHAEDRA Daphnis USA semi-double maroon red scented mid 120 cm/4 ft available in USA

PLUTO Daphnis USA semi-double red scented mid available in NZ

PORTE DE PRINTEMPS *see* KENSHUNMON

PRIDE OF TAISHO DYNASTY *see* TAISHO-NO-HOKORI

PRINCESS Saunders USA 1941 single pink/gold mid 90 cm/3 ft

TOP Mrs William Kelway

ABOVE *Paeonia delavayi*

Japan available in USA

PURPLE HEMP SCARF *see* GE JIN SI

QING SHAN GUAN XUE (the green mountain falls in love with the snow) China double white and pink mid 150 cm/5 ft available in France USA

RAPHAEL Kelway UK semi-double pink mid 120 cm/4 ft available in UK

RARE BLACK FLOWER *see* HEI HUA KUI

REDON Daphnis USA D-21 S pink mid 75 cm/2 ft 6 in available in NZ USA Germany

REINE DES VIOLETTES Fortune China 1840s double purple mid 120 cm/4 ft available in France Switzerland Germany

REINE DU PORTUGAL double purple red mid 70 cm/2 ft 4 in, available in Switzerland

RENOWN Saunders USA 1949 single red early mid 110 cm/3 ft 6 in available in USA

RIGHT ROYAL Saunders USA 1952 semi-double cream and pink mid 90 cm/3 ft available in USA

RUFFLED SUNSET Reath USA 1994 semi-double yellow-red mid 110 cm/3 ft 6 in, available in USA

SACRED MIRROR *see* IWATO-KAGAMI

SANG LORRAINE Lemoine France 1939 semi-double red scented late 120 cm/4 ft available in France

SATIN ROUGE Lemoine France 1926 double red mid 120 cm/4 ft available in France Germany Sweden

SAYGIO-SAKURA Japan semi-double red mid 120 cm/4 ft available in France

SHIMANE CHOJURAKU syn 'Ofujinishiki' Japan single or semi-double lavender-pink mid 120 cm/4 ft available in France Japan UK

SHINTENCHI (new heaven and earth) Japan pre-1931 single pink early 90 cm/3 ft available in Japan NZ USA

SHIUNDEN (palace of purple shadows, palais du nuage pourpre)

Japan double purple mid 120 cm/4 ft available in France Japan
Germany

SHIVUNANOBORI Japan single purple mid 120 cm/4 ft available in
France

SHUGYOKUDEN (palace of gems) Japan semi-double red mid
120 cm/4 ft available in France Germany Japan UK

SILHOUETTE REFLECTED ON WATER *see* MIZUKAGE

SILVER PINK WITH GOLD SCALES *see* YIN FEN JIN LIN

SILVER SAILS Saunders USA 1940 single yellow mid
111 cm/3 ft 6 in available in Germany NZ USA

SKY AT SUNRISE *see* ASAHI NO-SORA

LE SOLEIL *see* TAIYO

SOUVENIR DE DUCHER France double violet scented mid
150 cm/5 ft available in France Germany

SOUVENIR DE MADAME KNORR Van Houtte France 1853 double
pink mid 120 cm to 150 cm/4 ft to 5 ft available in France
Germany

SPRING CARNIVAL Saunders USA 1944 single yellow and pink
mid 120 cm/4 ft available in France

STOLEN HEAVEN Smirnow semi-double white early 150 cm/5 ft
available in USA

STRAWBERRY DELIGHT Reath USA 1997 double strawberry red
mid 100 cm/3 ft 4 in available in Germany USA

SUISHO HAKU Japan semi-double white early 120 cm/4 ft available
in NZ USA

SUMINO-ICHI (deepest ink) Japan semi-double black-red mid
120 cm/4 ft Germany Japan UK

SUMMER NIGHT Saunders USA 1949 semi-double pink and
yellow late 100 cm/3 ft available in NZ USA

SUNRISE Reath USA 1995 semi-double yellow and pink mid
120 cm/4 ft available in USA

SUNRISE IN SPRING *see* HARUNO AKEBONO

SUPERB Kelway UK semi-double red mid 120 cm/4 ft available in UK

Sumino-ichi

SURPRISE Lemoine France 1920 double yellow and pink mid 120 cm/4 ft available in France

SYLPHIDE Riviére France 1992 single rose-pink mid 90 cm/3 ft available in France.

TAISHO-NO-HOKORI (pride of Taishow dynasty) Japan 1936 semi-double to double red mid 150 cm/5 ft available in France Japan UK USA

TAIYO (great emperor, le soleil) Japan pre-1931 single to semi-double red early 120 cm/4 ft available in France Germany Japan NZ USA

TAMAFUYO (jewelled lotus) Japan pre-1919 semi-double pink fading to white early 120 cm/4 ft available in France Germany Japan UK USA

TEIKAN (emperor's crown, crown of the Mikado) Japan semi-double pink mid 120 cm/4 ft available in France Germany Japan NZ USA

TEMPLE ADORNED WITH MANY FLOWERS *see* GUNPODEN

TEN'I Japan semi-double blush early 150 cm/5 ft available in Germany Japan USA

THE CRICKET *see* HIGURASHI

THEMIS Daphnis USA semi-double pink early mid 90 cm/3 ft available in NZ USA

TIGER TIGER Saunders USA 1948 single red mid 120 cm/4 ft available in USA

TRIOMPHE DE VAN DER MAELAN Van der Maelen 1849 double pink mid 150 cm/5 ft available in France Germany

VESUVIAN Saunders USA 1948 double red weak stems early mid 75 cm/2 ft 6 in, available in NZ USA

WAUCEDAH PRINCESS Reath USA 1994 semi-double pink mid 110 cm/3 ft 10 in, available in NZ USA

WHITE JADE *see* BAI YU

WILHELMINE double red mid 150 cm/5 ft available in France Germany

WU LONG PENG SHENG (black dragon holds a splendid flower, precious offering from the black snake) China double red scented late 300 cm/10 ft available in Canada China France Japan UK

XU TA China double white free flowering mid to 70 cm/2 ft 4 in, available in USA

YACHIYOJISHI (immortal lion) Japan semi-double to double pale pink free flowering mid 150 cm/5 ft available in France Japan

YAN LONG ZI ZHU PAN (coiled dragon in the list grasping a purple pearl, plate of smokey purple pearl) China double maroon scented late 120 cm/4 ft available in China USA

YATSUKA JISHI Japan semi-double pink mid 70 cm/2ft 4 in, available in Switzerland

YIN FEN JIN LIN (silver pink with gold scales) China double pink scented mid 120 cm/4 ft available in Japan UK

YING LUO BAO ZHU (necklace of precious pearls) China double red-pink scented late 120 cm/4 ft available in China France Germany Japan USA

YOYO-NO-HOMARE (king of peonies) Japan double red-pink mid 120 cm/4 ft available in France Japan

ZENOBIA syn. ALEXANDRE de HUMBOLT double violet red mid 90 cm/3 ft available in France Germany

ZEPHYRUS Daphnis USA D-204 semi-double lavender mid 90 cm/3 ft available in NZ USA

ZHAOFEN (Zhao's pink) China single semi-double and double together on same plant pink late 250 cm/8 ft available in China France Japan UK USA

INTERSECTIONAL HYBRIDS
GENERAL LIST

BORDER CHARM Hollingsworth USA 1984 single to semi-double
yellow late mid 60 cm / 2 ft available in USA

HIDDEN TREASURE Seidl 1989 single or semi-double yellow mid
50 cm /1 ft 8in available in USA

LITTLE DARLIN Anderson USA 1986 single pink mid
50 cm /1 ft 8 in available in available in NZ USA

PRAIRIE CHARM Hollingsworth USA 1992 semi-double yellow very
early 75 cm / 2 ft 6 in available in Germany USA

ROSE FANTASY Seidl USA 1989 single pink mid 70 cm /2 ft 4 in
available in USA

SCARLET HEAVEN Anderson USA single red 70 cm /2 ft 4 in
available in NZ USA

TINGE OF YELLOW Anderson USA 1992 double or semi-double
mid 70 cm / 2 ft 4 in available in USA

VIKING FULL MOON Pehrson-Seidl USA 1989 semi-double yellow
early 75 cm / 2 ft 6 in available in USA

WHITE EMPEROR Seidl USA 1989 semi-double white early
75 cm /2 ft 6 in

YELLOW CROWN Itoh-Smirnow USA 1974 semi-double yellow
mid 90 cm / 3 ft available in USA

YELLOW DREAM Itoh-Smirnow USA 1974 semi-double yellow
scented mid 90 cm / 3 ft available in USA

YELLOW EMPEROR Itoh-Smirnow USA 1974 semi-double yellow
scented mid 90 cm /3 ft available in Switzerland USA

YELLOW HEAVEN -Smirnow USA 1974 semi-double yellow
scented mid 60 cm / 2 ft available in USA

HERBACEOUS PEONIES

KEY:

PLANT NAME IN BOLD TYPE = highly recommended.

* = American Peony Society Gold Medal

♉ = RHS Award of Garden Merit

Note unless otherwise described, the tree peonies listed here are lactiflora cultivars.

ALBERT CROUSSE

Very free flowering with full, flat flowers on strong stems.

CROUSSE, FRANCE 1893

DOUBLE PINK

FRAGRANT

LATE

95 CM / 3 FT 2 IN

AVAILABLE IN EUROPE CANADA UK USA

ALEXANDER FLEMING *see* DOCTOR ALEXANDER FLEMING

AMA-NO-SODE

Huge (up to 22 cm / 9 in) showy, mauve-pink flowers, apricot-yellow centre. Vigorous, free flowering.

JAPAN, PRE-1928

JAPANESE PINK, YELLOW

EARLY

110 CM /3 FT 10 IN

AVAILABLE IN CANADA

*AMERICA

Improved form of 'Burma Ruby' with large, deep, brilliant scarlet petals surrounding a boss of yellow stamens. Compact foliage.

RUDOLPH, USA 1976

SINGLE RED

EARLY TO MID

90 CM / 3 FT

AVAILABLE IN CANADA NZ UK USA

ANGEL CHEEKS

A tightly packed bomb of pale but glowing flesh pink, separated from paler guard petals by a narrow collar of pale yellow.

KLEHM, USA

DOUBLE PINK

FRAGRANT

MID

65 CM / 2 FT 2 IN

AVAILABLE IN CANADA JAPAN NZ UK USA

ARABIAN PRINCE

Deep crimson with a ring of gold stamens around the inner petals. Good autumn colour. Free flowering.

KELWAY, UK

SEMI-DOUBLE RED

VERY FRAGRANT

MID TO LATE

97 CM / 3 FT 3 IN

AVAILABLE IN UK

ASA GRAY

Strongly-scented, deep rose-pink flowers.
Free flowering.

CROUSSE, FRANCE 1886

DOUBLE PINK

VERY FRAGRANT

LATE MID

86 CM /2 FT 10 IN

AVAILABLE IN CANADA FRANCE NZ UK

AUGUSTE DESSERT

Rounded, clear pink petals pale to silvery
white at the margins. Good autumn colour.
Free flowering.

DESSERT, FRANCE 1920

SEMI-DOUBLE PINK

VERY FRAGRANT

MID TO LATE

76 CM / 2 FT 6 IN

AVAILABLE IN CANADA EUROPE NZ UK USA

AVANT GARDE

P. lactiflora x *P. wittmanniana* Large flowers
with pale mauve-pink petals darkening
towards the margins. Strong, dark red
stems.

LEMOINE, FRANCE 1907

SINGLE PINK

EARLY

90 CM / 3 FT

AVAILABLE IN CANADA FRANCE UK

BARONESS SCHRÖEDER

Very large globe-shaped white flowers with a
faint blush. Good cut flowers. Strong, free
flowering.

KELWAY, UK 1889

DOUBLE WHITE

FRAGRANT

MID TO LATE

90 CM / 3 FT

AVAILABLE IN NZ UK USA

BARRINGTON BELLE

Large flowers on strong stems. The central
staminoides are red or pink edged with
gold. Free flowering.

C G KLEHM, USA 1971

JAPANESE RED

MID

85 CM / 2 FT 9 IN

AVAILABLE IN CANADA FRANCE NZ USA

BIG BEN

Dark red, bomb-shaped flowers. Good cut
flowers.

AUTEN, USA 1943

DOUBLE RED

FRAGRANT

EARLY

75 CM /3 FT 6 IN

Bowl of Beauty

AVAILABLE IN USA

❦ BOWL OF BEAUTY
Anemone-flowered with wavy, cream-yellow staminoids on a saucer of bright pink guard petals.
HOOGENDOORN, HOLLAND 1949
JAPANESE PINK, CREAM
FRAGRANT
MID TO LATE
90 CM / 3 FT
AVAILABLE IN EUROPE UK USA

*BOWL OF CREAM
Very large cream-white, bowl-shaped flowers. Robust plant with bright green leaves.
C G KLEHM, USA 1963
DOUBLE WHITE
FRAGRANT
MID TO LATE
90 CM / 3 FT
AVAILABLE IN NZ UK USA

BREAK OF DAY
Magenta-pink, rose-like guard petals; darker staminoids lightly tipped with yellow.
MURAWSKA, USA 1947
JAPANESE PINK
MID
85 CM / 2 FT 9 IN
AVAILABLE IN CANADA NZ UK USA

BRIDESMAID *see* MARIE JACQUIN

BUNKER HILL
Midway between semi-double and double with rose-like crimson petals and yellow stamens. Robust. Good cut flower.
HOLLIS, USA 1906
DOUBLE RED
FRAGRANT
EARLY-MID
90 CM / 3 FT
AVAILABLE IN EUROPE UK SWEDEN

*BU-TE
'Isani-Gidui' x 'Tamate-Boku'. Large, rounded, slightly ruffled petals cupped around a mass of soft pale yellow staminoids.
WASSENBURG, USA 1954
JAPANESE WHITE
LATE
106 CM / 3 FT 8 IN
AVAILABLE IN GERMANY NZ SWEDEN SWITZERLAND USA

CHARLIE'S WHITE
Huge, bomb-shaped flowers flushed with yellow at the centre. Vigorous, tall enough for the back of the border; attractive dark green leaves. A popular cut flower, lasting well in cold storage.
C G KLEHM, USA 1951
DOUBLE WHITE

FRAGRANT

EARLY TO MID

UP TO 120 CM / UP TO 4 FT

AVAILABLE IN CANADA GERMANY NZ SWEDEN
UK USA

CHEDDAR CHARM

White guard petals around a large tuft of
golden petaloids. 'Cheddar Gold' is similar.
R KLEHM, USA 1992

JAPANESE WHITE

FRAGRANT

MID

90 CM / 3 FT

AVAILABLE IN USA

CHERRY HILL

Purplish-crimson flowers, almost double,
but open enough to show golden stamens
at the centre. Free flowering.
THURLOW, USA 1915

SEMI-DOUBLE RED

FRAGRANT

VERY EARLY

85 CM / 2 FT 9 IN

AVAILABLE IN FRANCE NZ UK USA

CHIFFON PARFAIT 'Monsieur Jules Elie' x
'President Taft'. Several globular, very full
pale pink flowers on every stem.
R KLEHM, USA 1981

DOUBLE PINK

FRAGRANT

VERY LATE

85 CM / 2 FT 9 IN

AVAILABLE IN NZ SWEDEN USA

CHOCOLATE SOLDIER

P. lactiflora x *P. officinalis*. Dark brownish-red
flowers with golden centres, usually
Japanese in form but occasional single or
double flowers appear.
AUTEN, USA 1939

JAPANESE DARK RED

EARLY

70 CM / 2 FT4IN

AVAILABLE IN FRANCE SWITZERLAND NZ UK
USA

CLAIRE DE LUNE 'Monsieur Jules Elie' x.
P. mlokosewitschii). A difficult cross. Rated
by Allan Rogers as the finest ivory-yellow
single. Rounded, slightly crinkled, cupped
petals, yolk-yellow stamens. Slender, strong
stems.
WHITE-WILD, USA 1954

SINGLE PALE YELLOW

FRAGRANT

VERY EARLY

70 CM TO 80 CM / 2 FT 4 IN TO 2 FT 6 IN

AVAILABLE IN CANADA EUROPE NZ UK USA

*CORAL CHARM

The sought after, peachy-coral colouring of
these huge, cupped flowers was achieved
comparatively recently. Deep coral buds

Claire de Lune

fade to a softer shade on opening.

WISSING, USA 1964

SEMI-DOUBLE CORAL PINK

EARLY

90 CM OR MORE / 3 FT OR MORE

AVAILABLE IN CANADA JAPAN NZ SWITZERLAND USA

CORAL SUNSET

(Lactiflora 'Minnie Shaylor'x *P. peregrina* 'Otto Froebel'. Considered by Roy Klehm to be the best coral. Prettily shaped rosettes, soft but intense colour.

WISSING-C G KLEHM, USA 1981

SEMI-DOUBLE CORAL PINK

EARLY

80 CM / 2 FT 8 IN

AVAILABLE IN NZ USA

CORNELIA SHAYLOR

Large, densely packed palest blush petals fade to white. The globe-shaped flowers are held on strong stems.

SHAYLOR, USA 1919

DOUBLE PINK

FRAGRANT

MID TO LATE

90 CM / 3 FT

AVAILABLE IN CANADA FRANCE NZ UK USA

COURONNE D'OR

A ring of narrow yellow staminoids separates an inner tuft of pale blush petals

from an outer ring of larger petals. Strong but not very pleasant scent. Vigorous, free flowering.

CALOT, FRANCE 1873

DOUBLE WHITE

FRAGRANT

MID

110 CM / 3 FT 10 IN

AVAILABLE IN CANADA EUROPE UK USA

CYTHEREA

P. lactiflora x *P. peregrina*. Large cup-shaped rose pink flowers on strong stems. Dense foliage. Long-lasting cut flower. Spreads by underground roots.

SAUNDERS, USA 1953

SEMI-DOUBLE PINK

EARLY-MID

75 CM / 2 FT 6 IN

CANADA SWITZERLAND UK USA NZ

DIANA PARKS

P. lactiflora x *P. officinalis*. Large, brilliant red flowers fade as they age. Excellent cut flowers.

BOCKSTOCE, USA 1942

DOUBLE RED

VERY FRAGRANT

EARLY TO MID

106 CM /3 FT 6 IN

AVAILABLE IN FRANCE JAPAN NZ USA

Couronne d'Or

DOCTOR ALEXANDER FLEMING
Bunker Hill' x 'Sarah Bernhardt'. Sweet-scented flowers with inward curving, vibrant pink petals.
FRANCE
DOUBLE PINK
FRAGRANT
MID
110 CM / 3 FT 10 IN
AVAILABLE IN CANADA FRANCE SWITZERLAND NZ UK USA

DOUGLAS BRAND
Huge (up to 25 cm / 10 in) flowers, clear water-melon red. In spite of their weight, the stout stems hold them upright. One of the best double reds.
TISCHLER, USA 1972
DOUBLE RED
LATE
80 CM / 2 FT 8 IN
AVAILABLE IN USA

♥ DUCHESSE DE NEMOURS
A much loved old favourite with relatively small, loosely double flowers, creamy white with yellow shadows at the centre. Sweetly scented, good cut flowers. Free flowering.
CALOT, FRANCE 1856
DOUBLE WHITE
VERY FRAGRANT
MID TO LATE
80 CM / 2 FT 8 IN

AVAILABLE IN CANADA EUROPE UK USA

EARLY SCOUT
A compact plant, inheriting rich green, fine-cut foliage from its parent *P. tenuifolia*. The cupped flowers hold a mass of golden stamens. Thrives in northerly latitudes.
AUTEN, USA 1952
SINGLE DARK RED
VERY EARLY
45 CM TO 60 CM / 1 FT 6 IN TO 2 FT
AVAILABLE IN EUROPE NZ USA

EARLY WIND-FLOWER
P. emodi x *P. veitchii*. Very different from other peonies and quite lovely: nodding, fragile-looking flowers like giant wood anemones on long stems above light green deeply-cut leaves. 'Late Windflower' follows seven to ten days later.
SAUNDERS, USA 1939
EARLY
90 CM / 3 FT
AVAILABLE IN EUROPE NZ USA

EDULIS SUPERBA
One that has stood the test of time in the garden and as a cut flower; rose pink, rose-scented, medium-sized flowers with a ring of large guard petals round ruffled petals at the centre. Free flowering.
LEMOINE, FRANCE 1824
DOUBLE PINK

Duchesse de Nemours

FRAGRANT

EARLY TO MID

90 CM / 3 FT

AVAILABLE IN EUROPE JAPAN NZ UK USA

ELLEN COWLEY

P. lactiflora x *P. peregrina*. Cupped flowers, a vibrant shade of orangey-pinky-red, with broad, rounded petals. A compact plant with elegantly dissected leaves. Vigorous and prolific.

SAUNDERS, USA 1940

SEMI-DOUBLE RED-PINK

EARLY

70 CM / 2 FT 4 IN

AVAILABLE IN CANADA GERMANY NZ USA

*ELSA SASS

Large, beautifully shaped flowers with faint pink and yellow shading at their hearts. Reliable, very free flowering.

SASS, USA 1930

DOUBLE WHITE

VERY LATE

75 CM / 2 FT 6 IN

AVAILABLE IN FRANCE NZ UK USA

EMPEROR OF INDIA

Dark, purple-pink guard petals surround a central tuft of self-coloured, yellow tipped staminoids. Free flowering.

KELWAY, UK 1901

SINGLE PINK

FRAGRANT

MID TO VERY LATE

90 CM / 3 FT

AVAILABLE IN UK

ETCHED SALMON

Very pretty, loosely ruffled flowers, soft coral with paler edges to the petals, held upright on a tidy plant.

COUSINS-R KLEHM, USA 1981

DOUBLE PINK

FRAGRANT

EARLY TO MID

90 CM / 3 FT

AVAILABLE IN NZ USA

ETINCELANTE

Long-lasting flowers with vivid pink petals narrowly edged with silver. Golden stamens in a big tuft. Vigorous and free flowering.

DESSERT, FRANCE 1905

SINGLE PINK

EARLY TO MID

90 CM / 3 FT

AVAILABLE IN FRANCE UK USA

FAIRY'S PETTICOAT

Very large, blush pink flowers fading to cream. A good cut flower.

C G KLEHM, USA

DOUBLE PINK

VERY FRAGRANT

EARLY

75 CM / 2 FT 6 IN

AVAILABLE IN CANADA NZ UK USA

❦ FELIX CROUSSE

A trusted favourite, although bettered by, for example, 'Felix Supreme'. Globe-shaped, glowing carmine flowers are carried in clusters. Free flowering, good cut flower.

CROUSSE, FRANCE 1881

DOUBLE RED

FRAGRANT

MID TO LATE

75 CM / 2 FT 6 IN

AVAILABLE IN CANADA EUROPE NZ UK USA

FELIX SUPREME

Larger than 'Félix Crousse', free flowering, strong, good cut flower.

KRIEK, USA 1955

DOUBLE RED

LATE

75 CM / 2 FT 6 IN

AVAILABLE IN CANADA EUROPE NZ UK USA

❦ FESTIVA MAXIMA

Beautiful, globe-shaped flowers open palest pink and fade to creamy white with a few crimson flecks and a warm, peachy glow at their hearts. Rose scented. Free flowering.

MIELLEZ, FRANCE 1851

DOUBLE WHITE

VERY FRAGRANT

MID

100 CM / 3 FT

AVAILABLE IN CANADA EUROPE JAPAN NZ UK USA

FIRELIGHT

P. lactiflora x *P. officinalis*, *P. mlokosewitschii* x *P. macrophylla*. Large rose pink flowers open flat and have flares of a darker shade. Long golden stamens.

SAUNDERS, USA 1950

SINGLE PINK

EARLY

110 CM / 3 FT 4 IN

AVAILABLE IN USA

FLAME

P. lactiflora x *P. peregrina*. Reliable plant with healthy foliage and vibrant, slightly orange pink flowers on strong stems. A good peony for a site in partial shade. Good cut flower. Very free flowering

GLASSCOCK, USA 1939

SINGLE PINK

EARLY

80 CM / 2 FT 8 IN

AVAILABLE IN EUROPE NZ UK USA

GARDENIA

Large, loosely double flowers open to show golden stamens, set off by dark foliage. The flowers have a faint blush, especially in shade.

LINS, USA 1955

Félix Crousse

Gleam of Light

DOUBLE WHITE

FRAGRANT

LATE

85 CM / 2 FT 10 IN

AVAILABLE IN CANADA FRANCE NZ USA

GERMAINE BIGOT

Large flowers opening flesh pink with a paler centre becoming creamy with red flecks. Attractive leaves colour well in autumn. A good cut flower. Free flowering.

DESSERT, FRANCE 1902

SEMI-DOUBLE PINK

FRAGRANT

MID TO LATE

90 CM / 3 FT

AVAILABLE IN UK

GLEAM OF LIGHT

Pretty cup-shaped flowers with clear pink rounded petals encircling short yellow petaloids. Delicious scent. Very free flowering.

KELWAY, UK

JAPANESE PINK, YELLOW

FRAGRANT

MID TO LATE

95 CM / 3 FT

AVAILABLE IN UK

GLOBE OF LIGHT

Bright rose-pink flowers with large golden-yellow centres. Good cut flowers. Long flowering season, good autumn colour, free flowering.

KELWAY, UK 1928

JAPANESE PINK

FRAGRANT

MID TO LATE

90 CM / 3 FT

AVAILABLE IN NZ UK

GLOWING CANDLES

Medium to large flowers with pale pink outer petals round a chamois coloured centre. Long in flower. Good in colder regions.

WILD, USA 1966

JAPANESE PINK, BUFF

LATE

90 CM / 3 FT

AVAILABLE IN CANADA USA

HONEY GOLD

Large creamy-white guard petals surround a mass of slender pale yellow petals. Long stems, good cut flower.

C G KLEHM, USA

DOUBLE WHITE AND YELLOW

FRAGRANT

LATE

75 CM / 2 FT 6 IN

AVAILABLE IN JAPAN NZ UK USA

Inspecteur Lavergne

A tried and trusted peony: shapely globular
flowers, a good strong crimson.

Doriat, France 1924

DOUBLE RED

FRAGRANT

MID

86 CM / 2 FT 10 IN

AVAILABLE IN EUROPE UK USA

Instituteur Doriat

A stunning sight in full flower. Masses of
deep cherry red flowers. Frilled, self-
coloured petaloids are enlivened by a
thread-like white rim. They almost hide the
large guard petals. Autumn colour.

Doriat, France 1925

JAPANESE RED

FRAGRANT

LATE

100 CM / 3 FT

AVAILABLE IN CANADA FRANCE UK

Irwin Altman

Large, symmetrical flowers, clear light red.
Flowers well when young.

Kelsey, USA 1940

DOUBLE RED

VERY FRAGRANT

LATE

80 CM / 2 FT 10 IN

AVAILABLE IN FRANCE GERMANY NZ USA

Isani-gidui (Isani jishi)

Classic Japanese form with large, rounded
outer petals guarding a dome of narrow,
crowded yellow petaloides. The scent is
sometimes described as 'medicinal'.

Japan pre-1928

JAPANESE WHITE, YELLOW

FRAGANT

LATE

85 CM / 2 FT 10 IN

AVAILABLE IN FRANCE UK USA

Jan van Leeuwen

Charmingly simple flowers, like 'Isani-gidui'
but smaller with stronger stems. Attractive
leaves. It apparently flowers mid-season in
Europe but very late in the USA.

van Leeuwen, Netherlands 1928

JAPANESE WHITE

MID OR VERY LATE

87 CM / 2 FT 11 IN

AVAILABLE IN GERMANY SWEDEN UK USA

Joy of Life

Large but fragile-looking flowers up to 25
cm / 10 in across with broad blush-pink
petals. Long flowering season.

Kelway, UK 1911

SEMI-DOUBLE PINK

FRAGRANT

MID TO VERY LATE

85 CM / 2 FT 10 IN

AVAILABLE IN UK

Instituteur Doriat

Joy of Life

JUNE ROSE

Large, almost double flowers, rose shaped with loosely held petals of a deep, bright pink, seen to advantage against dark green leaves.

JONES, USA 1938

SEMI-DOUBLE PINK

FRAGRANT

MID

78 CM / 2 FT 7 IN

AVAILABLE IN CANADA UK USA

*KANSAS SYN. KOJIMANO-HIKARI

One of the most reliable peonies for warmer climates. The colouring varies in intensity; the outer petals are marbled. Good cut flowers, free flowering.

BIGGER, USA 1940

DOUBLE RED

MID

90 CM / 3 FT

AVAILABLE IN CANADA EUROPE JAPAN NZ UK USA

KARL ROSENFIELD

Large, bright crimson globe-shaped flowers with inward-curving petals. Good cut flowers, free flowering.

ROSENFIELD, USA 1908

DOUBLE RED

MID TO LATE

78 CM / 2 FT 7 IN

AVAILABLE IN CANADA EUROPE JAPAN NZ UK

USA

KELWAY'S GLORIOUS

Legendary, and still considered one of the best. Huge saucer-shaped flowers are white with a warm cream centre and smell of roses. They are borne very freely on stout stems on healthy, dark green bushes, slow to establish but worth waiting for. Good cut flowers.

KELWAY, UK 1909

DOUBLE WHITE

VERY FRAGRANT

MID TO LATE

100 CM / 3 FT

AVAILABLE IN CANADA FRANCE NZ SWEDEN UK USA

KELWAY'S SUPREME

Large flowers with broad, blush-pink petals symmetrically arranged around small yellow centres are produced freely and continuously over a long period, side shoots prolonging the display.

KELWAY, UK 1892

SEMI-DOUBLE PINK

VERY FRAGRANT

MID TO VERY LATE

100 CM / 3 FT

AVAILABLE IN UK

KOJIMANO-HIKARI *see* KANSAS

TOP Kansas

ABOVE Kelways Supreme

Kelway's Glorious

KRINKLED WHITE

Large, deckle-edged, tissue-paper textured petals surround golden stamens. Drought resistant, good cut flower, free flowering.
BRAND, USA 1928
SINGLE WHITE
EARLY (UK) LATE (USA)
90 CM / 3 FT
AVAILABLE IN EUROPE NZ UK USA

LADDIE

P. peregrina 'Otto Froebel' x *P. tenuifolia*. A charming miniature with scaled-down flowers and fine-cut leaves. A pretty subject for the front of a border or rock garden. Better for warm regions than *P. tenuifolia* or 'Early Scout'
GLASSCOCK, USA 1941
SINGLE RED
VERY EARLY
30 CM / 1 FT
AVAILABLE IN CANADA UK USA

❧ LADY ALEXANDRA DUFF

A much loved old peony with pale mauve-pink outer petals and smaller central petals. Almost white with a few flecks of crimson at the heart of the flower. The flowers are born in clusters on each stem, giving a long flowering season.
KELWAY, UK 1902
DOUBLE PINK
VERY FRAGRANT

MID (UK) LATE (USA)
90 CM / 3 FT
AVAILABLE IN FRANCE CANADA NZ UK USA

LATE WIND-FLOWER

P. emodi x *P. beresowskii*. Aptly named peony with the charm of 'Early Windflower' but flowering seven to ten days later.
SAUNDERS, USA 1939
SINGLE WHITE
EARLY
90 CM / 3 FT
AVAILABLE IN NZ USA

❧ LAURA DESSERT

Classical many-petalled flowers open palest pink with a yellow glow at the heart, giving an overall impression of soft cream faintly flushed with apricot yellow. Rose scent. Free flowering.
DESSERT, FRANCE 1913
DOUBLE CREAM
VERY FRAGRANT
EARLY TO MID
90 CM / 3 FT
AVAILABLE IN CANADA EUROPE UK

LORD KITCHENER SYN. BALLIOL

Intense maroon-red flowers with small yellow centres, held in clusters well above dark green leaves.
KELWAY, UK 1907
SINGLE RED

Krinkled White

TOP Laura Dessert

ABOVE Lord Kitchener

VERY EARLY TO MID
90 CM / 3 FT
AVAILABLE IN EUROPE NZ UK

LOTUS QUEEN

Medium-sized flowers of great purity with
cream, rose-like outer petals guarding
slender yellow staminoids. Light scent.
MURAWSKA, USA 1947
JAPANESE WHITE
FRAGRANT
LATE (US) MID (UK)
90 CM / 3 FT
AVAILABLE IN NZ UK USA

LOVELY ROSE

P. lactiflora x *P. peregrina*. Deep rose-pink
petals fade to a paler shade. There are
distinctive white blotches at the base of
each petal. Free flowering.
SAUNDERS, USA 1942
SEMI-DOUBLE PINK
EARLY
75 CM / 2 FT 6 IN
AVAILABLE IN GERMANY UK USA

MADAME ANTOINE RIVIERE

Very large flowers with broad petals of
velvety garnet round a large boss of golden
stamens. Strong and remarkably free
flowering.
RIVIERE, FRANCE 1935
SINGLE RED

MID
120 CM / 4 FT
AVAILABLE IN FRANCE

MADAME CALOT

Large, very double bomb-shaped flowers,
pale pink to cream with a few crimson
flecks. Exceptionally fragrant, strong stems,
good for cutting, free flowering.
MIELLEZ, FRANCE 1856
DOUBLE PINK
VERY FRAGRANT
MID
80 CM / 2 FT 8 IN
AVAILABLE IN FRANCE UK USA

MADAME DE VERNEVILLE

Large outer petals and a full bomb of
smaller petals at the centre, white with a
hint of yellow, rose scented. Fast growing,
very free flowering
CROUSSE, FRANCE 1885
DOUBLE WHITE
FRAGRANT
EARLY
75 CM / 2 FT 6 IN
AVAILABLE IN UK NZ USA

MADAME DUCEL

Globes of pale flesh-pink petals. Compact,
free-flowering bush.
MECHIN, FRANCE 1880
DOUBLE PINK

Madame Calot

Madame Ducel

FRAGRANT

EARLY

60 CM / 2 FT

AVAILABLE IN GERMANY UK USA

MAHOGANY

P. peregrina 'Otto Froebel' x *P. lactiflora*.
Glossy mahogany petals surround large
golden-yellow stamens. Fresh, light green
leaves, good cut flower.

GLASSCOCK, USA 1937

JAPANESE RED

FRAGRANT

EARLY

70 CM / 2 FT 4 IN

AVAILABLE IN GERMANY SWITZERLAND USA

MANDARIN'S COAT

Medium-sized, symmetrical flowers with
vivid magenta petals around a big ball of
gold-tipped petaloids. In Allan Rogers'
words 'it has proven itself from Minnesota
to Oregon.'

MARX-ROGERS, USA 1978

JAPANESE PINK, YELLOW

LATE

60 CM / 2 FT

AVAILABLE IN CANADA GERMANY NZ USA

MARIE JACQUIN SYN. BRIDESMAID, WATERLILY

Pale pink petals fading to creamy white are
cupped around a tuft of yellow stamens.

The flowers, born in clusters, are
exceptionally highly scented. Long in flower.
Free flowering.

VERDIER, FRANCE

SEMI-DOUBLE PINK, WHITE

VERY FRAGRANT

MID

90 CM / 3 FT

AVAILABLE IN UK USA

MARY E NICHOLLS

Several large, elegant, rose-shaped blooms
to each stem. Very free flowering.

NICHOLLS, USA 1941

DOUBLE WHITE

VERY FRAGRANT

LATE

90 CM / 3 FT

AVAILABLE IN NZ USA

MISCHIEF

A pretty flower with very large wild rose
petals round a small cluster of yellow
stamens. A free flowering plant with a big
impact in full bloom.

AUTEN, USA 1925

SINGLE PINK

LATE

90 CM / 3 FT

AVAILABLE IN CANADA UK USA

**MISS AMERICA

Very large, pure white flowers open from
blush-pink buds to reveal yellow stamens.
Grows slowly into a large plant. Its good
health, the classical beauty of the flowers
and their scent have earned two gold
medals. Good in warmer climates. Free
flowering.

MANN-VAN STEEN, USA 1936

SEMI-DOUBLE WHITE

FRAGRANT

EARLY (UK) MID (US)

UP TO 120 CM /4 FT

AVAILABLE IN CANADA JAPAN NZ SWEDEN
SWITZERLAND UK USA

MISTRAL

Distinctive, deeply-cut petals give the
flowers a fragile air. They are light cherry red
with paler margins. Compact, free
flowering.

DESSERT, FRANCE 1905

SINGLE RED

FRAGRANT

MID

75 CM / 2 FT 6 IN

AVAILABLE IN UK

♛ MONSIEUR JULES ELIE
(FUJI IN JAPAN)

Everyone's idea of a peony and enduringly
popular. Large, unfading, clear, light rose-
pink flowers, sweetly scented, with rounded
outer petals holding a mass of smaller petals
curled in the style of a chrysanthemum.
Good for cutting. Free flowering.

CROUSSE, FRANCE 1888

DOUBLE PINK

FRAGRANT

MID TO LATE

80 CM / 2 FT 8 IN

AVAILABLE IN CANADA EUROPE JAPAN NZ UK
USA

MONTEZUMA

P. lactiflora x *P. peregrina*. One of the loveliest
early red singles. Rich scarlet flowers with
rounded petals are carried on strong stems.

SAUNDERS, USA 1943

SINGLE RED

FRAGRANT

EARLY

90 CM / 3 FT

AVAILABLE IN CANADA FRANCE NZ UK USA

*MOONSTONE

Pale blush fading to white with pink outer
petals gives an impression of white and pale
pink flowers on the same plant. Long
flowering season.

MURAWSKA, USA 1943

DOUBLE BLUSH

MID TO LATE

90 CM / 3 FT

AVAILABLE IN NZ USA

*Mrs Franklin D Roosevelt

A large, classically lovely peony with
rounded flowers of clear pale pink. Sweet
scent. Good cut flowers. Free flowering.
FRANKLIN, USA 1932
DOUBLE PINK
FRAGRANT
LATE
70 CM / 2 FT 4 IN
AVAILABLE IN EUROPE NZ USA

Myrtle Gentry

One of the most fragrant peonies. Huge
flowers open pale blush, fading almost to
white.
BRAND, USA 1925
DOUBLE PINK
VERY FRAGRANT
VERY LATE
90 CM / 3 FT
AVAILABLE IN FRANCE NZ USA

Nice Gal

Bright mauve-pink petals with silvered
margins are symmetrically arranged round
yellow stamens. Compact, dense, free
flowering.
KREKLER, USA 1965
SEMI-DOUBLE PINK
FRAGRANT
LATE
55 CM / 1 FT 10 IN
AVAILABLE IN CANADA NZ UK USA

**Nick Shaylor

Twice winner of the APS Gold Medal. Large,
loosely double flowers open pale flesh pink
and fade to white except at the heart.
Reliable but the heavy stems may need
support.
ALLISON, USA 1931
DOUBLE BLUSH
LATE
71 CM / 2 FT 5 IN
AVAILABLE IN CANADA GERMANY NZ UK USA

*Norma Volz

Another very beautiful blush peony, almost
white but with soft flesh tones. Sturdy but
sometimes fails to flower.
VOLZ, USA 1962
DOUBLE BLUSH
FRAGRANT
MID
90 CM / 3 FT
AVAILABLE IN CANADA GERMANY NZ USA

Nymphe

Fragile-looking flowers with warm flesh-pink
petals surrounding a ball of golden stamens.
Free flowering.
DESSERT, FRANCE 1913
SINGLE PINK
FRAGRANT
LATE
90 CM / 3 FT
AVAILABLE IN CANADA EUROPE UK USA

Mrs Frankin D Roosevelt

Nymphe

OLD FAITHFUL

Very well behaved. Strong stems hold the flowers well above healthy dark green foliage. Magnificent size and colour. Pure true red.

GLASSCOCK-FALK, USA 1964

DOUBLE RED

LATE

90 CM / 3 FT

AVAILABLE IN GERMANY NZ USA

♈ *P. MLOKOSEWITSCHII*

Velvety-green leaves overlaid with pinkish grey turn pinkish orangey brown in autumn. Ravishing cupped, soft yellow flowers. Not just to die for – to kill for.

MLOKOSEIWICZ, CAUCASUS 1900

SINGLE YELLOW

VERY EARLY

75 CM / 2 FT 6 IN

AVAILABLE IN EUROPE UK USA

P. OFFICINALIS 'ALBA PLENA',
♈ *P. OFFICINALIS* 'ROSEA PLENA',
♈ 'RUBRA PLENA'

Double white, pink and red forms of the European peony, an old cottage garden favourite. The heavy heads may need support. The red is stronger than the pink and white forms. A slow starter but not difficult in well-drained soil. Good cut flower. Free flowering.

EUROPE

DOUBLE WHITE, PINK, RED

EARLY

60 TO 70 CM / 2 FT TO 2 FT 4IN

AVAILABLE IN NZ SWEDEN UK USA

♈ *P. PEREGRINA* 'OTTO FROEBEL' SYN. SUNSHINE

The Red Peony of Constantinople. Deeply-cut glossy dark green leaves set off clear, glowing red flowers with yellow centres.

PRE-1889

SINGLE RED

EARLY

50 CM / 1 FT 8 IN

AVAILABLE IN EUROPE UK USA

PAEONIA TENUIFOLIA 'RUBRA PLENA'

Worth growing for its finely-cut, ferny foliage as well as its flowers. The single species is worthwhile, too. Both prefer a cold climate.

DOUBLE RED

EARLY

20 CM / 8IN

AVAILABLE IN EUROPE UK USA

PALADIN

P. lactiflora x *P. peregrina*. Vibrant red flowers open from unusual, pointed buds over a tidy mound of foliage.

SAUNDERS, USA 1950

SEMI-DOUBLE RED

EARLY TO MID

TOP *Paeonia officinalis* 'Rubra Plena'

ABOVE Paladin

60 CM / 2 FT

AVAILABLE IN CANADA EUROPE USA

*PAULA FAY

Vivid mauve-pink flowers, strong stems,
fresh-looking light green leaves. Good cut
flower.

FAY USA 1968

SEMI-DOUBLE PINK

 FRAGRANT

EARLY

75 CM / 2 FT 6 IN

AVAILABLE IN CANADA EUROPE JAPAN NZ UK
USA

PETER BRAND

A shapely, cupped flower, rich, deep ruby
red. Excellent autumn colour.

SEIT, HOLLAND 1937

DOUBLE RED

FRAGRANT

MID

90 CM / 3 FT

AVAILABLE IN EUROPE UK USA

*PILLOW TALK

Full, fluffy, well-rounded flowers, a pretty
shade of light rose pink. Glossy green
leaves. Strong, free flowering.

C G KLEHM, USA 1973

DOUBLE PINK

FRAGRANT

MID

65 CM TO 80 CM / 2 FT 2 IN TO 2FT 10 IN

AVAILABLE IN GERMANY CANADA JAPAN NZ
SWEDEN UK USA

POSTILION

Stunning great flowers, glowing scarlet red
on a strong plant.

SAUNDERS, USA 1941

SEMI-DOUBLE RED

VERY FRAGRANT

EARLY

90 CM / 3 FT

AVAILABLE IN EUROPE CANADA NZ UK USA

PRAIRIE MOON

Archangel x Laura Magnuson. One of the
loveliest and most reliable peonies.
Sometimes single, occasionally loosely
double but usually semi-double, large,
fragile-looking, pale clear yellow.

FAY, USA 1959

SEMI-DOUBLE YELLOW

EARLY TO MID

80 CM / 2 FT 8 IN

AVAILABLE IN GERMANY NZ USA

PRINCESS MARGARET

Like a cabbage rose with cup-shaped
flowers of rich rose pink.

MURAWSKA, USA 1960

DOUBLE PINK

FRAGRANT

LATE

75 CM / 2 FT 6 IN

AVAILABLE IN EUROPE CANADA NZ USA

RASPBERRY SUNDAE

A vanilla bombe with a ring of narrow petals
sits on a saucer of pale pink guard petals,
topped with a large tuft of darker pink
petals (the raspberry sauce).

C G KLEHM, USA 1968

DOUBLE PINK, CREAM

FRAGRANT

LATE (US) MID (UK)

90 CM / 3 FT

AVAILABLE IN CANADA GERMANY NZ UK USA

*RED CHARM

P. lactiflora x P. officinalis 'Rubra Plena'.
Large, dome-shaped, rich crimson flowers,
much admired. Long flowering season.

GLASSCOCK, USA 1944

DOUBLE RED

MID (US) EARLY (UK)

90 CM / 3 FT

AVAILABLE IN CANADA EUROPE NZ UK USA

REINE HORTENSE SYN. PRESIDENT TAFT

Beautiful flowers, uniform pale flesh pink
flecked with crimson at the centre. Grey-
green leaves, red flower stems. Good cut
flower. Free flowering.

CALOT, FRANCE 1857

DOUBLE PINK

FRAGRANT

MID TO LATE

82 CM / 2 FT 9 IN

AVAILABLE IN CANADA EUROPE UK USA

REQUIEM

Waxy white petals round a huge boss of
golden yellow in-curved stamens. Free
flowering.

SAUNDERS, USA 1941

SINGLE WHITE

FRAGRANT

MID

95 CM / 3 FT 6IN

AVAILABLE IN GERMANY NZ SWITZERLAND USA

ROSE HEART SYN. BESS BOCKSTOCE

ROSEDALE

P. lactiflora x P. officinalis. Semi-double or
double clear rose-red flowers. Good cut
flower, compact, free flowering.

AUTEN, USA 1936

DOUBLE TO SEMI-DOUBLE

LATE RED

UP TO 75 CM / UP TO 2 FT 6 IN

AVAILABLE IN EUROPE NZ USA

ROSELETTE

A peony with P. lactiflora, P. mlokosewitschii
and P. tenuifolia in its ancestry. Large, open
cups, clear pink crinkled petals.

SAUNDERS, USA 1950

SINGLE PINK

EARLY

Reine Hortense

90 CM / 3 FT

AVAILABLE IN FRANCE NZ UK USA

SALMON GLOW

Unusual large, single or semi-double
flowers: translucent pale salmon petals fade
to cream pink. Vigorous, free flowering but
the stems need support.

GLASSCOCK, USA 1947

SINGLE PINK

EARLY

85 CM / 2 FT 9 IN

AVAILABLE IN CANADA FRANCE USA

❦ SARAH BERNHARDT

An old favourite: very beautiful large
flowers, rosy pink, paler at the petal
margins. Free-flowering, but weak stemmed
and out-classed by the modern 'Chiffon
Parfait'.

LEMOINE, FRANCE 1906

DOUBLE PINK

VERY LATE

90 CM / 3 FT

AVAILABLE IN CANADA EUROPE JAPAN NZ UK
USA

SCARLET O'HARA

A popular and robust peony, better than
most in poor conditions. Large, rounded
scarlet petals enclose a tidy ring of golden
stamens. Some scent. Long in flower.

GLASSCOCK-FALK, USA 1956

SINGLE RED

FRAGRANT

EARLY (UK) MID (US)

90 CM / 3 FT

AVAILABLE IN EUROPE NZ UK USA

*SEA SHELL

One of the best single peonies. Soft, mauve-
pink flowers born over a long period on a
strong plant. Good cut flower.

SASS, USA 1937

SINGLE PINK

FRAGRANT

LATE

90 CM / 3 FT

AVAILABLE IN EUROPE NZ USA

SHAWNEE CHIEF

Medium-sized flowers on strong stems, the
outer petals much larger than those at the
centre. Long-lasting shiny green leaves.
Vigorous and prolific.

BIGGER, USA 1940

DOUBLE DARK RED

MID

90 CM / 3 FT

AVAILABLE IN FRANCE USA

SHIRLEY TEMPLE

Large, lightly-scented flowers, white with
cream and blush shadows, opening from
pink buds. Strong stems, long flowering
season, good cut flower, free flowering.

UNKNOWN ORIGIN

DOUBLE CREAM WHITE

FRAGRANT

MID

83 CM / 2 FT9IN

AVAILABLE IN CANADA EUROPE UK USA

SOLANGE

Beautiful domed flowers with pale cream
petals shading to buff and apricot at the
centre. Sometimes the buds fail to open.

LEMOINE, FRANCE 1907

DOUBLE BLUSH

FRAGRANT

LATE

85 CM / 2 FT 10 IN

AVAILABLE IN CANADA EUROPE NZ UK

SWORD DANCE

Showy flowers with brilliant red guard
petals and a large bunch of cream petaloids
shading to pink at their base. Good in warm
areas.

AUTEN, USA 1933

JAPANESE RED, CREAM

LATE

90 CM / 3 FT

AVAILABLE IN CANADA USA

TOP BRASS

High-centred bomb with white guard petals,
a ruff of narrow yellow petals and a central
tuft of cream and pale pink. Honey scent,

reliable, long in flower.

C G KLEHM, USA 1968

DOUBLE CREAM

FRAGRANT

LATE (US) MID (UK)

70 CM / 2 FT 4 IN

AVAILABLE IN CANADA NZ UK USA

VIVID ROSE

Large rounded flowers, luminous rose pink.
Good cut flowers.

C G KLEHM USA 1952

DOUBLE PINK

VERY FRAGRANT

VERY LATE

60 TO 70 CM / 2 FT TO 2 FT 4 IN

AVAILABLE IN NZ USA

VOGUE

Huge flowers on long, strong stems. Rose-
pink petals with silvery undersides. Very
free flowering.

HOOGENDOORN, NETHERLANDS, 1949

DOUBLE PINK

VERY FRAGRANT

MID

80 CM / 2 FT 9 IN

AVAILABLE IN CANADA FRANCE UK USA

*WALTER MAINS

P. lactiflora x *P. officinalis*. Large Japanese
flowers on a strong plant. Dark red guard
petals, red and white petaloids edged with

Vogue

gold.
MAINS, USA 1957
JAPANESE RED
EARLY
80 CM / 2 FT 9 IN
AVAILABLE IN CANADA NZ UK USA

*WESTERNER
Light pink guard petals, masses of long, soft yellow petaloides. Strong plants.
BIGGER, USA 1942
JAPANESE PINK, YELLOW
LATE (US) MID (UK)
90 CM / 3 FT
AVAILABLE IN EUROPE UK USA

*WHITE CAP
Showy flowers with cream and pale pink petaloids in a bowl of raspberry red guard petals, held well above the leaves.
WINCHELL, USA 1956
JAPANESE RED, CREAM
LATE
80 CM / 2 FT 9 IN
AVAILABLE IN CANADA EUROPE NZ USA

WHITE INNOCENCE
P. emodi x. *P. lactiflora*. The tallest known herbaceous peony. Plenty of white flowers, small but beautiful; unusual, tightly curled greenish stamens. Needs support.
SAUNDERS, USA 1947
SINGLE WHITE

MID
150 CM / 5 FT
AVAILABLE IN GERMANY NZ USA

☙ WHITLEYI MAJOR SYN. ALBA GRANDIFLORA, THE BRIDE
Imported from China by a London nurseryman (Whitley); thought to be the closest cultivated peony to the wild *P. lactiflora* from which so many peonies are bred. Large, scented flowers in clusters. Good autumn colour.
WHITLEY, UK 1808
SINGLE WHITE
FRAGRANT
EARLY
95 CM /3 FT 2 IN
AVAILABLE IN UK

WILFORD JOHNSON
Large rose-pink flowers on strong stems. Dense foliage, robust, free flowering.
BRAND, USA 1966
DOUBLE PINK
LATE
70 CM / 2 FT 4 IN
AVAILABLE IN NZ USA

HERBACEOUS PEONIES: GENERAL LIST

A B FRANKLIN Franklin USA 1928 double white with flesh shading
late available in USA

A LA MODE R Klehm USA 1981 single white and gold scented,
early 85 cm/34 in, available in NZ UK USA Canada Sweden

ABALONE PINK Krekler/Klehm 1978 single pink early
65 cm/26 in, available in USA

ADOLPHE ROUSSEAU Dessert-Mechin 1890 semi-double red
unpleasant scent early to mid 95 cm/38 in, available in Canada
Europe USA

ADONIS Sass USA 1930 double pink mid 90 cm/3 ft
available in USA

ADORABLE Nicholls-Wild USA 1962 double pink free flowering
mid 90 cm/3 ft available in NZ

AFTERGLOW Kelway UK double pink scented late 120 cm/4 ft
available in UK

ALESIA Lemoine France 1927 double cream white scented very late
90 cm/3 ft available in France USA

ALEXANDER WOOLCOTT Saunders USA 1941 semi-double red
early 65 cm/2 ft 2 in, available in USA

ALEXANDRE DUMAS Guérin France 1862 double pink and cream
scented free flowering mid 90 cm/3 ft available in France

ALICE CROUSSE Calot France 1872 double pink scented mid
90 cm/3 ft available in France

ALICE HARDING Lemoine France 1922 double cream white
scented late 90 cm/3 ft available in France UK USA

ALICE ROBERTS Krekler USA Japanese pink mid 90 cm/3 ft USA

ALMA HANSEN Cooper 1946 double white late 110 cm/3 ft 10 in
available in France

AMABILIS double pink mid 90 cm/3 ft available in France

AMERICA Rudolph 1976 USA single red some scent, early

70 cm/28 in, available in Germany Sweden NZ UK USA

ANGELO COBB FREEBORN Freeborn USA 1943 double coral-red
early to mid 90 cm/3 ft available in Canada France UK USA

ANGELUS Auten USA 1933 single pale pink early available in USA

ANN BERRY COUSINS Cousins-R Klehm USA 1972 semi-double
pink early 70 cm/2 ft 4 in, available in Germany NZ USA

ANN COUSINS Cousins USA 1946 double white scented mid to
late 70 cm/2 ft 4 in, available in France Canada Germany NZ
Sweden USA

ANNISQUAM Thurlow-Stranger USA 1951 double pink some scent
mid 80 cm/32 in, available in USA

ANTWERPEN unknown origin single pink some scent mid
80 cm/32 in, available in Canada Europe Switzerland USA

ARCHANGEL Saunders USA 1950 single white early
80 cm/2 ft 8 in, available in Germany USA

ARGENTINE Lemoine France 1924 double cream-white scented
late 70 cm/28 in, available in Canada UK USA

ARMISTICE Kelsey 1938 double rich pink scented late mid
90 cm/3 ft available in NZ USA

ATHENA Saunders USA 1955 single white and pink early
60 cm/2 ft available in Germany USA

ATTAR OF ROSES Murawska USA 1951 double pink scented early
mid 90 cm/3 ft available in USA

AUGUSTIN D'HOUR syn. for General McMahon

AUREOLE Hollis 1905 Japanese pink scented autumn colour early
to mid 86 cm/3 ft available in Canada UK

AUTENS Auten USA 1816 double crimson scented very early
90 cm/3 ft available in NZ UK USA

AVALANCHE Crousse France 1886 double white scented free
flowering mid to late 90 cm/3 ft available in Europe NZ USA

AZTEC Nicholls 1941 Japanese red-pink free flowering early
100 cm/3 ft available in France

BALLERINA Kelway UK double blush pink scented early to mid

TOP Argentine

ABOVE Barrymore

90 cm/3 ft available in UK

BALLIOL syn. for Lord Kitchener

BANNER BRIGHT Franklin USA semi-double pink mid
70 cm/2 ft 4 in, available in USA

BARBARA Polish origin Japanese bright pink on pink late
80 cm/2 ft 8 in, available in UK NZ

BARRYMORE Kelway UK Japanese palest blush scented mid to late
85 cm/2 ft 10 in, available in UK

BATTLE FLAG Nicholls USA 1941 Japanese red, red and gold
centre mid available in USA

BEAUTY'S QUEEN Kelway UK semi-double white scented mid to
late 86 cm/34 in, available in UK

BEERSHEBA Kelway UK single rose pink scented early
110 cm/4 ft available in UK

BELLE CENTER Mains USA 1956 semi-double dark red early
60 cm to 75 cm/2 ft to 2 ft 6 in, available in France UK USA

BELLEVILLE Harold Wolfe/Hollingsworth USA 1998 Japanese
mauve pink mid to late 120 cm/4 ft available in USA

BESS BOCKSTOCE syn.Rose Heart Bockstoce USA 1955 double
pink and white scented mid 60 cm/24 in,
available in Canada NZ USA

BEST MAN Klehm USA double red late 80 cm/2 ft 6 in,
available in Canada Germany NZ Sweden USA

BETTER TIMES Franklin USA 1942 double pink mid
70 cm/2 ft 4 in, available in Canada Germany USA

BEV Krekler USA 1975 double pink scented mid
90 cm/3 ft available in Germany USA

BLANCHE KING Brand USA 1922 double pink some scent late
90 cm/3 ft available in France

BLAZE Orville Fay USA 1972 single red early 75 cm/2 ft 6 in,
available in Europe NZ Sweden USA

BLUSH QUEEN Hoogendoorn Netherlands 1949 double white mid
97 cm/3 ft 3 in, available in Canada France NZ UK USA

BLUSHING PRINCESS Saunders-Reath USA 1991 semi-double pale
    pink early 90 cm/3 ft available in USA

BOB KREKLER Krekler USA 1965 Japanese pink and yellow mid
    95 cm/3 ft 4 in, available in USA

BONANZA Franklin USA 1947 double red mid 90 cm/3 ft available
    in France Sweden NZ USA

BOSSUET Miellez France double magenta pink mid 100 cm/3 ft
    available in France

BOUQUET PERFECT Tischler USA 1987 Japanese vivid pink mid
    to late 60 cm/2 ft available in USA

BRAVURA Saunders USA 1943 single red with yellow centre mid
    90 cm/3 ft available in NZ USA

BRAVURA SUPREME Krekler USA single red, mid 85 cm/2 ft 10 in,
    available in USA

BRIDAL GOWN Klehm USA 1981 double white mid 75 cm/
    2 ft 6 in, available in NZ UK USA

BRIDAL ICING Klehm USA 1981 double white some scent free
    flowering mid to late 70 cm/2 ft 4 in, available in NZ

BRIDAL SHOWER Klehm USA 1981 double white mid 90 cm/3 ft
    available in Germany NZ

BRIDAL VEIL Kelway UK double pink mid to late 90 cm/3 ft
    available in Germany UK

BRIDE'S DREAM Krekler USA 1965 Japanese white and pale yellow
    free flowering late 90 cm/3 ft available in USA Canada

BRIGHT KNIGHT Glasscock USA 1947 semi-double blood red early
    90 cm/3 ft available in Canada Europe NZ UK USA

BRIGHTNESS Glasscock USA 1947 single red very early
    65 cm/2 ft 2 in, available in USA

BRITISH BEAUTY Kelway UK 1889 double pink scented late
    90 cm/3 ft available in UK

BRITISH EMPIRE Kelway UK 1901 Japanese deep rose red, gold
    centre scented mid-late 76 cm/2 ft 6 in, available in UK

BROTHER CHUCK Klehm USA double blush pink mid

TOP British Beauty

ABOVE Captivation

70 cm/2 ft 4in, available in USA

BUCCANEER Saunders USA 1929 single red very early
70 cm/2 ft 4 in, available in NZ

BUCKEYE BELLE Mains USA 1956 semi-double red early
85 cm/2 ft 10 in, available in NZ Sweden UK USA

BURMA MIDNIGHT R Klehm USA 1980 single or semi-double red
mid 90 cm/3 ft available in USA

*BURMA RUBY Glasscock USA 1951 single bright red scented early
70 cm/2 ft 4 in *see* 'America' available in Canada NZ USA

BUTCH Krekler USA 1959 semi-double reddish pink scented early
90 cm/3 ft available in UK USA

BUTTER BOWL Rosenfield 1955 Japanese pink/yellow scented mid
90 cm/3 ft available in Canada NZ UK USA

CALYPSO Kelway UK 1925 Japanese pink darker pink centre
scented mid to late 95 cm/3 ft 4 in available in UK

CAMELLIA Saunders USA 1942 double white highly scented early
90 cm/3 ft available in Germany USA

CAMPAGNA Saunders USA 1941 single white early up to
50 cm/1 ft 8 in, available in NZ USA

CANDY HEART Bigger USA 1961 double white mid
80 cm/2 ft 8 in, available in USA

CAPITOL DOME Bigger USA 1979 double white early mid
80 cm/2 ft 8 in, available in USA

CAPTIVATION Kelway UK single rose pink scented mid
110 cm/3 ft 6 in, available in UK

CARDINAL'S ROBE Saunders USA 1940 semi-double red early
90 cm/3 ft available in Germany NZ USA

CARINA Saunders USA 1944 semi-double red free flowering early
70 cm/2 ft 4 in, available in Gemany USA

CARMEN Lemoine France 1898 double rose red scented mid to late
83 cm/2 ft 9 in, available in Germany UK

CARNIVAL Kelway UK double carmine pink, cream and rose centre
scented mid 90 cm/3 ft available in UK

CAROL Bockstoce USA 1955 double dark crimson early 60 cm to 75 cm/2 ft to 2 ft 6 in, available in Germany NZ UK USA

CAROLINA MOON Auten USA 1940 double white late 90 cm/3 ft available in Sweden USA

CARRARA Bigger USA 1952 Japanese white with yellow centre mid 110 cm/3 ft 10 in, available in France Germany NZ

CASABLANCA Lins 1942 double white scented mid 100 cm/3 ft available in France USA

CASCADE Kelway UK Japanese pink scented mid to late 90 cm/3 ft available in UK

CATHEDRAL double pink scented free flowering mid 80 cm/2 ft 8 in, available in NZ

CHALICE Saunders USA 1929 single cream very early 120 cm/4 ft available in Europe USA

CHARLEMAGNE Crousse France 1880 double white flushed with pale lilac very late 80 cm/2 ft 8 in available in UK

CHARLES BURGESS Krekler USA 1963 Japanese red, gold-tipped centre mid 75 cm/2 ft 6 in, available in Canada Germany Sweden USA

CHARM Franklin USA 1931 Japanese dark red, red and yellow centre scented 90 cm/3 ft available in NZ UK USA

CHEDDAR CHEESE C G Klehm USA 1973 double cream strongly scented mid 90 cm/3 ft available in Europe NZ Sweden USA

CHEDDAR GOLD R Klehm USA 1971 double white strongly scented mid 75 cm/2 ft 6 in, available in Canada Germany NZ Sweden USA

CHEDDAR SUPREME R Klehm USA Japanese white scented mid 83 cm/2 ft 9 in, available in Germany NZ USA

CHEDDAR SURPRISE R Klehm USA 1980 semi-double to double white scented mid75 cm/2 ft 6 in, available in NZ USA

CHERRY ROYAL Wild USA 1967 double pink mid 80 cm/2 ft 8 in, available in Canada Germany USA

CHERRY RUFFLES Hollingsworth USA 1996 semi-double red free

flowering mid 70 cm/2 ft 4 in, available in USA

CHESTINE GOWDY Brand USA 1913 double silver pink scented
free flowering autumn colour mid-late 95 cm/3 ft 2 in,
available in UK USA

CHIEF JUSTICE Auten USA 1941 semi-double deep red late
85 cm/2 ft 10 in, available in Canada Europe USA

CHIEF WAPELLO Smith 1971 double dark red mid to late
90 cm/3 ft available in USA

CHINOOK Marx/Rogers USA 1981 double blush scented very late
available in NZ USA

CHIPPEWA Murawska 1943 double red early 110 cm/3 ft 10 in,
available in Canada France NZ USA

CINCINNATI Krekler USA 1962 double pink mid 80 cm/2 ft 8 in,
available in Canada NZ USA

CIRCUS CLOWN Wild USA 1970 Japanese rose pink and yellow
mid 90 cm/3 ft available in USA

CLAIRE DUBOIS Crousse France 1886 double pink mid
90 cm/3 ft available in France UK

CLAUDIA Saunders USA 1944 single or semi-double pink early
95 cm/3 ft 2 in, available in Canada USA

CLEMENCEAU Dessert France 1920 double pink some scent very
late 95 cm/3 ft 2 in, available in Europe

CLOUD CAP Bigger USA 1974 double blush white mid
70 cm/2 ft 2 in, available in USA

COLETTE THURILLET Rivière France 1988 Japanese magenta with
yellow centre mid 110 cm/3 ft 10 in, available in France

COLOR MAGNET Hollingsworth USA 1994 single violet pink free
flowering mid 120 cm/4 ft available in USA

COMANCHE Bigger USA 1957 Japanese red mid 90 cm/3 ft
available in USA

COMMAND PERFORMANCE Hollingsworth USA 1996 double red
mid 75 cm/2 ft 6 in, available in USA

COMMANDO Glasscock USA 1944 double dark red early

95 cm/3 ft 2 in, available in NZ USA

CONSTANCE SPRY Saunders USA 1941 semi-double red mid
85 cm/2 ft 10 in, available in NZ USA

CONVOY Glassscock USA 1944 double red early 80 cm/2 ft 8 in,
available in USA

COPELAND'S YELLOW Seidl/Allan NZ 1987 double cream yellow
early 65 cm/2 ft 2 in, available in NZ

CORA STUBBS Krekler Japanese pink and cream mid
110 cm/3 ft 6 in, available in Canada Germany NZ USA

CORAL FAY Fay USA 1973 single to semi-double crimson pink
early 75 cm/2 ft 6 in, available in Europe NZ UK USA

CORAL 'N GOLD Cousins-R Klehm USA 1981 single or semi-
double coral pink early 75 cm/2 ft 6 in, available in Canada
Germany NZ Switzerland USA

CORAL QUEEN Sass USA 1937 double pale pink late
70 cm/2 ft 2 in, available in USA

CORAL SUPREME Wissing USA 1964 semi-double coral pink early
80 cm/2 ft 8 in, available in Canada NZ USA

CORAL TIDE Khlem USA single pink mid 85 cm/2 ft 10 in

COUNTESS OF ALTAMONT Kelway UK 1905 single blush pink
scented mid 95 cm/3 ft 2 in, available in Germany UK

COURAGE Bigger USA 1968 double white mid 90 cm/3 ft available
in USA

CREAM DELIGHT Reath USA 1971 single cream early to mid
70 cm/2 ft 4 in, available in Germany USA

CREAM PUFF Marx/Rogers USA 1981 Japanese blush mid
90 cm/3 ft available in NZ USA

CREAM SAUCER Seidl/Allan NZ 1987 single cream very early
70 cm/2 ft 4 in, available in NZ

CRIMSON GLORY Sass USA 1937 Japanese red scented very late
100 cm/3 ft available in Germany UK

CRUSADER Glasscock USA 1940 semi-double red early
80 cm/2 ft 8 in, available in Germany USA

TOP LEFT Countess of Altamont   TOP RIGHT Dayspring   ABOVE Daystar

DAD Glasscock-Krekler USA semi-double red early 95 cm/3 ft 2 in, available in NZ USA

DAINTY LASS Glasscock 1935 Japanese pink and yellow very early 85 cm/2 ft 10 in, available in Germany USA

DAKOTA Auten USA 1941 single red early 85 cm/2 ft 10 in, available in USA

DANDY DAN Auten USA 1946 semi-double red early 63 cm/2 ft 1 in, available in Canada Germany UK USA

DAUNTLESS Glasscock USA 1944 single red early 90 cm/3 ft available in Germany USA

DAVID HARUM Brand USA 1907 double red mid 90 cm/3 ft available in NZ USA

DAWN PINK Sass USA 1946 single pink early to mid 90 cm/3 ft available in Germany USA

DAWN GLOW Saunders-Hollingsworth USA 1986 single white flushed with mauve scented early 90 cm/3 ft available in USA

DAYSPRING Kelway UK single pink early 73 cm/2 ft 5 in, available in Germany UK

DAYSTAR Kelway UK (name may be invalid) double pink with paler centre scented mid-late 95 cm/3 ft 2 in, available in UK

DAYSTAR Saunders USA 1849 single pale yellow very early 90 cm/3 ft available in USA

DAYTON Krekler USA 1962 double deep pink late 80 cm/2 ft 8 in available in USA

DEAREST Pehrson/Hollingsworth USA 1992 single white veined with pink early 90 cm/3 ft available in USA

DECORATIVE Kelway UK single bright pink scented free flowering autumn colour mid 90 cm/3 ft available in UK

❦ DEFENDER Saunders USA 1929 single dark crimson early 90 cm/3 ft available in UK USA

DELAWARE CHIEF Hollingsworth USA 1984 double red early mid 80 cm/2 ft 8 in, available in USA

DINNER PLATE Klehm USA 1968 double pink scented free

flowering late 90 cm/3 ft available in Canada NZ UK USA

DO TELL Auten USA 1946 Japanese pale pink with darker centre,
early 80 cm/2 ft 8 in, available in France NZ UK USA

DOCTEUR H BARNSBY Dessert France 1913 double pink late
83 cm/2 ft 9 in, available in UK

*DOLORODELL Lins USA 1942 double pink late 90 cm/3 ft
available in France NZ USA

DOREEN Sass USA 1949 Japanese pink, yellow centre scented mid
80 cm/2 ft 8 in, available in Canada NZ UK USA

*DORIS COOPER Cooper USA 1946 double pink scented very late
90 cm/3 ft available in France NZ USA

*DOUGLAS BRAND Tischler USA 1972 double red mid
80 cm/2 ft 8 in, available in Canada USA

DR F R HUXLEY Brand USA 1936 double white mid
80 cm/2 ft 8 in, available in USA

DR F G BRETHOUR Sass USA 1938 double white scented late
85 cm/2 ft 10 in, available in USA

DR L W POLLOCK *see* LEE W POLLOCK

DRAGON'S NEST Auten USA 1933 Japanese or double red mid
95 cm/3 ft 5 in, available in Canada Germany

DRESDEN Kelway UK single white autumn colour early to late
90 cm/3 ft available in Germany UK

DRESDEN PINK Wild USA 1957 double pink late
85 cm/2 ft 10 in, available in Germany USA

DULUTH Franklin USA 1931 double white late 90 cm/3 ft available
in USA

DUNSTAN DREAM McArthur NZ double pink scented late
95 cm/3 ft 4 in, available in NZ

DURER Goos-Koenemann 1910 Japanese white mid
80 cm/2 ft 8 in, available in Germany Switzerland

EARLY DAYBREAK Saunders USA 1949 single white early
75 cm/2 ft 6 in, available in USA

EARLY GLOW Hollingsworth USA 1992 single white early

75 cm/2 ft 6 in, available in USA

EARLYBIRD Saunders USA 1939 single red fine-cut leaves very early
53 cm/1 ft 9 in, available in NZ USA

EASTERN STAR Bigger USA 1975 double white late
85 cm/2 ft 10 in, available in USA

ECHO Saunders USA 1951 single pale pink early 63 cm/2 ft 1 in,
available in Germany USA

EDGAR JESSUP Bockstoce USA 1958 double red mid 90 cm/3 ft
available in Canada, France USA

EDITH CAVELL Kelway UK 1916 double white scented mid
80 cm/2 ft 8 in, available in France UK

EDMUND SPENCER origin unknown double mauve pink mid to
late 90 cm/3 ft available in UK

EDWIN C SHAW Thurlow 1919 double pink scented mid to late
80 cm/2 ft 8 in, available in France USA

ELISE RENAULT Doriat France 1927 double mauve early
85 cm/2 ft 10 in, available in France

ELIZA LUNDY Krekler USA 1975 double deep red similar to 'Red
Charm' early 60 cm/2 ft available in NZ USA

ELIZABETH FOSTER Saunders USA 1941 single pink early mid
80 cm/2 ft 8 in, available in USA

ELIZABETH PENINGER Nicholls Wild USA1958 double pink mid
to late 100 cm/3 ft 6 in, available in France

ELLA CHRISTIANSEN Brand USA 1925 double pink free flowering
mid 85 cm/2 ft 10 in, available in USA

ELLA CHRISTINE KELWAY Kelway UK 1898 double pale mauve
pink scented early to mid 90 cm/3 ft available in UK

ELSIE PICKET Tischler USA 1967 double pink mid
85 cm/2 ft 10 in, available in USA

EMMA KLEHM C G Klehm USA 1951 double pink scented very
late 60 cm/2 ft available in Europe NZ USA

ENTICING 1955 double pink late 90 cm/3 ft available in France

EVELYN TIBBITS Krekler USA 1965 Japanese white scented mid

90 cm/3 ft available in NZ

EVENING WORLD Kelway UK 1928 Japanese coral pink and
white, blush centre scented very late 90 cm/3 ft available in UK

EVENTIDE Glasscock USA 1945 single pink early 100 cm/3 ft
available in NZ USA

FAIRBANKS Auten USA 1945 Japanese blush very late
90 cm to 95 cm/3 ft to 3 ft 2 in, available in Germany USA

FAIRFIELD Hollingsworth USA 1998 single red mid 120 cm/4 ft
available in USA

FAIRY PRINCESS Glasscock-Falk USA 1945 single red early
55 cm/1 ft 10 in, available in NZ USA

FANCY NANCY Auten USA 1944 Japanese pink with pink centre
mid 80 cm/2 ft 8 in, available in Germany NZ USA

FANTASTIC Tischler USA 1972 Japanese pink with pink centre mid
80 cm/2 ft 8 in, available in Germany USA

FASHION SHOW Kelway UK double deep pink scented mid-late
87 cm/2 ft 11 in, available in UK

FAVORITA Auten USA 1956 single red early 80 cm/2 ft 8 in,
available in France USA

FEATHER TOP Wild USA 1967 Japanese rose red mid
90 cm/3 ft available in Canada Europe USA

FEERIE Cayeux France 1990 single scarlet pink early
85 cm/2 ft 10 in, available in France

FESTIVA POWDER PUFF Klehm USA double white mid
85 cm/2 ft 10 in, available in NZ

FESTIVA SUPREME R Klehm USA 1981 double white scented mid
85 cm/2 ft 10 in, available in USA

FEU D'ARTIFICE Rivière France 1986 Japanese red on red free
flowering mid 120 cm/4 ft available in France

FIBRIO GOLD Gilbertson USA Japanese white and gold free
flowering mid 75 cm/2 ft 6 in, available in USA Canada

FIRE OPAL Marx-Rogers 1984 double red late 90 cm/3 ft
available in USA

Fashion Show

FIREBELL Mains 1959 double red early 85 cm/2 ft 10 in,
  available in Canada Germany USA

FIRELIGHT Saunders USA 1950 single pink very early
  75 cm/2 ft 6 in, available in Germany USA

FIRST LADY Klehm USA double pink mid 80 cm/2 ft 8 in, Canada
  France Germany NZ Sweden USA

FLAG OF WAR Kelway UK 1899 single maroon-red scented
  autumn colour very early 100 cm/3 ft available in UK

FLORENCE ELLIS Nicholls USA 1948 double pink scented mid
  90 cm/3 ft available in Germany NZ UK

FLORENCE NICHOLLS Nicholls USA 1938 double white mid
  80 cm/2 ft 8 in, available in Germany Switzerland NZ USA

FOKKER Ruys Netherlands 1928 double red mid 80 cm/2 ft 8 in
  available in Germany Switzerland

FRANCES MAINS Mains 1955 double pink mid 90 cm/3 ft
  available in France USA

FRANCES WILLARD Brand USA 1907 double white some scent
  free flowering mid 85 cm/2 ft 10 in, available in Germany USA

FRANCOIS ORTHEGAT Parmentier France 1850 double red mid
  90 cm/3 ft available in Canada

FRANK KEITH Moots 1962 semi-double red mid 100 cm/3 ft
  available in France

FRIENDSHIP Glasscock-Falk 1955 single pink free flowering very
  early 70 cm/2 ft 4 in, available in USA

FRINGED IVORY Klehm USA double white mid 85 cm/2 ft 10 in,
  available in Germany USA

FUYAJO Japanese red with buff-edged red petaloides mid
  110 cm/4 ft available in France

GAIL TISCHLER Brand USA 1964 Japanese pink gold and pink
  centre late available in USA

GARDEN GLORY Auten 1956 double red free flowering late
  90 cm/3 ft available in USA

GARDEN LACE Hollingsworth USA 1992 Japanese pink and yellow

free flowering mid 90 cm/3 ft available in USA

GARDEN PEACE Saunders USA 1941 single white scented early 85
cm/2 ft 10 in, available in Germany NZ USA

GAY CAVALIER Glascock USA 1944 single red very early
75 cm/1 ft available in Germany USA

GAY PAREE Auten USA 1933 Japanese pink cream late
110 cm/3 ft 10 in, available in Canada Europe USA NZ

GAYBORDER JUNE Hoogendoorn Netherlands 1949 double pink
mid 90 cm/3 ft available in France UK USA

GENE WILD Cooper USA 1956 double pale pink mid or late
55 cm/1 ft 10 in, available in Europe Germany USA

GENERAL MACMAHON Calot France 1867 (formerly 'Augustin
d'Hour') double red mid 90 cm/3 ft available in Canada

GEORGIANA SHAYLOR Shaylor USA 1908 double pale pink
scented mid 80 cm/2 ft 8 in, available in France USA

GERRY Glasscock-Klehm USA 1988 double red free flowering early
mid 80 cm/2 ft 8in, available in USA Canada

GERTRUDE ALLEN Nicholls/Wild USA 1958 Japanese white and
yellow late 90 cm/3 ft available in USA

GILBERT BARTHELOT Doriat France 1931 double pink, scented
mid 90 cm/3 ft available in France UK

GILDED SPLENDOR Japanese pink cerise, gold-edged centre mid
85 cm/2 ft 10 in, available in NZ

GLAD TIDINGS McArthur NZ double plum red very late
85 cm/2 ft 10 in, available in NZ

GLOIRE DE CHARLES GOMBAULT Gombault France 1866 double
pink scented mid 100 cm/3 ft available in France Sweden

GLORY HALLELUJAH C G Klehm USA double rose red scented
late 83 cm/2 ft 11 in, available in Canada Germany
NZ Sweden UK USA

GLOWING RASPBERRY ROSE Cousins-R Klehm USA 1981 double
raspberry red early 80 cm/2 ft 8 in, available in Germany
NZ USA

GO DAIGO Millet France 1926 Japanese lilac with yellow centre
early 90 cm/3 ft available in France

GOLD STANDARD Rosenfield USA 1934 Japanese white scented
mid 90 cm/3 ft available in NZ

GOLDEN BRACELET Brand USA 1939 double cream mid available
in Canada

*GOLDEN GLOW Glasscock USA 1935 single pink early
65 cm/2 ft 2 in, available in Sweden USA

GOLDILOCKS Gilbertson 1975 double pale yellow some scent early
70 cm/2 ft 4 in, available in Germany NZ USA

GOLLY Krekler USA 1966 double pale pink mid 85 cm/2 ft 10 in
available in NZ USA

GRACE LOOMIS Saunders USA 1920 double white scented late
90 cm/3 ft available in France UK

GREEN LOTUS Krekler-Klehm USA semi-double green-striped
white early 70 cm/2 ft 4 in, available in USA

GROVER CLEVELAND Terry 1904 double crimson some scent late
mid 90 cm/3 ft available in France USA

*HANSINA BRAND Brand USA 1925 double pink late 90 cm/3 ft
available in USA

HARI-AI-NIN Babcock 1929 Japanese red mid 90 cm/3 ft
available in Germany NZ Sweden Switzerland

HAWAII Murawska USA 1960 Japanese or double pink mid
85 cm/2 ft 10 in, available in NZ

HEIDI Tischler USA 1972 Japanese pink mid 64 cm/2 ft 2 in,
available in NZ USA

HELEN HAYES single Murawska USA 1943 double pink scented
mid 88 cm/2 ft 9 in, available in UK USA

HELEN MATTHEWS Saunders/Krekler USA 1953 semi-double red
early 60 cm/2 ft available in NZ

HELEN SEARS Smith/Krekler USA 1928 Japanese pale lavender
pink mid to late 90 cm/3 ft available in NZ

HENRI POTIN Doriat France 1924 Japanese deep pink and yellow

highly scented late 85 cm/2 ft 10 in, available in
Canada France USA

HENRY BOCKSTOCE Bockstoce USA 1955 double red early
75 cm/2 ft 6 in, available in Canada USA

HENRY SASS Sass USA 1948 double white free flowering late mid
available in USA

HENRY ST CLAIR Brand USA 1941 double red mid 90 cm/3 ft
available in USA

HERITAGE Saunders USA 1950 double scarlet red some scent early
90 cm/3 ft available in Canada Germany NZ USA

HERMIONE Sass USA 1932 double pink scented late 90 cm/3 ft
available in NZ USA

HIAWATHA Franklin USA 1931 double deep red late 90 cm/3 ft
available in UK USA

HI-MABEL Bockstoce USA 1961 semi-double pink early
110 cm/3 ft 10 in, available in France NZ USA

HIGHLIGHT Auten-Wild USA 1952 double red late mid
75 cm/2 ft 6 in, available in Germany USA

HIT PARADE Nicholls 1965 Japanese pink mid 110 cm/3 ft 10 in,
available in Germany USA

HONOR Saunders USA 1941 single or semi-double pink free
flowering early 90 cm/3 ft available in France UK USA

HOOSIERLAND C G Klehm USA 1968 semi-double red mid
70 cm/2 ft 4 in, available in NZ USA

HORIZON Saunders USA 1943 single white early 90 cm/3 ft
available in Canada NZ UK USA

HOT CHOCOLATE Sass USA 1971 Japanese red, red and gold
centre mid 85 cm/2 ft 10 in, available in Canada NZ

ILLINI BELLE Glasscock USA 1941 semi-double red early
90 cm/3 ft available in Canada Germany Sweden NZ UK USA

ILLINI WARRIOR Glasscock-Falk USA 1955 single red early
75 cm/2 ft 6 in, available in Canada France UK USA

IMPERIAL PARASOL Marx-Rogers USA 1979 Japanese pink and

white late 70 cm/2 ft 2 in, available in USA

INSTITUTEUR DORIAT Doriat France double pink scented mid 75 cm/2 ft 6 in, available in Germany UK

ISRAEL Krekler USA 1975 single dark red early 75 cm/2 ft 6 in, available in NZ USA

IVORY JEWEL Klehm USA 1981 single white mid to late 75 cm/2 ft 6 in, available in NZ

IVORY VICTORY Klehm USA double white scented free flowering mid 80 cm/2 ft 8 in, available in USA

JACQUELINE HANRATTY Gardner pre-1951 double red early mid available in USA

JACQUES DORIAT Doriat France 1928 Japanese pink with yellow centre late 100 cm/3 ft available in France

JAMES KELWAY Kelway UK 1900 double blush pink scented mid 100 cm/3 ft available in France UK

JAMES PILLOW Pillow USA 1936 double pink scented late 90 cm/3 ft available in Germany NZ USA

JAMES R MANN Thurlow USA 1920 double pink scented mid 90 cm/3 ft available in UK USA

JANICE Saunders USA 1939 single or semi-double pink some scent mid 85 cm/2 ft 10 in, available in Canada Germany

JAPPENSHA-IKHU (JAPAN SHUAKI) Japan Japanese pale pink mid 80 cm/2 ft 8 in, available in NZ

JAY CEE Klehm USA 1959 double pink late 80 cm/2 ft 8 in, available in Canada USA

JAYHAWKER Bigger USA 1949 double pink scented mid 110 cm/3 ft 6 in available in NZ USA

JEAN E BOCKSTOCE Bockstoce USA 1933 double wine red early 85 cm/2 ft 10 in, available in NZ USA

JEANNE D'ARC Calot France 1858 double pink scented mid 90 cm/3 ft available in France UK

JOHN GARDNER Gardner pre-1951 Japanese red with gold-edge, red centre late mid available in USA

JOHN HARVARD Auten USA 1939 semi-double red very early tall
available in USA. 'John Harward' (below) may be the same.

JOHN HARWARD Auten USA 1939 single to semi-double red early
to mid 120 cm/4 ft available in France USA

JOHN HOWARD WIGELL Wigell 1942 double deep pink early to
mid 75 cm/2 ft 6 in, available in Europe USA

JOHNNY Japanese red-pink and gold mid 80 cm/2 ft 8 in, available
in Switzerland NZ

JOSEPH CHRISTIE Rosenfield 1929 double white scented mid
90 cm/3 ft available in NZ

JUDY BECKER Sass USA 1941 double very dark red late
60 cm/2 ft available in USA

KAKODEN Japan introduced 1955 semi-double to double white
mid 55 cm/1 ft 10 in, available in NZ USA

KAMONO KEROGANA single red mid 85 cm/2 ft 10 in,
available in NZ

KARATZU single garnet red mid 110 cm/3 ft 10 in,
available in France

KAREN GRAY Krekler USA 1965 Japanese fuchsia red and cream
mid 90 cm/3 ft available in Canada France NZ USA

KATHERINE HAVEMEYER Thurlow 1921 double pink free
flowering late 85 cm/2 ft 10 in, available in France

KATHRYN FONTEYN double blush pink fading to white scented
mid 90 cm/3 ft available in France NZ UK

KAY TISCHLER Brand-Tischler USA 1964 Japanese pink, pink-
tipped yellow centre mid available in USA

KELWAY'S BRILLIANT Kelway UK 1928 Japanese red scented mid
to late 90 cm/3 ft available in UK

KELWAY'S FAIRY QUEEN Kelway UK 1927 semi-double coral pink
scented mid to late 78 cm/1 ft 7 in, available in Switzerland UK

KELWAY'S LOVELY Kelway 1905 double pink scented late
100 cm/3 ft available in UK

KELWAY'S MAJESTIC Kelway 1928 Japanese raspberry red on red

scented early to very late 100 cm/3 ft available in NZ UK

KEVIN Krekler USA 1975 double pink mid 85 cm/2 ft 2 in, available in NZ

KICKAPOO Auten USA 1931 single red scented late 90 cm/3 ft available in France

KING OF ENGLAND Kelway UK 1901 Japanese red mid 78 cm/1 ft 7 in, available in Germany NZ

KNIGHTHOOD Kelway double red scented mid to late 75 cm/2 ft 6 in, available in UK

KOJIKI Millet France 1926 single pink late 110 cm/3 ft 6 in, available in France

LA FIANCEE Dessert France 1902 single white, mid 85 cm/2 ft 10 in, available in France

LA FRANCE Lemoine France 1901 double pink scented free flowering late 78 cm/2 ft 7 in, available in Canada Europe

LA LORRAINE Lemoine France 1901 double white scented mid 75 cm/2 ft 6 in, available in NZ USA

LA PERLE Crousse France 1886 double pale pink highly scented free flowering mid 78 cm/2 ft 7 in, available in NZ USA

LADY KATE Vories 1924 double pink, late 120 cm/4 ft available in NZ

LADY ORCHID Biggar USA 1942 double pink, late 110 cm/3 ft 10 in, available in Canada France Switzerland UK USA

LANCASTER IMP Klehm USA double white free flowering mid to late 65 cm/2 ft 2 in, available in NZ

LARGO Vories 1929 Japanese pink, pink and yellow centre mid 90 cm/3 ft available in Canada Germany NZ Sweden USA

LAURA MAGNUSON Saunders USA 1941 semi-double pink mid 60 cm/2 ft available in USA

LAVENDER MIST G McArthur NZ single lavender early 95 cm/3 ft available in NZ

LAVON Hollingsworth USA 1993 double pink and yellow scented

Kelways Majestic

late mid 120 cm/4 ft available in USA

L'ECLATANTE Calot France 1860 double red scented late to very
late 90 cm/3 ft available in Canada France UK

LE CHARME Eliason 1964 Japanese pink and buff-yellow late to
150 cm/5 ft available in USA

LE CYGNE Lemoine France 1907 double white scented free
flowering early 69 cm/2 ft 3 in, available in UK USA

LE JOUR Shaylor USA 1915 single white mid 90 cm/3 ft
available in USA

LE PRINTEMPS Lemoine France 1905 single cream yellow early
80 cm/2 ft 8 in, available in Canada France Sweden

LEGION OF HONOUR Saunders USA 1941 single scarlet red early
70 cm/2 ft 4 in, available in Germany

LIBERATOR Saunders USA 1940 single red early 90 cm/3 ft
available in France

LIEBCHEN Murawska USA 1959 single pink mid 90 cm/3 ft
available in NZ Sweden USA

LIGHTS OUT Klehm USA single dark red early 90 cm/3 ft available
in USA

LILAC TIMES Lins 1958 Japanese lilac pink with lilac centre late
70 cm/2 ft 4 in, available in France NZ

LILLIAN WILD Wild USA 1930 double white late 90 cm/3 ft
available in Canada UK USA

LITTLE RED GEM Reath USA 1988 single red very early
38 cm/15 in, available in Germany USA

LOIS KELSEY Kelsey 1934 semi-double white slightly scented mid
90 cm/3 ft available in Germany NZ UK USA

LONGFELLOW Brand USA 1907 double red late 60 cm/2 ft
available in USA

LORA DEXHEIMER Brand USA 1913 double red mid 90 cm/3 ft
available in UK USA

LORD AVEBURY Kelway UK 1904 double or semi-double red
scented mid to late 90 cm/3 ft available in Germany UK

LORD CAVIN Klehm USA double white with red stripes mid
90 cm/3 ft available in Canada France Germany NZ UK USA

LORELEI Hollingsworth USA 1996 double apricot pink scented
mid 65 cm/2 ft 2 in, available in USA

LORETTA FRANK Franklin USA 1953 single pink early 90 cm/3 ft
available in USA

LOTTIE DAWSON REA Rea USA 1939 double white late
90 cm/3 ft available in NZ USA

LOTUS BLOOM Saunders USA 1943 semi-double pink early
95 cm/3 ft available in NZ USA

LOUIS BARTHELOT Doriat France 1927 double white slightly
scented mid 90 cm/3 ft available in Germany UK USA

LOUIS VAN HOUTTE Calot France 1867 double red mid
90 cm/3 ft available in France USA

LOUISE LOSSING Lossing 1943 double white scented mid
110 cm/3 ft 10 in, available in Canada France

LOUISE MARX Marx-Rogers USA 1981 Japanese white scented
prolific mid to late up to 120 cm/4 ft available in NZ USA

LOVELY LOUISE Murwaska 1962 double pale pink scented mid
80 cm/2 ft 8 in, available in France

LOWELL THOMAS Rosenfield USA 1934 double or semi-double
red late 60 cm/2 ft available in France Germany Sweden
UK USA

LUCKY Krekler-Klehm USA Japanese red and yellow mid
75 cm/2 ft 6 in, available in USA

LUDOVICA Saunders USA 1941 semi-double pink very early
58 cm/1 ft 11 in, available in Canada Germany NZ USA

LULLABY Pehrson USA 1974 double blush, very late 120 cm/4 ft
available in NZ USA

LYRIC Kelway UK 1894 double mauve pink scented mid
90 cm/3 ft available in UK

MADAME BOULANGER Neuheiten double pink late 90 cm/3 ft
available in France

Louis van Houtte

MADAME BUTTERFLY Franklin USA 1933 Japanese purple pink
  mid 100 cm/3 ft available in Germany NZ USA

MADAME CLAUDE TAIN Doriat France 1927 double white scented
  late 87 cm/2 ft 11 in, available in Canada Europe UK USA

MADAME DE VATRY Guérin 1863 double blush scented free
  flowering 80 cm/2 ft 8 in, available in Switzerland

MADAME EDOUARD DORIAT Doriat France 1924 double white
  highly scented mid 110 cm/3 ft 10 in, available in France

MADAME EMILE DEBATENE Dessert/Doriat France 1927 double
  pink late 90 cm/3 ft available in Germany NZ UK

MADAME FURTADO Guérin France 1856 double mauve-pink mid
  90 cm/3 ft available in France

MADAME GEISSLER Crousse France 1880 double pale pink
  scented mid 90 cm/3 ft available in France

MADAME HENRY FUCHS Rivière France 1955 Japanese red with
  red and gold centre late 90 cm/3 ft available in France

MADAME JULES DESSERT Dessert France 1909 double pink
  scented free flowering mid to late 110 cm/3 ft 10 in,
  available in France

MADELON Dessert France 1922 double pink scented late
  90 cm/3 ft available in Canada Germany

MADYLONE Van Loon 1966 double pale pink late
  80 cm/2 ft 8 in, available in NZ Sweden USA

MAESTRO Auten USA 1957 double red mid 85 cm/2 ft 10 in,
  available in NZ

MAGENTA GEM Krekler-Klehm USA single magenta mid
  60 cm/2 ft available in USA

MAI FLEURI Lemoine France 1905 single blush early 70 cm/2 ft
  available in Canada Germany Sweden UK

MANKATO Brand USA 1936 single white free flowering mid
  available in USA

MANY HAPPY RETURNS Hollingsworth USA 1990 double red
  prolific early mid 75 cm/2 ft 6 in, available in Germany NZ USA

MARCELLA Lins USA 1952 double white mid 75 cm/2 ft 6 in,
available in USA

MARIE CROUSSE Crousse France 1892 double pink scented free
flowering mid 88 cm/2 ft 11 in, available in Canada Europe

MARIE FISCHER Fischer 1973 single pale blush very early
83 cm/2 ft 9 in, available in NZ

MARIE LEMOINE Lemoine France 1869 double white sweet scent
late 90 cm/3 ft available in Canada UK

MARIETTA SISSON Sass 1933 double pink highly scented early
80 cm/2 ft 8 in, available in USA

MARSHMALLOW BUTTON Klehm USA double white scented, mid
60 cm/2 ft available in USA

MARSHMALLOW PUFF Klehm USA double white, mid
70 cm/2 ft available in USA Canada

MARTHA BULLOCH Brand USA 1907 double pink scented late
mid 120 cm/4 ft available in Germany USA

MARY BRAND Brand USA 1907 double red mid 70 cm/2 ft
available in Germany USA

MARY EDDY JONES Nicholls USA 1961 double pink scented early
mid available in Canada

MARY JO LEGERE Pehrson USA 1978 double pink available in NZ

MATILDA LEWIS Saunders USA 1921 double maroon autumn
colour late 90 cm/3 ft available in UK USA

MAY APPLE Wolf-Bigger USA 1977 single pink early
75 cm/2 ft 6 in, available in NZ USA

MAY MUSIC Saunders USA 1973 single apricot buff early
90 cm/3 ft available in Germany USA

MAY TREAT Krekler 1978 single coral pink late 90 cm/3 ft available
in USA

MEADOW LARK Bigger USA 1977 Japanese pink and yellow late
80 cm/2 ft 10 in available in USA

MESSAGERE Lemoine France 1909 single white, early 90 cm/3 ft
available in Canada

MIKADO Japan 1893 Japanese magenta red with gold centre late
110 cm/3 ft 10 in, available in France NZ USA

MINNIE SHAYLOR Shaylor USA 1919 semi-double white mid to
late 90 cm/3 ft available in NZ USA

MINUET Franklin 1931 double pink late 100 cm/3 ft
available in NZ USA

MISS ECKHARDT Van der Meer Netherlands 1928 double pink
scented mid 90 cm/3 ft Europe UK USA

MISS MARY Krekler USA 1967 single red mid 85 cm/2 ft 10 in,
available in USA

MISSIE'S BLUSH Bainum/Hollingsworth 1994 double blush fading
to white mid 80 cm/2 ft 8 in, available in USA

MISTER ED C G Klehm 1980 double blush scented late (US) early
(UK) 70 cm/2 ft 4 in, available in Canada Germany NZ Sweden
UK USA

MONSIEUR ADAM MODZELEWSKY Doriat 1935 double red with
white petal margins early 120 cm/4 ft available in France

MONSIEUR MARTIN CAHUZAC Dessert France 1899 double red
mid 90 cm/3 ft available in Canada Germany Sweden Switzerland
UK USA

MOON OVER BARRINGTON R Klehm double white scented mid
65 cm/2 ft 4 in available in Germany USA

MOON RIVER C G Klehm USA semi-double pale pink some scent
mid 70 cm/2 ft available in Europe NZ USA

MOONRISE Saunders USA 1949 semi-double white, yellow centre
scented early 70 cm/2 ft available in Canada Germany NZ USA

MOONSHINE semi-double pale yellow early 90 cm/3 ft
available in NZ

MOTHER'S CHOICE Glasscock USA 1950 double white late
75 cm/2 ft 6 in, available in Germany Canada NZ UK USA

MR ED *see* MISTER ED

MR G F HEMERICK Van Leeuwen USA 1930 Japanese pink late
75 cm/2 ft 6 in, available in Germany NZ Sweden UK USA

*MRS A M BRAND Brand USA 1925 double white scented late
90 cm/3 ft available in USA

MRS BRYCE FONTAINE Brand USA 1916 double dark crimson mid
85 cm/2 ft 10 in, available in USA

MRS EDWARD HARDING Shaylor USA 1918 double white mid
90 cm/3 ft available in Canada Europe UK

MRS EUCLID SNOW Brand USA double blush mid
80 cm/2 ft 8 in, available in NZ

MRS FRANK BEACH Brand USA 1925 double white scented free
flowering late short available in USA

*MRS J V EDLUND Edlund USA 1929 double white scented late or
very late up to 120 cm/4 ft available in Europe UK USA

MRS JAMES KELWAY Kelway UK 1936 double white late
available in USA

MRS LIVINGSTON FARRAND Nicholls 1935 double salmon pink
very late 95 cm/3 ft available in Germany NZ USA

MT ST HELENS Marx-Rogers USA 1981 double dark red good scent
late 90 cm/3 ft available in USA

MY LOVE Hollingsworth USA 1992 double white late mid
90 cm/3 ft available in USA

MY PAL RUDY Klehm USA 1952 double pink scented mid
93 cm/3 ft available in Canada Germany NZ UK USA

MYRA MACRAE Tischler USA 1967 double pale lavender pink late
75 cm/2 ft 6 in, available in Germany USA

MYRON D BIGGER Bigger USA 1966 double blush white late
65 cm/2ft 4 in. available in USA

MYRTLE TISCHLER Franklin/Tischler USA 1963 double pink mid
80 cm/2ft 10 in, available in Canada Germany USA

NANCY NICHOLLS Nicholls USA 1941 double blush scented
prolific very late 90 cm/3 ft available in Germany NZ UK USA

NATALIE Saunders USA 1939 semi-double pink early 60 cm/2 ft
available in Canada Germany

NELLIE SHAYLOR Shaylor USA 1919 Japanese red and cream late

available in Canada NZ USA

NEON Nicholls 1941 Japanese neon pink, gold-tipped red centre mid 110 cm/3 ft 10 in, available in Europe USA

NIGHTWATCH Saunders USA 1950 semi-double dark red early mid 80 cm/2 ft 10 in, available in USA

NIPPON BEAUTY Auten 1927 Japanese red with red centre late 120 cm/4 ft available in Canada France USA

NIPPON BRILLIANT Auten 1933 Japanese red, red and yellow centre late 110 cm/3 ft 10 in, available in France

NIPPON GOLD Auten USA 1929 Japanese pink and yellow late available in USA

NOEMIE DEMAY Calot France 1867 double pink scented mid 85 cm/2 ft 10 in, available in France

NOSEGAY Saunders USA 1950 single pink, early 70 cm/2 ft 4 in, available in Canada USA

NOVA Saunders USA 1950 single pale green yellow very early 75 cm/2 ft 6 in, available in USA

O SHU KEN ('O Sho Kun') white early to mid 80 cm/2 ft 8 in, available in NZ Switzerland

OPAL HAMILTON Nicholls-Wild USA 1957 Japanese pink and yellow mid 90 cm/3 ft available in Canada Europe USA

ORANGE GLORY Auten 1956 single scarlet red early, 120 cm/4 ft available in France

ORANGE LACE Bigger USA 1966 Japanese pale pink, yellow and pink centre late 85 cm/2 ft 10 in, available in USA

ORPEN Kelway UK Japanese purple red scented late 85 cm/2 ft 10 in, available in UK

PADDY'S RED single red mid 90 cm/3 ft available in NZ

♆ P. CAMBESSEDESII single pink early 45 cm/1ft 6 in, available in UK

P. EMODI single white very early 100 cm/3 ft available in NZ

♆ P. OBVATA single pink mid 60 cm/2 ft available in UK

♆ P. OBVATA var. ALBA single white mid 55 cm/1ft 10 in,

available in UK

P. OFFICINALIS single red mid 60 cm/2 ft available in NZ
Switzerland

❦ *P. OFFICINALIS* 'ANEMONIFLORA ROSEA' single purple-pink
mid 45 cm/1ft 6in available in UK

P. OFFICINALIS subsp.*VILLOSA* single red early 45 cm/1 ft 6 in,
available in USA

P. PEREGRINA single red early 50 cm/1 ft 8 in,
available in NZ Switzerland UK

P. x *SMOUTHII* single crimson scented cut-leaved early
45 cm/1 ft 6 in, available in Germany Switzerland USA

P. TENUIFOLIA single dark red fine-cut leaves early 50 cm/1 ft 8 in,
available in NZ Sweden Switzerland

P. TENUIFOLIA 'FLORE PLENA' double red fine-cut leaves early
50 cm/1 ft 8 in, available in NZ

P. VEITCHII single purple autumn colour early 50 cm/1 ft 8 in,
available in Sweden Switzerland USA

P. VEITCHII var. *WOODWARDII* single pink early 30 cm/1 ft
available in Sweden Switzerland

P. WITTMANNIANA single pale yellow or cream early
80 cm/2 ft 8 in, available in Switzerland

PAGEANT Saunders USA 1941 single pink yellow centre early
90 cm to 120 cm/3ft to 4 ft available in Germany NZ USA

PAREE FROU FROU Klehm USA Japanese pink on pink scented
early 80 cm/2 ft 8 in, available in NZ

PARTY DRESS Krekler USA single red early 30 cm/1 ft
available in NZ

PASTEL GEM Bigger USA 1979 double pale cream pink late mid
90 cm/3 ft available in USA

PAT VICTOR Krekler USA Japanese white and yellow late
85 cm/2 ft 10 in, available in USA

PATRIOT Saunders USA 1943 single blood red early
90 cm/3 ft available in Canada USA

PAUL BUNYAN Lins 1955 double pink very late 90 cm/3 ft
available in Canada France NZ Switzerland USA

PAUL M WILD Wild USA 1964 double red late (US) mid (UK)
95 cm/3 ft 2 in, available in NZ USA Europe UK

PEACH DELIGHT Smirnov USA 1978 semi-double peach pink mid
to late 110 cm/3 ft 10 in, available in NZ

PEPPERMINT Nicholls-Wild USA 1958 double pale pink late mid
90 cm/3 ft available in Canada USA

PETITE RENEE Dessert France 1899 Japanese pink yellow white
mid to late 85 cm/2 ft 10 in, available in Germany Sweden USA

PETTICOAT FLOUNCE R Klehm USA 1985 double pink early
85 cm/2 ft 10 in, available in Canada Germany NZ USA

PHILIPPE RIVOIRE Rivière France 1911 double dark red scented
late 75 cm/2 ft 6 in, available in Europe USA

PHILOMELE Calot France 1861 Japanese or double pink scented
autumn colour free flowering mid 75 cm/2 ft 6 in,
available in UK

PHYLLIS KELWAY Kelway UK 1908 semi-double rose pink some
scent mid 80 cm/2 ft 8 in, available in USA

PICO Freeborn USA 1934 single white mid 90 cm/3 ft
available in Canada Germany USA

PICOTEE Saunders USA 1949 single white and pink early
45 cm/1 ft 6 in, available in NZ USA

PINAFORE Bigger USA 1991 Japanese pink with pink centre mid
75 cm/2 ft 6 in, available in USA

PINK CAMEO Bigger USA 1954 double pink mid 75 cm/2 ft 6 in,
available in UK USA

PINK CHALICE Saunders USA single pink late 110 cm/3 ft 6 in,
available in France

PINK CRESCENDO Hollingsworth USA 1984 double pink late
90 cm/3 ft available in USA

PINK DERBY Bigger USA 1966 double pink and white mid available
in USA

PINK FORMAL Nicholls USA 1953 double pink late mid
90 cm/3 ft available in Canada Germany NZ USA

PINK HAWAIIAN CORAL R Klehm 1981 double coral pink scented
early 90 cm/3 ft available in Canada Germany NZ USA

PINK LEMONADE C G Klehm USA 1951 double pink and yellow
scented mid 90 cm/3 ft available in Germany NZ Sweden USA

PINK PARASOL SURPRISE R Klehm USA 1992 double pink cream
and yellow highly scented early 75 cm/2 ft 6 in, available in USA

PINK PARFAIT C G Klehm USA 1975 double pink some scent late
95 cm/3 ft 2 in, available in Canada Germany NZ UK USA

PINK POM POM Reath USA 1991 double pink late 90 cm/3 ft
available in USA

PINK PRINCESS formerly 'Pink Dawn' single pale pink mid
95 cm/3 ft 2 in, available in Germany NZ UK USA

PINK WONDER Bigger USA 1950 double pink free flowering late
mid 90 cm/3 ft available in USA

PLAINSMAN Bigger USA 1949 Japanese blush with yellow centre
free flowering mid 90 cm/3 ft available in NZ USA

POLAR STAR Sass USA 1932 Japanese white and yellow late mid
100 cm/3 ft available in USA

POLLY SHARP Carol Warner 1997 single pink fading to white mid
to late 65 cm/2 ft 2in, available in USA

PRAIRIE FIRE Brand USA 1932 Japanese deep pink and red mid
80 cm/2 ft 8 in, available in France USA

PRAIRIE BELLE Bigger USA 1945 semi-double cream-pink fading to
white mid 120 cm/4 ft available in USA

PRESIDENT LINCOLN Brand USA 1928 single red late
110 cm/3 ft 10 in, available in France USA

PRESIDENT TAFT Blaauw USA 1909 double pink free flowering
late 90 cm/3 ft available in Germany NZ

PRESIDENT WILSON Thurlow 1918 double mauve pink scented
mid 120 cm/4 ft available in France

PRIAM Sass USA 1930 double red mid 120 cm/4 ft

available in USA

PRIDE OF SOMERSET Kelway UK single red late 85 cm/2 ft 10 in,
available in UK

PRIMEVERE Lemoine France 1907 double white anemone form
highly scented free flowering mid 88 cm/2 ft 11 in,
available in UK USA Switzerland

PRINCESS BRIDE Klehm USA double white early 70 cm/2 ft
available in USA

QUALITY FOLK Krekler USA 1973 single pink early
40 cm/1 ft 4 in, available in NZ

QUEEN ELIZABETH Kelway UK single pink scented early
82 cm/2 ft 9 in, available in UK

QUEEN OF HAMBURG Sass USA 1937 double pink free flowering
late mid 90 cm/3 ft available in USA

QUEEN OF SHEBA Sass USA 1937 double pink late 90 cm/3 ft
available in UK USA

R A NAPIER Brand USA 1939 double pink and white late mid
90 cm/3 ft available in USA

RASPBERRY CHARM Wissing-R Klehm semi-double red early
90 cm/3 ft available in Germany USA

RASPBERRY ICE C G Klehm 1980 double rose red mid 90 cm/3 ft
available in NZ USA

RAY PAYTON Krekler USA Japanese red, yellow-edged centre mid to
late 95 cm/2 ft 10 in, available in Canada NZ Sweden

RED BEAUTY Auten USA 1956 semi-double red early
75 cm/2 ft 6 in, available in NZ

RED COMET Auten USA 1956 double red mid 90 cm/3 ft available
in NZ USA

RED GLORY Auten USA 1937 semi-double red early 90 cm/3 ft
Europe USA

RED GRACE Glasscock USA 1980 double red mid 70 cm/2 ft4in
Canada Germany NZ USA

RED RED ROSE Saunders USA 1942 semi-double red mid

75 cm/2 ft 6 in, available in Canada Europe USA

RED VELVET Auten USA 1945 single red late 85 cm/2 ft 10 in, available in Germany

REINE DELUXE Klehm USA double pink free flowering mid available in Canada NZ

REINE SUPREME Klehm USA 1985 double pink red stripes scented mid 85 cm/2 ft 10 in, available in NZ USA

REWARD Saunders USA 1941 single red some scent early 70 cm/2 ft 4 in, available in Canada USA

RICHARD CARVEL Brand 1913 double crimson red highly scented free flowering very early 85 cm/2 ft 10 in, available in France USA

RIGOLOTTE (also listed as Rigolette Rigoloto) Doriat France 1931 Japanese dark red mid 90 cm/3 ft available in France

RIVIDA Harrell-Varner 1985 single lavender pink late 75 cm/ 2 ft 6 in, available in NZ

ROBERT Gardner pre-1951 double dark pink late 120 cm/4 ft available in USA

ROBERT W AUTEN Auten USA 1948 semi-double dark red early 75 cm/2 ft 6 in, available in Canada Germany Switzerland USA

ROSABEL Sass USA 1937 double red free flowering mid 85 cm/2 ft 10 in, available in USA

ROSALIE Auten USA 1927 double rose red mid to 60 cm/2 ft available in USA

ROSE GARLAND Saunders USA 1943 single rose pink early 85 cm/2 ft 10 in, available in USA

ROSE HEART *see* BESS BOCKSTOCE

ROSE MARIE Auten/Glasscock USA 1936 double dark red early mid 75 cm/2 ft 6 in, available in NZ

ROSE OF DELIGHT Kelway UK 1925 single bright pink scented early to mid 90 cm/3 ft available in UK

ROSE PEARL Bigger USA double pink scented late 75 cm/2 ft 6 in, available in USA

ROSE SHAYLOR Shaylor USA 1920 double pink some scent mid

Rose Garland

70 cm/2 ft available in Germany USA

ROSY CHEEK Saunders USA 1943 semi-double rose pink early
78 cm/2 ft 7 in, available in Canada Germany USA

ROY PEHRSON'S BEST YELLOW Pehrson-Laning USA 1982 single
yellow early 85 cm/2 ft 10 in, available in USA

ROYAL ROSE Reath USA 1980 semi-double pink early
85 cm/2 ft 10 in, available in Germany NZ USA

ROZELLA Reath USA 1991 double pink 79 cm/
2 ft 7 in, available in Germany USA

RUSHLIGHT Saunders USA 1950 single cream early 90 cm/3 ft
available in Canada Germany UK USA

RUTH CLAY Kelsey 1935 double red 80 cm/2 ft 8 in,
available in Switzerland USA

RUTH ELIZABETH Brand USA 1936 double red late
75 cm/2 ft 6 in, available in France USA

SALMON BEAUTY Glasscock-Auten USA 1939 double pink mid
90 cm/3 ft available in NZ

SALMON CHIFFON Rudolph/R Klehm USA 1981 single salmon
pink early 85 cm/2 ft 10 in, available in Canada Germany
NZ USA

SALMON DREAM Reath USA 1979 semi-double pale salmon pink
mid 85 cm/2 ft 10 in, available in NZ

SALMON GLORY Glasscock USA 1947 double salmon pink early
85 cm/2 ft 10 in, available in Canada NZ USA

SALMON SURPRISE Cousins-R Klehm USA 1986 single salmon
pink early 75 cm/2 ft 6 in, available in Germany USA

SANCTUS Saunders USA 1955 single white early 60 cm/2 ft
available in Europe USA

SANDRA MARIE Hollingsworth USA 1998 semi-double pale pink
scented mid to late 70 cm/2 ft available in USA

SCHAFFE Krekler USA 1965 double pink scented late mid
65 cm/2 ft 2 in, available in Germany USA

SHAWNEE ROSE Bigger USA 1979 double pink mid

110 cm/3 ft 10 in, available in USA

SHAYLOR'S SUNBURST Allison 1931 Japanese white yellow some
scent early 90 cm/3 ft available in Canada Germany USA

SHOW GIRL Hollingsworth USA 1984 Japanese pink and cream
yellow mid 100 cm/3 ft available in Germany USA

SILVER SHELL Wild USA 1962 double white some scent early mid
73 cm/2 ft 5 in, available in USA

SKY PILOT Auten USA 1939 Japanese pink yellow centre mid
120 cm/4 ft available in France USA

SNOW MOUNTAIN Bigger USA 1940 double white late
90 cm/3 ft available in Germany USA

SNOW SWAN R Klehm USA 1987 single white mid
85 cm/2 ft 10 in, available in USA Canada

SOPHIE Saunders USA 1940 single pink early mid 65 cm/2 ft 2 in,
available in NZ

SOUVENIR D'A MILLET Millet France 1924 double red highly
scented mid to late 63 cm/2 ft 1 in, available in France

SOUVENIR DE LOUIS BIGOT Dessert France 1913 double rose
scented mid to late 63 cm/2 ft 1 in, available in Canada
France USA

SOUVENIR D'HARAUCOURT single white mid 70 cm/2 ft available
in France

*SPARKLING STAR Bigger USA 1953 single dark pink early
75 cm/2 ft 6 in, available in USA

SPELLBINDER Bigger USA 1960 single white mid to late
80 cm/2 ft 8 in, available in NZ

SPRINGFIELD Krekler USA 1962 double pink scented free
flowering mid 70 cm/2 ft 4 in, available in Canada Germany USA

STARDUST Glasscock-Falk USA 1964 single white early
80 cm/2 ft 8 in, available in Germany NZ USA

STARLIGHT Saunders USA 1949 single cream yellow very early
65 cm/2 ft 2 in, available in Canada Germany Sweden USA

STREPHON Kelway UK single pink mid to late 90 cm/3 ft

available in UK

SUNLIGHT Saunders USA 1950 single pale yellow very early
46 cm/1 ft 6 in, available in USA

SUNNY SIDE UP Bigger USA 1979 Japanese white with yellow
centre mid 110 cm/3 ft 10 in, available in USA

SUPERIOR Reath USA 1984 single salmon pink, yellow centre early
90 cm/3 ft available in USA

SUSIE Q Klehm USA double pink some scent mid
60 cm/2 ft available in Germany NZ USA

SWEET SIXTEEN Klehm USA 1972 double pink scented mid
70 cm/2 ft 4 in, available in Germany NZ UK USA

TAMATE-BOKU unknown origin Japanese pink very late
90 cm/3 ft available in Canada Germany UK

TANGO Auten USA 1956 single orange-red early75 cm/2 ft 6 in,
available in Germany USA

TEMPEST Auten USA 1931 double crimson free flowering mid
90 cm/3 ft available in France USA

THE FAWN Wright double pink mid 85 cm/2 ft 10 in,
available in NZ USA

THE MIGHTY MO Wild USA 1950 double red early
70 cm/2 ft 4 in, available in Germany NZ Sweden USA

THERESE Dessert France 1904 double pink scented free flowering
mid 78 cm/2 ft 7 in, available in Canada UK USA

THUMBELINA Krekler/ R Klehm USA single pink early
40 cm/1 ft 3 in, available in USA

TISH Tischler USA 1972 Japanese red late 90 cm/3 ft
available in NZ USA

TOKIO unknown origin pre-1910 Japanese pink mid 90 cm/3 ft
available in Canada Germany USA

TOM ECKHARDT Krekler USA 1965 Japanese pink scented mid
75 cm/2 ft 6 in, available in Canada NZ

TOPEKA GARNET Bigger USA 1975 single dark red free flowering
mid 75 cm/2 ft 6 in, available in Germany NZ USA

Strephon

TOPEKA STATUE Bigger USA 1991 Japanese white, yellow centre
mid 90 cm/3 ft available in USA

TORO-NO-MAKI unknown origin pre-1928 Japanese white some
scent mid up to 85 cm/2 ft 10 in, available in Europe USA

TORPILLEUR Dessert France 1913 Japanese violet red scented mid
90 cm/3 ft available in Germany USA

TOURANGELLE Dessert France 1910 double pale pink free
flowering mid to late 95 cm/3 ft available in USA

TRAFFORD W BIGGER Bigger USA 1966 Japanese dark red, dark
red gold-tipped centre mid 90 cm/3 ft available in USA

TRIOMPHE DE L'EXPOSITION DE LILLE Calot France 1865
double pink late 68 cm/2 ft 3 in, available in Germany
Switzerland

TRUTH Bigger USA 1968 double white mid 75 cm/2 ft 6 in,
available in USA

TULAGI Lins 1945 Japanese red with red centre mid 90 cm/3 ft
available in France

TWITTERPATED Krekler-Klehm semi-double pink/red streaks early
80 cm/2 ft 8 in, available in USA

VELVET PRINCESS Bigger USA 1977 double dark red mid
75 cm/2 ft 6 in, available in USA

VICTOR HUGO syn. of 'Félix Crousse'

VIOLET DAWSON Klehm USA 1991 Japanese white and gold mid
80 cm/2 ft 8 in, available in USA

VIRGINIA DARE Newhouse 1939 single white free flowering mid
75 cm/2 ft 6 in, available in NZ

VIVID GLOW Cousins-R Klehm USA pre-1988 single rose pink
early 1m/3 ft available in Germany USA

WALTER E WIPSON Murawska USA 1956 double white very late
75 cm/2 ft 6 in, available in NZ USA

WALTER FAXON Richardson USA 1904 double pink free flowering
80 cm/2 ft 8 in, available in NZ Switzerland USA

WALTER MARX Marx/Rogers USA 1981 single white scented late to

120 cm/4 ft available in NZ USA

WEST ELKTON Krekler USA 1958 Japanese red mid 90 cm/3 ft
available in NZ

WHITE CHARM Glasscock-Falk USA 1964 double white late mid
70 cm/2 ft 4 in, available in NZ USA

WHITE FROST Reath USA 1991 double white late-mid
75 cm/2 ft 6 in, available in NZ USA

WHITE IVORY Klehm USA 1981 double white scented mid
85 cm/2 ft 10 in, available in Canada NZ

WHITE SANDS Wild & Son USA 1968 Japanese white scented late
mid 90 cm/3 ft available in Canada NZ USA

WHITE WINGS Hoogendoorn Netherlands 1949 single white some
scent mid to late 80 cm/2 ft 8 in, available in Germany NZ
Sweden Switzerland UK USA

WHOPPER C G Klehm USA 1980 double pink scented mid
85 cm/2 ft 10 in, available in Germany USA

WIESBADEN Goos-Koenemann 1911 double pink scented early
80 cm/2 ft 8 in, available in Europe UK

WILBUR WRIGHT Kelway UK 1909 single very dark red mid to late
90 cm/3 ft available in Germany

WINDCHIMES Reath USA 1984 single pink very early 90 cm/3 ft
available in Germany NZ USA

WINNIFRED DOMME Brand USA 1913 double dark red mid
60 cm/2 ft available in USA

WRINKLES AND CRINKLES Wild USA 1971 double pink scented
mid 70 cm/2 ft available in Germany USA

ZULU WARRIOR Glasscock USA 1929 single dark red medium
early 85 cm/2 ft 10 in, available in USA

ZUZU Krekler USA 1955 semi-double pink some scent mid
85 cm/2 ft 10 in, available in Germany NZ UK USA

PART FOUR

GROWING
PEONIES

CHAPTER 10

WHERE AND HOW
TO PLANT PEONIES
HERBACEOUS PEONIES

CHOOSING THE RIGHT SITE

P EONIES ARE AMONG THE EASIEST of all herbaceous plants to grow. In James
Kelway's words, 'You cannot very well kill them. They are as tough as a
Scotch thistle, as hardy as paving stones and as full of vigour as a common
marigold.' They *are* tough, and completely hardy, but they have one essential
climatic requirement: they need a cold winter period of dormancy every year. With
very few exceptions they will tolerate hard frosts (zones 2 through 7) and intense
summer heat, but they will not grow in very mild, semi-tropical or tropical areas.
Their survival in zone 8 depends on how cold the winter gets, which is usually a
question of altitude. Research has shown that herbaceous peonies need about 600
hours of winter temperatures below 0°C (32°F). Caprice Farm Nursery, one of the
most successful peony nurseries in the USA is in zone 8, in an area where the winter
temperature hardly ever drops below –4°C (25°F). Peonies have also been known to
grow and flower successfully in zone 9, in parts of southern California and Texas.

Zoning is a fairly crude way of describing local climates. The growing conditions in
a particular spot are influenced by so many factors, and some of them can be
manipulated. If you are in zones 8 or 9, give your peonies the best possible chance
by planting them on the cool east or north side of a building or wall, or in shade cast

by trees or shrubs, so that the hot afternoon sun cannot reach them. Plant with the eyes (the buds of the new shoots) only just below the surface. Keep the root area cool with a thick mulch during the summer, and remove the mulch to expose the roots to cold air in winter. Increase your chances of success by choosing early single, semi-double or Japanese varieties (they are bred from species with warmer natural habitats), and give them plenty of water during the hot summer months.

Peonies are not choosy about soil, doing quite well in poor conditions, particularly on chalk, but the ideal is a well-drained, rich and slightly alkaline soil. Avoid planting them right under a tree or close to a hedge; the roots will rob the peonies of food and water. Peonies tolerate spells of drought quite well, but watering during dry spells in spring will ensure big flowers. The one situation they will not endure is one where their roots are in water-logged soil. If the soil is poorly drained, improve it by digging in plenty of organic material and coarse grit. Some shelter from the wind is desirable, especially if you don't intend to stake each plant; on the other hand a fairly open position will allow air to circulate around the plants, preventing the development of fungal diseases. As with roses, it is not advisable to plant peonies in soil where peonies have been growing before. In such a situation, replace the soil to a depth of 90 cm (3 ft).

Some experts recommend planting peonies in full sun, others advocate light shade, and some insist that they will thrive in quite dense shade. Some common sense is needed when interpreting such conflicting advice. In cold northern climates with short summers, peonies need all the sun they can get. In Finland, for example, they do best in raised beds in full sun. In general, most peony varieties flower more prolifically in the sun, but very hot summer sun will bleach out the colours of red and pink varieties so in warm climates shade from the midday sun is a positive advantage. In shade the individual blooms last longer so the flowering season is prolonged, but there will probably be fewer flowers on each plant. If late frosts are a problem in your garden, shade from the early morning sun is definitely advisable; it is not so much the frost that damages flower buds as the rapid thaw early in the day.

The English writer Margery Fish whose gardening books are very down-to-earth and clearly written from experience, wrote in *Gardening in the Shade*, 'Most gardening books recommend that peonies should be planted in full sun, but I know many gardens where they grow well in shade and that is the way I like to grow mine. For

TOP *P. peregrina*, noted by Margery Fish as doing well under trees.

ABOVE 'Sarah Bernhardt' thrives in cold sites.

her, *P. mlokosewitschii* thrived under a laburnum and elsewhere in her Somerset garden it flowered well under a large phlomis. Her description reminded me that although the flowers of 'Molly-the-Witch' are fleeting, they are followed by crimson autumn leaves and seed pods opening to show a brilliant cerise lining. Mrs Fish also recommended *P. officinalis* as a reliable ground cover plant for woodland, the ratio of flower to leaf giving the plants just the right degree of informality for a semi-wild situation, and she noted that the single blood red *P. peregrina* 'Sunshine' looked well under trees in her own garden and flowered under an ilex at nearby Tintinhull. William Robinson also suggested planting herbaceous varieties under trees, on the margin of a shrubbery, in long grass 'and indeed almost any rough place'. But he conceded that the choicest double forms deserve 'the best cultivation in beds and borders'.

Although most species do well in semi-wild situations, there are exceptions. *P. cambessedesii* from the Balearic islands and *P. clusii* from Crete need tender loving care, a place in the sun, extra well-drained soil and shelter from cold winds.

PEONIES FOR WARM SITES
Big Ben, Bowl of Beauty, Carol, Dawn Pink, Kansas, Kelway's Glorious, Laddie, Lady Alexandra Duff, Miss America, Mt St Helen's (Zone 8), Picotee (Zone 8), Sword Dance.

PEONIES FOR VERY COLD SITES
Most lactifloras and hybrids don't mind how cold it gets. The following do well in Canada or Finland in Zones 2 and 3: Duchesse de Nemours, Early Scout, Glowing Candles, Lady Alexandra Duff, Madame de Verneville, Marie Crousse, *P. tenuifolia* 'Rubra Plena', Red Charm, Sarah Bernhardt, Stardust.

BUYING HERBACEOUS PEONIES
Some garden centres sell peonies in containers, but they do not offer a wide choice of varieties, and the chances of getting good, strong examples of the plants you want, correctly labelled, are better if you order direct from a peony specialist. There is an international list on page 368. Suppliers send out bare-rooted plants in autumn, the correct time of year to plant. But they deal with orders in rotation, and if you order

late your plants may not arrive until winter has set in and the ground is under snow or too frozen to dig. So send for your catalogue early, make your choice and get your order in.

When they arrive the tubers should be plump and moist with between three and five eyes. The eyes are the buds from which the plant's shoots will develop in spring. If the tubers are dry and shrivelled or have no eyes, send them back. Don't be disappointed if your peonies don't do much in the first year. Even the strongest, healthiest young plants may not flower until one or two years after planting.

If the roots are dry on arrival, soak them in water for a few hours. If you are unable to plant them at once, replace them in the packing material and keep it damp. They will keep like this for up to fourteen days, but if you have to wait longer before planting, dig a trench and heel them in or plant them temporarily in pots of compost.

WHEN TO PLANT
Although the leaves wither in autumn, root growth goes on under the ground, and will continue until winter sets in. Early autumn planting allows the plant to establish itself in its new position. In China herbaceous peonies are traditionally planted in the seventh moon of the lunar year and tree peonies in the eighth. All agree that spring planting is often a recipe for disaster.

PREPARING THE GROUND
Once they are established, peonies will continue to flower for many decades with very little attention. It seems only fair to repay their generosity in advance by getting them off to the best possible start. Unless you are preparing a whole bed or border, dig a separate hole for each plant, 60 cm (24 in) in diameter and 45 cm (18 in) deep, putting the soil to one side. Put two spadefuls of well-rotted farmyard manure (traditionally, cow manure is recommended) and a good handful of bonemeal or general fertilizer into the hole and fork it into the soil at the bottom of the hole. The peony's roots must not be in direct contact with manure, so cover the manure with a layer of soil at least 5 cm (2 in) deep.

If you are making a whole border, treat it as described above, starting with a trench at one end of the border and working methodically through to the other end.

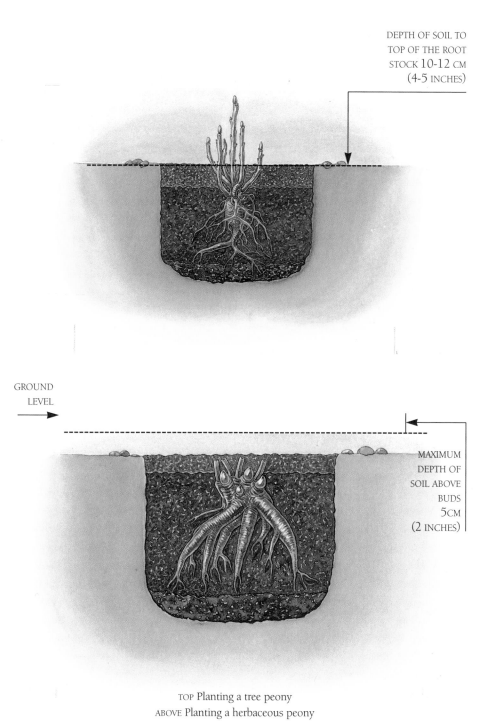

DEPTH OF SOIL TO
TOP OF THE ROOT
STOCK 10-12 CM
(4-5 INCHES)

GROUND
LEVEL

MAXIMUM
DEPTH OF
SOIL ABOVE
BUDS
5CM
(2 INCHES)

TOP Planting a tree peony
ABOVE Planting a herbaceous peony

TOP A fourteen-year-old plant of the tree peony 'Yu Ban Bai' (jade plate white) flourishing in the shade of a tree at Cricket Hill Garden, USA.

ABOVE The versatile tree peony 'Luoyang Hong' (Luoyang red) does well in both warm and cold sites. Shown here at Cricket Hill, USA.

PLANTING

Whether you are putting in new plants or dividing existing specimens, take as much trouble planting each peony as you would with a highly-prized, expensive shrub – you only have to do it once. Space individual plants 90-120 cm (3-4 ft) apart or plant in groups of three of a kind at 60 cm (2 ft) apart with 90-120 cm (3-4 ft) between groups. These distances look impossibly big on the ground but it is important not to plant too close. The plants need air circulating around them to minimize the risk of fungal diseases, and in time they will fill the allotted space.

Set the peony root in position in the hole with the eyes facing upwards. They should be just 5 cms (2 ins) below ground level in cold areas, 3 cm (1.5 in) or less in warm climates. If necessary put more soil into the hole to raise the level. I cannot emphasize too strongly that the most important rule for success is *not to plant the root too deep*. When you are sure that it is at the correct depth, return the rest of the soil to the hole and tread it in firmly. It is a common fault not to plant firmly enough. Press the soil really firmly onto the roots with the toe of your boot. Finish with a mulch of bark or mushroom compost to keep the weeds at bay and to retain moisture in the soil, but keep the mulch clear of the central crown of the plant.

TREE PEONIES

CHOOSING THE RIGHT SITE

Tree peonies thrive in similar conditions to herbaceous peonies but they are not quite so hardy, and are more shade tolerant, definitely preferring a site shaded from the midday sun. The ideal position would provide a few hours of sun in the morning and a few hours again towards the end of the day.

TREE PEONIES FOR WARM SITES

Bai Yu (white jade), Er Qiao (twin beauty), Fen Dian Bai (phoenix white), Hu Hong (Hu's red), Lan Tian Yu (blue sky jade), Luoyang Hong (Luoyang red), Qing Long Wo Mo Chi (green dragon lying on a Chinese inkstone), Shan Hu Tai (coral terrace), Sheng Dan Lu (Taoist stove filled with the pills of immortality), Ying Luo Bao Zhu (necklace with precious pearls), Zhao Fen (Zhao's pink), Zhi Hong (rouge red),

Zhuang Yuan Hong (number one scholar's red), Zi Lan Kui (Grand Duke dressed in blue and purple).

TREE PEONIES FOR VERY COLD SITES (ZONES 3, 4)
Luoyang Hong (Luoyang red), Shan Hu Tai (coral terrace), Supreme Pink, Wu Long Peng Sheng (black dragon holds a splendid flower).

BUYING TREE PEONIES
Tree peonies are expensive because the process of propagation is difficult and slow. Like herbaceous peonies they are available from specialist nurseries by mail order, in autumn and spring and, in some areas, through the winter. They can also sometimes be found in containers at plant centres. They survive quite well out of the ground. In China they used to be shipped bare-rooted from cool mountain districts to the cities of the south when the flower buds were already well developed. However those plants were invariably thrown away after flowering. For more long-term success, look for plants with one or more strong, stout stems and a vigorous root system. If the roots are dry on arrival, soak them in water for a few hours.

PLANTING
Follow the method given above for herbaceous peonies, but plant tree peonies deeper, with the grafting point 10-12 cm (4-5 in) below the soil surface. You can identify the graft by a ridge on the stem and a change in the bark texture above and below it. Planting distances vary between 1.2 m and 1.8 m (4 and 6 ft) according to the species or variety.

GROWING TREE PEONIES IN POTS
In early autumn choose good strong plants to pot up. The container should be at least 30 cm (12 in) wide and high, and should have adequately functioning drainage holes. Put a layer of broken crocks or large pebbles at the bottom of the pot, then add a layer of general purpose compost. Put the peony in the pot, making sure the grafting point will be at least 8 cm (3 in) below the surface. Fill in with compost and firm it well around the roots.

If you want the plants to flower early, leave the pots outdoors so they can benefit

TOP 'Ying Luo Bao Zhu' (necklace with precious pearls)
at Cricket Hill, USA.

ABOVE 'Qing Long Wo Mo Chi' (green dragon lying on a Chinese inkstone)
growing at Cricket Hill Gardens, USA.

347

TOP 'Zhao Fen' (Zhao's pink) is happy in warm climates and easy to grow
in a container. Shown growing here at Cricket Hill Gardens, USA.

ABOVE 'Zhu Sha Lei' (cinnabar ramparts) does well in a pot.
Photographed in the Cricket Hill Gardens, USA.

from the cold winter weather and bring them in to the greenhouse or a cool room indoors in January. When flower buds appear remove all except one on each stem. Dead-head as the flowers fade. When flowering is over, the pots can be sunk into the ground outdoors. Feed them during the summer either once with a slow-release granular fertilizer or fortnightly with a liquid plant food. The plants can remain in their pots for several years, until they grow out of them. After about three years, re-pot in fresh compost, in a slightly bigger pot than before.

In China, tree peonies intended to flower between December and April are dug up 60-70 days before the flowering date, stripped of their leaves and aired for two days until the roots are soft. They are then packed and shipped to their final destination. Between 40 and 60 days before the flowering date (depending on the variety) they are potted up. They can be brought on to flower even earlier by storing them at an artificially cold temperature, and flowering can be delayed by artificially prolonging the dormant period.

RELIABLE CHINESE TREE PEONIES FOR POT CULTURE
Bai Yu, Hu Hong, Lan Tian Yu, Luoyang Hong, Wu Long Peng Sheng, Zhao Fen, Zhu Sha Lei.

CHAPTER 11

AFTERCARE, TROUBLE-SHOOTING AND PROPAGATION

THE SAME GENERAL RULES APPLY to both herbaceous and tree peonies as to most garden plants, and they are mostly a matter of common sense. They take a few years to get established and then they usually thrive with very little attention. They often survive in neglected gardens: evidence of a robust constitution.

WATERING

If the spring and summer after planting are very dry seasons, water herbaceous peonies copiously at intervals, allowing the ground to become fairly dry between waterings. Water young tree peonies regularly during dry spells for the first few years but do not allow the soil to become waterlogged.

FEEDING

If the planting positions have been well prepared with manure and bonemeal as described on page 342, it should not be necessary to feed your herbaceous peonies for several years after planting. Thereafter, every few years they may benefit from a top dressing of bonemeal or general fertilizer, specially in very free-draining soil where the nutrients tend to be leached out when it rains. But use fertilizer sparingly; over feeding can cause problems, burning the plant or encouraging lots of thin, non-flowering shoots. Put the fertilizer on when the plants have finished flowering in early summer. This is when they need food to build up flowering shoots for the following year. An annual spring mulch of compost or leaf mould helps retain moisture around the roots.

Heavy flowers leaning out of a border onto the pathway are
an acceptable sign of an informal style. *Dean Hole's Garden, Rochester*
by Ernest Arthur Rowe, 1862-1922.

Young tree peonies will benefit from an annual spring feed with a general fertilizer or a mulch of farmyard manure. If older, established plants perform poorly, treat them in the same way to get them going again.

STAKING

In some gardens, heavy flowers leaning out of a border on to a pathway are perfectly acceptable signs of an informal style of gardening. In others this is not appropriate. The flowers of the taller kinds of double herbaceous peony will flop to the ground if they are not supported, specially in windy places, and specially after rain. Various manufactured metal or plastic supports are available, and most gardeners have their favourite types. Simple metal hoops or half-hoops with a diameter of about 45 cm (18 in) can be pushed into the ground to the required height for each plant. If ready-made ones are not available, they can be made up for you by an ironworker, an investment that should last many years. Avoid supports painted a strong shade of green. Contrary to popular belief, matt black is the most unobtrusive colour in the garden.

My own requirements are that plant supports should be as nearly invisible as possible, and as natural as possible. I find that a circle of twiggy hazel branches pushed into the soil works well. It may be old-fashioned but it is effective. Put the branches in place when the plant is still only about 30 cm (12 in) high, taking care to avoid piercing the peony roots. As the leaves grow they will hide the twigs. I sometimes have to supplement this arrangement by tying individual stems in full bloom to a slim bamboo cane.

If you want to avoid using supports altogether, choose short varieties with strong stems, specially any from the following list:

HERBACEOUS PEONIES FOR WINDY SITES
Argentine, Calypso, Dayspring, Early Scout, Gardenia, Jan van Leeuwen, Laddie, Madame Calot, Madame Ducel, Montezuma, Old Faithful, *P. officinalis*, *P. tenuifolia* 'Rubra Plena'

In windy areas tree peonies also need firm staking. Use taller metal half or whole hoops, or attach the main stem to a sturdy wooden stake, using a rubber tree tie.

TOP LEFT Short, sturdy peonies for windy sites:
'Calypso' at The Peony Gardens, Lake Hayes, New Zealand.

TOP RIGHT 'Madame Calot'at Green Cottage, Lydney, Gloucestershire.

ABOVE 'Madame Ducel' at Green Cottage, Lydney, Gloucestershire.

PRUNING

If you want specially large blooms to cut for the house, or to exhibit at a horticultural show, you should disbud your peonies. This involves removing any secondary, side buds from each stem while they are still very small, leaving just one main bud to develop at the stem's tip. Apart from that, the only pruning herbaceous peonies need is dead heading the flower heads as they fade, and cutting the dying foliage off at or just below ground level in the autumn. Leave a few seed heads to develop if you want them for decoration, or if you are collecting the seeds for propagation.

In theory tree peonies need no pruning either, apart from dead heading, but in practise they can become leggy, bearing their flowers out of sight at the tops of scrawny stems. This can be avoided by careful pruning to produce a shapely plant. In China and Japan they do this as a matter of course, in early summer after flowering. Using sharp secateurs, remove weak or overcrowded stems from the base. Taking out the oldest one third of stems each year will encourage a constant supply of vigorous stems to grow from the base. Some stems can be shortened to maintain a well-clothed, rounded shape. If a healthy-seeming plant fails to flower or to make new stems from below ground, it may be worth administering shock treatment by cutting it down to just 15 cm (6 in) high in the autumn: a case of kill or cure.

MOVING PEONIES

It is a fairly well-known but misunderstood fact that peonies do not like to be moved. But from time to time even in the most carefully planned gardens a plant may be in the wrong place, and the owner would like to change its position. Perhaps it is at odds with a new colour scheme for a herbaceous border; perhaps the peony is not thriving and might do better in a sunnier or shadier place. It is true that if a herbaceous peony has been established for three years or more it will resent disturbance if it is dug up and moved in its entirety. The thing to do is to dig it up and divide the root to make several new plants. You may have to wait a year or two for them to flower, but they ought to thrive as well as any other newly planted peony. The correct time and method is described below under 'Propagation by Division.'

TROUBLE-SHOOTING

One of the wonderful things about peonies is that the subject of 'pests and diseases' can be dealt with in just a few paragraphs. Among the pests that plague gardeners, the nuisance of maurauding rabbits and deer is on the increase. It is good to be able to report that peonies are immune, probably because their stems and flowers contain bitter-tasting phenol compounds.

The worst pests are nematodes, also called root gall eelworms, microscopic soil-dwelling insects which attack the roots. If a peony's young shoots are spindly and sickly, dig up the plant and look at the roots. Irregular, gnarled roots with pea-sized swellings are a sign of nematode infestation. Burn the plant and its near neighbours and replace the soil. If the plants are new, you may have bought the pest with the plants, so notify the supplier and ask for your money back. There is another, less virulent soil pest, the garden symphylan. It is unlikely to be a problem if you always plant in autumn, never in spring.

The chief enemy of peonies is botrytis, a fungus causing stems and buds to wilt, turn brown and wither just before the buds open. Tidy gardening helps to prevent it; when you cut down the stems in autumn pick up any dead leaves and debris from the ground around the peonies and burn the lot or bag it up and remove it. Damp air and wet leaves encourage botrytis, so plant your peonies at least 90 cm (3 ft) apart so that drying breezes can circulate around them. If you need to water during dry spells, water the ground not the leaves. In a wet spring, inspect the plants regularly and remove diseased stems, cutting back into healthy growth. To be absolutely sure to guard against botrytis, spray with an appropriate fungicide at regular intervals from the time the shoots first emerge. Effective preparations come and go on the market. Use whatever is currently recommended and follow the manufacturer's instructions.

PROPAGATION FROM SEED

Many herbaceous peonies do not produce seed at all, and from those that do the chances of getting a worthwhile plant are about one in a thousand. But the species do come true from seed and for patient gardeners with a special interest in them, growing species from seed can be a fascinating and economical way of building up a collection. Patience is necessary because it may be five years or more before you get a flower on your young plants. Tree peonies of the Suffruticosa group produce plenty of viable seed and the seed occasionally carried on hybrid tree peonies has produced important new forms in the past and is worth experimenting with.

The best results come from fresh seed, gathered and sown as soon as it is ripe, so check this with your supplier. If you gather seed from your own plants, do it when the pods have cracked open and the seeds are still sticky. Clean them in a 10% solution of household bleach and rinse in clean water, discarding any soft or shrivelled seeds.

The seeds can be sown outdoors directly into a well-dug and raked, weed-free seed bed or in trays or pots of general purpose compost. They can be left to themselves in winter, but in spring and summer make sure the soil or compost is moist. But guard against over-watering. The seeds may not germinate in the first year. Two years after germination the little plants are ready to be lined out in autumn in rows 30-40 cm (12-16 in) apart and grown on until they reach the flowering stage.

PROPAGATION BY DIVISION

Division of the crown is the usual, very easy method for producing new plants of herbaceous peonies. Plants are usually ready to be divided four years after planting, and occasionally they have put on enough growth after three years. Unlike most other herbaceous plants they can also be left for very many years without deteriorating.

In early autumn lift the plant with a fork being careful not to damage the big tuberous roots. Hose the roots down to clean them. If you leave them in the shade for three or four hours they will soften and become easier to divide. Cut the roots with a sharp knife into pieces each with at least three eyes (shoots). This will give you plants about the same size as those a reliable nursery would send out. Like those from the nursery, your new plants may not flower in their first season, but they should do so in the second year. The very first flowers are often untypical of the variety, so don't worry if they are not as you expect. By the second year of flowering they should have settled down.

Tree peonies are not so easy to propagate. The usual techniques are layering (with a rather low rate of success) and grafting, usually on to a herbaceous 'nurse' root. Grafting requires specialized technical skill and I shall not try and describe it.

In China tree peonies as well as herbaceous are often propagated by division. In the case of tree peonies this is something of a lottery; success is by no means guaranteed, but it is worth a try. The divisible material develops around the point where the parent plant was grafted. It can be encouraged to form by a good annual mulch of garden compost. In early autumn, after the equinox and before the first frost, a four-year-old parent plant is dug up and the roots and stem thoroughly washed. The plant is left in a shady place for one or two days for the roots to soften, then roots with three or more buds are detached with a sharp knife. It is a wise precaution against infection to dust the cut surfaces with fungicide before planting the divisions. 15 cm (6 in) of soil is then mounded over each plant to protect it from frost

PROPAGATION BY CUTTINGS

Cuttings can be taken from tree peonies in early autumn using strong one or two-year-old shoots 10-15 cm (4-6 in) long. They are dipped in a rooting preparation then pushed into sand up to two thirds their length, watered well and protected under a cloche or plastic tunnel. Fifty per cent is considered a good success rate.

Whatever method you use, it is worth having a go at propagating your favourite peonies. Nothing else gives one quite the same happy sense of achievement as success in producing new plants.

APPENDIX A

WHERE TO SEE PEONIES:

AN INTERNATIONAL LIST OF
PEONY GARDENS AND COLLECTIONS.

N.B. Many of the gardens listed are in private ownership. Unless regular opening hours are advertised, please always write or telephone before you visit.

CANADA

*Peony flowering season from
late May to late June*

Alberta: Devonian Botanic Garden, University of Alberta, Edmonton, Alberta T6G 2E1. Tel 403 987 3054, fax 403 987 4141.

Manitoba: Assiniboine Park, Winnipeg.

Ontario: Brickman's Botanical Gardens, Wartburg, RR1, Sebringville, Ontario N0K 1X0. Tel 519 393 6223, fax 519 393 5239.

Cedar Valley Botanic Gardens, Brighton, Ontario. Tel 613 475 0535.

Edwards Gardens, 777 Lawrence Avenue East, Don Mills, Ontario M3C 1P2. Tel 416 445 1552.

Kiwi Gardens, Harper Road, RR7, Perth,

Ontario K7H 3C9. Tel 613 267 7384, fax 613 264 0278.

Maplelawn, 529 Richmond Road, Ottawa.

Mount Pleasant Cemetery, Mepham Memorial Peony Garden, 375 Mt Pleasant Road, St Clair, Toronto, Ontario.

Niagara Parks Commission School of Horticulture, PO Box 150, Niagara Falls, Ontario L2E 6T2. Tel 416 356 8554.

Royal Botanical Gardens, PO Box 399, Hamilton, Ontario L8N 3H8. Tel 416 527 1158:

The Sandra Cornett Collection of peonies in Barbara Laking Memorial Garden, 680 Plains Road West on Route 2, 35 miles south of Toronto.

Quebec: Montreal Botanical Gardens, 4101 Sherbrooke Street East, Montreal, Quebec H1X 2B2. Tel 514 872 1454. On Route 138 near metro station Pie IX.

Pépinière Charlevoix Inc., 391 boul. Mailloux, Rivière-Malbaie, Quebec G5A 1N6. Tel 418 439 4646, fax 418 439 4647.

CHINA

Many cities in northern and central China have Tree Peony Gardens in public parks. The following is just a selection. The main flowering season is the last two weeks of April

Beijing: Beijing Botanical Garden has a Tree Peony Garden with 5,500 tree peonies (230 varieties) and 2,500 herbaceous peonies (200 varieties). The Garden is in two parts, the northern at Sleeping Buddha Temple Road, Western Suburbs and the southern at 20, Nanxingcun, Xianshan, Beijing.

The Imperial Garden's Tree Peony Garden in the Forbidden City.

Jing Shan Park's Tree Peony Garden.

Zhongshan Park's Tree Peony Garden.

Heze: Shandong Province: Annual International Tree Peony Fair from 20 to 28 April.

Caozhou Hundred Flower Garden.

Ancient and Modern Tree Peony Garden.

Caozhou Tree Peony Garden (combining Zhao Lou garden owned by the Zhao family who have grown and bred peonies for generations, Li Ji garden and He Lou garden).

Lanzhou: Gansu Province: Peace Tree Peony Garden where 'Black Swan' peony originated. Flowering season is in May

Luoyang: Henan Province. Annual Peony Festival from 15 to 25 April.

Tree peony garden in Wang Cheng Park, the site of the capital of the Eastern Zhou Dynasty (770-256 BC) 19,800 plants of 320 different varieties.

Beauty of the Empire Tree Peony Garden (200,000 plants, 400 varieties), on a hillside at a higher elevation, therefore a little later coming into flower.

Pengzhou: Sichuan Province: Pengzhou, or Tianpeng, was famous for its peonies during the Tang Dynasty.

Dan Jing Shan Tree Peony Garden. 10,000 plants, 200 varieties, some very old of local origin.

Shanghai: Shanghai Botanical Garden, Longwu Road, Shanghai. 120 tree peony varieties.

Taiyuan: Shanxi Province: Twin Pagoda Monastery Peony Garden. Home of 'Purple Cloud Fairy' peonies.

Xian: Shaanxi Province: Xian Botanical Garden, Cuiha Road. 200 tree peony varieties.

Yan'an: Shaanxi Province: Thousand Flower Mountain Tree Peony Garden. 30,000 plants, 12 local varieties.

FINLAND

Flowering season from about 20 May to mid-July.

Rea Peltola and Vesa Koivu, Puutarha Metsan reunassa, Palsilantie 63, 17800 Kuhmoinen, Finland. Tel 03 555 1345. Garden under construction, to open in 2002.

FRANCE

Flowering season from mid-April until the end of May.

Alsace-Lorraine: Jardin Botanique, Col de Saverne, 67700 Saverne, Alsace. Tel 88 91 10 14. Peony collection.

Jardin Botanique du Montet, 100 Rue du Jardin Botanique 54600, Villers lès Nancy. Tel 03 83 41 47 47, fax 03 83 27 86 59. Part of the University, the plant collections include peony species and varieties

Auvergne-Limousin: Parc Victor-Thuillat, Limoges.

Jardin des Croisades, Château de Bosséol, 63270 Vic-le-Comte, Puy-de-Dôme. Tel 73 69 00 84.

Bourgogne-Franche-Comte: Abbaye de Fontenay, 21500 Montbard, Côte-d'Or. Tel 80 92 15 00, fax 80 92 16 88.

Château de Bussy-Rabutin, 21150 Bussy-le-Grand. Tel 03 80 96 00 03.

fax 03 80 96 09 46.

Bretagne-Pays de Loure: Jardin des Plantes, Place Mendes-France, 49000 Angers.

Centre-Poitou-Charente: Parc Floral d'Apremont, Apremont-sur-Allier, 18150 La-Guerche-sur-l'Aubois. Tel 02 48 80 41 41, fax 02 48 80 45 17.

Jardin Botanique, Boulevard Tonnele, 37000 Tours. Peony collection.

Ile de France-Paris: Parc de Courson, Bruyères-le-Châtel, Essonne. Tel 01 64 58 90 12, fax 01 64 58 97 00.

St Jean de Beauregard, 91940 St Jean de Beauregard, Essone. Tel 03 60 12 00 01,. fax 03 60 12 56 31. Peony walk.

Château de Thoiry, 78770 Thoiry-en-Yvelines. Tel 01 34 87 52 25, fax 01 34 87 54 12. Gardens restored since the 1970s include a long peony and daylily border made by the Vicomtesse de la Panouse.

Languedoc-Rousillon: Bambuseraie de Prafrance, 30140 Générargues par Anduze. Tel 66 61 70 47, fax 66 61 64 15. Peonies as well as bamboos.

Normandie: La Vallée des Jardins, Boulevard Weygand, Caen. Peony collection.

Jardins Claude Monet, 27620 Giverny, Eure. Tel 02 32 51 28 21, fax 02 32 51 54 18.

Provence-Côte-d'Azur: Villa Noailles, 59 Avenue Guy de Maupassant, Grasse 06130, Alpes Maritimes. Tree peony garden.

Rhône-Alpes: Les Horticules, Maison des Princes, 01800 Perouges, Ain.

Parc de la Tête d'Or, Place Leclerc, 69459 Lyon. Tel 04 78 89 53 52, fax 04 78 89 15 90. 300 peony varieties.

GERMANY

Flowering season from May to June. (The German name for peony, Pfingstrose, means rose of Pentecost or Whitsun.)

Weihenstephan, Bavaria. Weihenstephan Horticultural Garden. 26km north of Munich via A11. 5 ha. Headquarters of the International Shrub Register, but the main collections are hardy perennials. 250 cultivars of *Paeonia lactiflora*.

HOLLAND

Flowering season May and June.

Pépinière Joghmanshof, Laageinde 3, Kapel-Avezaath. Tel 0344 661415 or 0345 651600.

ITALY

Flowering season mid-April to the end of May.

Giardino Botanico Hanbury, La Mortola, Ventimiglia, Italy. Tel and fax 0184 229507

JAPAN

The flowering season is from late April to late June

Note: in the addresses given *shi* and *machi* = city; *ken* = prefecture; *dera* and *ji* = temple; *jima* = island. *Botan* = tree peony; *Shyakuyaku* = herbaceous peony.

Fukushima-ken: Iwase Pasture Kagamiishi-machi Fukushima-ken. Tel 248-62-6789. Train to Kagamiishi station on JR Touhoku line then 5 minutes by car. 3,500 herbaceous peonies in 150 varieties.

Kamakura Snow Peony Garden Tsuruyoaka Hachinman-gu.

Sukagawa Botan Park Sukagawa-shi, Fukushima-ken Tel 2487-3-2422. Train to Sukagawa on JR Touhoku line then 10 minutes by bus. Collection of medicinal peonies from the Edo period: 3,500 plants of 180 varieties.

Ibaraki-ken: Choufuku-ji Daigo-machi Ibaraki-ken. Tel 2957-4-0417 Train to Kamiogawa station on JR Suigun line then 7 minutes walk. A famous collection of herbaceous peonies.

Tsukuba Peony Garden, 500 Wakaguri
Kukizaki-machi, Inashiro-gun, 300-12
Ibaraki-ken. Tel 298-76-3660, fax 298-76-
4004. 3,500 tree peonies of 213 varieties
and 3,000 herbaceous peonies of 100
species.

Iwate: Hanaizumi-cho Iwate. 4,000
peonies.

Kanagawa: Machida Botan-En. Train to
Machida station on Odakyuu line then bus
to Yakushiike then 10 minutes walk. Or
train to Tsurukawa station via
Honmarchida. 1.4ha with 745 peony
plants of 122 varieties on north side of
Yakushiike park.

Manshoin Temple, West Harima. Tel 07915-
4-0158. Train to Kamigori Station by JR
Sanyo Main Line then 20 minutes by car.
2,000 peonies of 100 varieties.

Ryukokuji Temple, Tajima. Tel 0796-44-
0005. Train to Ebara Station on JR Bantan
Line, bus to Arawaka, then 3 minuntes
walk. 1,000 peonies of 90 varieties, grown
here since 1841.

Nagano-ken: Hase-dera Sakurai-shi
Nagano-ken. Tel 7444-7-7001. Train to
Hase-dera station on Kintetsu/Osaka line
then 15 minutes walk. The main temple of
Shingonshyuu and Japan's most famous
peony park with 7,000 tree peonies of 150

varieties.

Sekkou-ji Taima-machi Nagano-ken. Tel
745-48-2031. Train to Nijyou Jinjaguchi
station on Kintetsu/Osaka line then 20
minutes walk, or 10 minutes walk from
Taima-dera (see below). A few rare *Botan*
varieties.

Senju Botan-en Kamiishizu. 2,000 plants of
70 varieites at the western foot of the Yoro
Mountains.

Taima-dera, Taima-machi Nagao-ken. Tel
745-48-2008. Train to Taima-dera station
on Kintetsu/Osaka line then 10 minutes
walk. Japan's second most famous peony
park after Hase-dera.

Shimane-ken: Daikon-jima Yatsuka-machi
Shimane-ken. Tel 852-76-2236. Train to
Matsue station on JR Sanyou line then 40
minutes by bus. Or train to Yonago on
Sanyou line, then bus. Daikon Island is
Japan's biggest centre for the production
of tree peonies.

Shizuoka-ken: Kasuisai Botan Park Fukoroi-
shi Shizuoka-ken. Tel 5384-2-2121. Train
to Jukoroi station on JR Toukaido line then
15 minutes by bus. One of three *ensyuu*
sanzan temples, once frequented by the
shogun Tokugawa Ieyasu. 2,500 plants of
120 varieties.

Yokatuji Temple, Hanshin. Tel 0795-66-
0935. From JR/Kobe Electric Railway

Sanda Station take bus to Yotakuji. Famous for its Iris Garden, the temple also has about 1,000 peonies.

NEW ZEALAND

Tree peonies flower from the last week in September to the third week in November. Herbaceous peonies flower from the last week in October to mid-December. They peak during the second half of November

Canterbury: Craigmore Homestead, RD2 Timaru. Tel 03 6122 9840, fax 03 612 9890.

Marsal Paeonies, Old South Road, R D Dunsandel . Tel and fax 64 3 325 4003.

The Terraces, Leithfield, Amberley RD1 North Canterbury. Garden attached to peony nursery is open by appointment or on special open days in flowering season.

Otago: The Peony Gardens, 231 Lake Hayes Road, RD1 Queenstown. Tel and fax 03 442 1210.

UNITED KINGDOM

Flowering season unpredictable but roughly from late April to mid-June.

Bedfordshire: Toddington Manor, Toddington LU5 6HJ. Tel 01525 872576.

Cambridgeshire: Cambridge University Botanic Garden, Bateman Street, Cambridge CB2 1JF. Collection includes peony species.

Dorset: Portesham House, Portesham, Weymouth DT3 4HE. Tel 01305 871300. Small but choice collection of tree and herbaceous peonies.

Gloucestershire: Green Cottage, Redhill Lane, Lydney GL15 6BS. Tel 01594 841918. Visits by appointment only. Mrs Margaret Baber has the National Collection of *Paeonia lactiflora* pre-1915 varieties.

Hidcote Manor Gardens, Hidcote Bartrim, Chipping Campden GL55 6LR. Tel 01386 438333. National Trust garden has part of the National Collection of peonies, with 20 species and about 40 varieties of herbaceous peony.

Kent: Penshurst Place, Tonbridge TN11 8DG. Owned by the Viscount de Lisle's family, this historic garden has a peony border 120 m long.

Leicestershire: Burrough House, Melton Mowbray. Tel 01664 454226. Peony border.

Scotland: Kingscroft, Elie Fife KY9 1BY. Tel and fax 01333 330642. Mr and Mrs R Mitchell hold a National Collection of tree and herbaceous peony species. Visits by appointment only.

Royal Botanic Garden, Edinburgh EH3 5LR.

Comprehensive collection of peony species displayed in mixed plantings, including a tree peony moved from Alexander Duncan's (see page 84) garden at Arbroath.

Shropshire: Cruckfield House, Ford, Shrewsbury. Tel 01743 850222.

Hodnet Hall, Market Drayton TF9 3NN. A circular garden of peonies followed by shrub roses.

Somerset: Kelways Ltd. Langport TA10 9SL. Britain's foremost peony nursery for more than a hundred years has 600 herbaceous varieties in Peony Valley and a well planted display garden.

Staffordshire: Arbour Cottage, Napley. Tel 01630 672852. Tree and herbaceous peonies on acid soil.

Surrey: Royal Botanic Garden, Kew, Richmond TW9 3AB. Mixed collection of species and herbaceous varieties.

Sussex: Highdown, Goring-by-Sea BN12 6NY. Sir Frederick Stern's garden, now owned by Worthing Borough Council, still has some of his original collection including *Paeonia rockii*.

Wiltshire: The Courts Holt, Near Trowbridge, Wiltshire BA14 6RR. Tel 01225 782340

Worcestershire: Spetchley Park, Near Worcester WR5 1RS (Mr and Mrs R J

Berkeley). About fifty varieties of herbaceous peonies used in mixed and herbaceous borders in the Edwardian tradition. Ellen Willmott, the distinguished gardener and rosarian, was related to the Berkeleys and involved with planning the garden.

USA

Flowering times vary from east to west and north to south, so check before you visit. Further information may be obtained from The American Peony Society, 250 Interlachen Road, Hopkins, Michigan, 55343. Tel 612 938 4706

Connecticut: Bellamy-Ferriday House, 9 Main Street N, Box 181, Bethlehem, CT 06751. Tel 203 266 7596.

Cricket Hill Garden, 670 Walnut Hill Road, Thomaston, CT 06787. Tel 860 283 1042. Chinese tree peonies.

Hillside Gardens, 515 Litchfield Road (Route 272), Norfolk, CT. Tel 860 542 5345.

White Flower Farm, Litchfield, CT 06759. On Route 63, three miles south of Litchfield. Tel 800 411 6159.

Delaware: Winterthur Museum and Gardens, Winterthur DE 19735. Tel 302 888 4600.

Distict of Columbia: US National
Arboretum, 3501 New York Avenue, NE,
Washington, D.C. 20002. Tel. 202 245
2726, fax 202 245 4575.

Illinois: Klehm Nursery, Route 5, Box 197
Penny Road, South Barrington, IL 60010-
9390. Tel 847 551 3710, fax 847 551
3722.

Lake of the Woods Botanic Garden, PO Box
336, Mahomet, IL 61853. Tel 217 586
4630. 75 miles south of Chicago on State
Route 47, half mile from I-74.

Kansas: Botanica, 701 Amidon, Wichita,
KS 67203. Tel 316 264 0448.

Maryland: Cylburn Arboretum, 4915
Greenspring Avenue, Baltimore, MD
21209. Tel 410 396 0180. Tree peony
collection. Horticulture centre in mansion.

Hampton Hall, 535 Hampton Lane,
Towson, MD 21286. Tel 410 823 1309.

London Publik House and Gardens, 839
Londontown Road, Edgwater, MD 21037.
On State Route 253, seven miles south of
Annapolis. Tree peonies. Tel 410 222
1919.

Massachusetts: Arnold Arboretum of
Harvard University, The Arborway, Jamaica
Plains, MA 02130. Tel 617 524 1718.
South of US 20, ten miles west of Boston.

Glen Magna, 57 Forest Street, Danvers,
MA 10923. Tel 978 774 9165.

Longfellow House, 105 Brattle Street,
Cambridge, MA 02138. Tel 617 876
4491.

Naumkeag, Prospect Hill Road, Stockbridge,
MA 01262. Tel 413 298 3239.

Newbury Perennial Gardens, 65 Orchard
Street, Byfield, MA 01922. Tel 978 462
1144.

Sedgwick Gardens, 572 Essex Street, Beverly,
MA 01915. On State Route 22, thirty
miles north-east of Boston. Individual
gardens include a tree peony garden.
Tel 978 921 1944.

Tower Hill Botanic Garden, 11 French
Drive, Boylston, MA 01505. Tel 508 869
6111.

The Vale, The Lyman Estate, 185 Lyman
Street, Waltham, MA. Tel 781 893 7232.

Weston Nurseries, East Main Street,
Hopkinton, MA 01748. Tel 508 435
3414. Display gardens include peonies in
mixed plantings.

Michigan: Nichols Arboretum, University
of Michigan, 430 E University, Ann Arbor,
MI 48109-1115. Tel 734 763 5832.

New Jersey: Acorn Hall, 68 Morris Avenue,
Morristown, NJ 07960. Junction of State
Route 24, I-187 and US 202, 30 miles
west of New York City. Tel 973 267 3465.

Frelinghuysen Arboretum, 53 E. Hanover
Avenue, Morristown, NJ 07960. Tel 973

326 7600.

Skylands Botanical Garden, PO Box 3302 Ringwood, NJ 07456. 1 mile north of Ringwood which is on State Route 511, 40 miles west of New York City. Tel 973 962 9534. Individual gardens include a tree peony garden.

New York: Brooklyn Botanic Garden, 1000 Washington Avenue, Brooklyn, New York 11225. Tel 718 623 7200.

Cary Arboretum, Institute of Ecosystems, Route 44A (Box R) Milbrook NY 12545-0178. Tel 914 677 5358.

Clermont State Historic Site, 1 Clermont Avenue, Germantown, NY 12526. Tel 518 537 4240.

Cornell Plantations, 1 Plantations Road, Ithaca, NY 14850. Tel 607 255 3020. Cornell University estate including American Peony Society's Garden.

Ellwanger Garden, 625 Mount Hope Avenue, Rochester., NY. On US 20, 21 miles west of Schnectady. Address for information: Landmark George Landis Arboretum, Esperance, NY 12066. Tel 518 875 6935.

Jacques Marchais Museum of Tibetan Art, 338 Lighthouse Avenue, Staten Island, NY 10306. Tel 718 987 3478, fax 718 351 0402.

New York Botanical Garden, 200th Street and Southern Boulevard, Bronx, NY 10458. Tel 718 817 8700. 58 varieties of herbaceous peonies on the east side of the Conservatory.

Old Westbury Gardens, PO Box 430, Old Westbury, NY 11568. On Long Island, exit 39S Long Island Expressway 30 miles from New York City. Tel 516 333 0048.

Root Glen, 107 College Hill Rd, Clinton, NY 13323. On State Route 12B, nine miles south of Utica.

Landmark Society of Western New York, 133 South Fitzhugh Street, Rochester NY 14608. Tel 716 546 7029.

Wave Hill, Independence Avenue and West 249th Street, Riverdale, New York 10471. Tel 718 549 3200.

New Hampshire: Rundlet-May House, 364 Middle Street, Portsmouth, NH 03801. Tel 603 436 3205.

Ohio: Fellows Riverside Gardens, 816 Glenwood Avenue, Youngstown, OH 44502. Tel 330 740 7116.

Gardenview Horticultural Park, 16711 Pearl Road, US 42, Strongsville, OH 44136. Fourteen miles south-west of Cleveland, on US 42, 1.5 miles south of junction with State Route 82. Tel 440 238 6653.

Inniswood Botanical Garden, 940 Hempstead Road, Westerville, OH 43018. Twelve miles north of Columbus, off State

Route 3, north of exit 29 of I-270 loop. 200 varieties of peony. Tel 614 895 6216.

Kingwood Center, 900 Park Avenue West, Mansfield, OH 44906. State Route 430, 1 mile south of US 30, three miles west of Mansfield. 400 peony varieties. Tel 419 522 0211.

Stan Hywet Hall, 714 North Portage Path, Akron, OH 44303. Off State Route 18, four miles north-west of Akron. Tel 330 836 9075. 300 varieties of peony.

Toledo Zoo, 2700 Broadway, Toledo, OH 43609. On US 24, two miles south-west of Toledo. Tel 419 385 4040.

Pennsylvania: Hershey Gardens, Information Center, 400 W. Hersheypark Drive, Hershey, Pa 17033. On US 422, 90 miles west of Philadelphia, 15 miles east of Harrisburg. 100 varieties of peony. Tel 717 534 3492.

Longwood Gardens, PO Box 501, Rte 1, Kennet Square, PA 19348-0501. On US 1, 30 miles south-west of Philadelphia, 12 miles north of Wilmington. Tel 610 388 1000.

Scott Arboretum, Swarthmore College, Swarthmore, PA 19081. On State Route 320, 12 miles west of Philadelphia. Tree peonies. Tel 610 328 8025.

Rhode Island: Shakespeare's Head, 21 Meeting Street, Providence, RI 02903. Tel (Providence Preservation Society) 401 831 7440.

Tennessee: Cheekwood, Forrest Park Drive, Nashville, TN 37205. Off US 70, 8.5 miles south-west of Nashville. Tel 615 352 5310.

Vermont: Hildene, Route 7A, Manchester., VT 05254. Tel 802 362 1788.

Virginia: André Viette Nursery, PO Box 1109, Fisherville, VA 22939. On Route 608, 2.5 miles north of Route 250. Display gardens include peony border. Tel 540 943 2315, fax 540 943 0782.

Wisconsin: Boerner Botanical Gardens, 5879 South 92nd Street, Hales Corner, WI 53130. Tel 414 425 1130.

APPENDIX B

Where To Buy Peonies:

AN INTERNATIONAL LIST OF PEONY NURSERIES.

CANADA

British Colombia: Piroche Plants Inc. (wholesale only) 20542 McNeil Road, Pitt Meadows, BC V3Y 1Z1. Tel 604 465 7101. fax 604 465 7103. 96 tree peonies, about 100 herbaceous.

Ontario: Brickman's Botanical Gardens, Wartburg, RR1, Sebringville, Ontario N0K 1X0. Tel 519 393 62233, fax 519 393 5239. 94 herbaceous.

Connon Nurseries, 383 Dundas Street East, PO Box 1218, Waterdown, Ontario L0R 2H0. Tel 905 689 4631, fax 905 689 3554. 12 herbaceous.

Gardenimport Inc. PO Box 760 Thornhill, Ontario L3T 4A5. Tel 905 731 1950, fax 905 881 3499. 12 herbaceous.

Hortico, 723 Robson Road, RR1, Waterdown, Ontario L0R 2H1. Tel 905 689 6984, fax 905 689 6566. Small selection of tree peonies, 46 herbaceous.

Kiwi Gardens, Harper Road, RR7, Perth, Ontario K7H 3C9. Tel 613 267 7384, fax 613 264 0278. Un-named tree peonies sold by colour, about 20 herbaceous.

Whitehouse Perennials, RR2, Almonte, Ontario K0A 1A0. Tel 613 256 3406, fax 613 256 6827. 26 herbaceous varieties.

Quebec: Pépinière Charlevoix Inc, 391 boul. Mailloux, Rivière-Malbaie, Quebec G5A 1N6. Tel 418 439 4646, fax 418 439 4647. 30 herbaceous varieties.

FINLAND

Rea Peltola and Vesa Koivu, Puutarha Metsan reunassa, Palsilantie 63, 17800 Kuhmoinen, Finland. Tel 03 555 1345. Peonies for sale from year 2002

FRANCE

Pivoines Rivière, 'La Plaine', 26400 Crest (Drome). Tel 04 75 25 44 85 fax 04 75 76 77 38. 99 tree peonies, 135 herbaceous varieties.

GERMANY

Albrecht Hoch, Potsdamerstrasse 40, D
14163 Berlin. Tel (030) 802 62 51, fax
802 62 22. 6 Itersectional hybrids, 7 tree
peonies, 120 herbaceous.

Staudengartner Heinz Klose, Rosenstrasse
10, D 34253 Lohfelden. Tel 0561 51 55
55, fax 0561 51 51 20. 23 species and
their forms, 650 herbaceous varieties.

Wolfgang Linneman, Rheindorfer Strasse
49, D-53225 Bonn. Tel 0049 228 471448,
fax 0049 228 471247. Very
comprehensive, connoisseur's list of
Chinese and Japanese tree peonies.

Werner Simon, Staudenweg 2, D-97828
Marktheidenfeld. Tel 9391 3516.

Staudengartnerei Grafin von Zeppelin,
Laufen/Baden D 79295 Sulzburg. Tel
07634 69716, fax 07634/6599. 5 species,
90 herbaceous, 16 tree peonies.

HOLLAND

Pépinière Joghmanshof, Laageinde 3, Kapel-
Avezaath. Tel 0344 661415 or 0345
651600.

JAPAN

Kotobuki bussan, 880, Futago, Yatsuka-cho,
Yathuka-gun, Shimane Prefecture, Japan
690-1406. Tel 81 852 762555, fax 81 852
762100.

NEW ZEALAND

Canterbury: Craigmore Peonies
Partnership, RD2 Timaru. Tel 03 6122
9840, fax 03 612 9890.

Marsal Paeonies, Old South Road, R D
Dunsandel, Canterbury. Tel and fax 03
325 4003. 16 tree peonies, 9
intersectional hybrids, over 120
herbaceous.

The Terraces Paeony Nursery, 50 Terrace
Road, Leithfield, Amberley, RD1 North
Canterbury. Tel 03 314 9006, fax 03 314
9078. 70 herbaceous.

Otago: Omeo Peonies, 6 Hawley Road,
Alexandra. Tel and fax 03 449 2097. More
than 50 herbaceous.

The Peony Gardens, 231 Lake Hayes Road,
RD1 Queenstown. Tel and fax 03 442
1210. 25 tree peonies, 86 herbaceous.

SWEDEN

Hermann Krupke, Guldsmedsgardens
Plantskola, Hov, 524 95 Ljung, Sweden.
Tel 0513-500 40

SWITZERLAND

Frei, Weinland-Stauden, Breitenstrasse 5,
CH-8465 Wildensbuch ZH. Tel 052/319
12 30 fax 052/319 10 15. 15 species, 56
herbaceous varieties, 30 tree peonies.

UNITED KINGDOM

Cheshire: Phedar Nursery, Bunkers Hill, Romiley, Stockport SK6 3DS. Tel 0161 430 3772. Peony species and Chinese tree peonies.

Cornwall: Burncoose and Southdown Nurseries, Gwennap, Redruth Cornwall TR16 6BJ. Tel 01209 861112, fax 01209 860011. Tree peonies sold by colour, and a few herbaceous varieties.

Essex: Langthorns Plantery, High Cross Lane West, Little Canfield, Dunmow, Essex CM6 1TD. Tel and fax 01371 872611. A few herbaceous varieties.

Norfolk: Bressingham Plant Centres, Diss, Norfolk IP22 2AB. Tel 01379 687468, fax 01379 688034.

Scotland: Oriental Leaves, Woodwell Farmhouse Nurseries, Rait, Perthshire PH2 2RZ, Tel 01821 670754, fax 01821 670744. Chinese tree peonies.

Somerset: Kelways Limited, Barrymore Farm, Langport, Somerset TA10 9EZ. Tel 01458 250521, fax 01458 253351. Wide selection of species and their forms, tree and herbaceous peonies.

Scotts Nurseries (Meriott) Ltd, Meriott, Somerset TA16 5PL. Tel 01460 72306, fax 01460 77433. A few tree peonies and more than 18 herbaceous varieties.

Surrey: Garden Style, Wrecclesham Hill, Farnham, Surrey GU10 4JX. Tel 01252 735331, fax 01252 735269. Tree peonies as specimens in pots.

Sussex: Coombland Gardens, Coneyhurst, Billingshurst, West Sussex RH14 9DG. Tel 014403 741727, fax 01403 741079. Peony species.

West Midlands: David Austin Roses, Bowling Green Lane, Albrighton, Wolverhampton WV7 3HB. Tel 01902 373931, fax 01902 372142. Wide selection of species and their forms, tree and herbaceous peonies.

USA

South Carolina: Wayside Gardens, Hodges, S. Carolina 29695. Tel 800 845 1124.

Connecticut: White Flower Farm, Litchfield CT 06759. Tel 860 567 8789,. 20 herbaceous varieties.

Cricket Hill Garden, 670 Walnut Hill Road, Thomaston, CT 06787. Tel 860 283 1042. Specialists in Chinese tree peonies, over 80 varieties.

Illinois: Klehm Plants c/o Beaver Creek Nursery, 6604 Randall Road, Poplar Grove, IL 61065-9005. Tel 815 737 8760.

Van Hoorn Nurseries Inc., PO Box 814, Island Lake, IL 60042. Tel 888 467 8271. fax 847 526 7668. 11 herbaceous varieties.

Massachusetts: Weston Nurseries, East Main Street, Hopkinton, MA 01748. Tel 508 435 3414. Seven varieties of herbaceous peonies.

Michigan: Reath's Nursery, County Road 577, N 195 Vulcan, Michigan 49892. Tel 906 563 9777. 80 tree peonies, 110 herbaceous.

Minnesota: Busse Gardens, 5873 Oliver Avenue SW, Cokato, MN 55321 Tel 800 544 3192.

Sevald Nursery, 4937 Third Avenue South, Minneapolis, MN 55409. Tel 612 822 3279.

Missouri: Hollingsworth Nursery, RR3, Box 27, Maryville, MO 64468. Tel 660 562 3010, fax 660 582 8688. About 50 herbaceous varieties offered for sale from a collection of 450.

Gilbert H. Wild & Son Inc., 1112 Joplin Street, Sarcoxie, MO 64862-0338. Tel 417 548 3514 fax 417 548 6831. 90 herbaceous varieties.

New York: Van Bourgondien Bros. 245 Route 109, PO Box 1000, Babylon, NY 11702-9004. Tel 800 437 7501 fax 516 669 1228. 13 tree peonies, mixed un-named herbaceous varieties.

Oregon: Brothers Herbs and Peonies Inc. (Rick Rogers), 27015 SW Ladd Hill Road, Sherwood, OR 97140. Tel 503 625 3613 or 625 7548, fax 503 625 16567. Tree peonies.

Caprice Farm Nursery, 15425 SW Pleasant Hill Road, Sherwood, OR 97140. Tel 503 625 7241, fax 503 625 5588. 45 herbaceous varieties.

Virginia: André Viette Nursery, PO Box 1109, Fisherville, VA 22939. Tel 540 943 2315, fax 540 943 0782. Six tree peonies, 125 herbaceous.

Granville Hall, 7294 Shackleford Avenue, Gloucester, VA 23061. Tel 804 693 3919. A few herbaceous varieties.

Washington: A & D Peony and Perennial Nursery, 6808 180th S E, Snohomish, Washington 98296. Tel 360 668 9690. Tree peonies and herbaceous.

Wisconsin: Anderson Peony Garden, W6658 Sunset Lane, Fort Atkinson, WI 53538. Tel 920 563 2927. Specialist breeders of the rare and sought-after Intersectional (Ito) Hybrids, offering 16 varieties.

BIBLIOGRAPHY

IN CHINESE:

Liu Xiang, *Zhongguo Mudan*, [Chinese Tree Peonies] Henan Science and Technology Press, Henan, China, 1995. 130 pages, 250 colour photographs.

He Xiaoyao (chief editor), *Luoyang Mudan Tu Pu*, [A Treatise on the Mudan Peony of Luoyang] China Pictorial Publishing House, 1998. 147 pages, 200 colour photographs.

Wang Lianyang, *Zhongguo Mudan Pinzhong Tuzhi*, [A Pictorial Record of Chinese Tree Peony Varieties] China Forestry Press, 1997. 213 pages, 400 colour photographs.

Xiao Bo Qing, *The Tree Peony in Caozhou*, Shanghai People Fine Art Press, Shanghai, China, 1992. 233 pages, 500 colour photographs.

IN ENGLISH:

The American Garden Guide Book , Evans & Co., New York.

American Cottage Gardens, Brooklyn Botanic Gardens, 1990.

Bean, W J, *Trees and Shrubs Hardy in the British Isles*, 8th edn, John Murray, 1970.

Culpepper, Nicolas, *Complet Herball and English Physician*, Enlarged, 1653.

Farrer, R J, *On the Eaves of the World*, Arnold, London 1917.

Fish, Margery, *Cottage Garden Flowers*, Collingridge, 1961.

Fish, Margery, *Gardening in the Shade*, Collingridge, 1964.

Fortune, Robert, *Wanderings in China*, John Murray, 1847.

National Gardens Scheme, *Gardens of England and Wales Open for Charity*, 1998.

Gerard, John, *The Herball or Generall Historie of Plantes*, ed. Th. Johnson, London, 1636.

Goody, Jack, *The Culture of Flowers*, Cambridge University Press, 1993.

Graham, Dorothy, *Chinese Gardens*, George G Harrap & Company Ltd, London, 1938.

Hadfield, Miles, *A History of British Gardening*, John Murray, London 1979.

Hanmer, Sir Thomas, *The Garden Book of Sir Thomas Hanmer Bart* (1659), London, 1933.

Harding, Alice, *The Peony*, Sagapress Inc./Timber Press Inc., Portland, Oregon, 1995.

Haworth-Booth, Michael, *The Moutan or Tree Peony*, Constable, London, 1963.

Jekyll, Gertrude, *Colour Schemes for the Flower Garden*, Country Life, 1908.

Jellicoe, Geoffrey and Susan, Goode, Patrick, Lancaster, Michael, *The Oxford Companion to Gardens*, OUP, 1986.

Kelway, James, *Garden Paeonies*, Eyre and Spottiswoode, 1954.

Kessenich, Greta M, *The American Tree Peony*, The American Peony Society, 1988.

Keswick, Maggie, *The Chinese Garden, History, Art & Architecture*, Academy Editions, 1978.

Klehm, R G, *The Peony*, Batsford, London, 1993.

Lancaster, Roy, *Travels in China*, The Antique Collectors' Club, London, 1989.

Page, Martin, *The Gardener's Guide to Growing Peonies*, David & Charles Publishers, Newton Abbot, Devon, UK and Timber Press, Inc., 1997.

Pereire, Anita and van Zuylen, Gabrielle, *Private Gardens of France*, Weidenfeld & Nicolson, 1983.

Pope, Clara Marie, *Species and Varieties of the Genus Paeonia,* 1822.

Quest-Ritson, Charles, *The English Garden Abroad*, Viking, 1992.

Raven, Sarah, *The Cutting Garden*, Frances Lincoln, 1996.

Rawson, Jessica, *Chinese Ornament – the Lotus and the Dragon*, British Museum Publications, 1984.

Robinson, William, *The English Flower Garden*, John Murray, 1893.

Robinson, William, *The Wild Garden*, John Murray, 1870.

Rogers, Allan, *Peonies*, Timber Press Inc., Portland, Oregon 1955.

Royal Horticultural Society, *The Plant Finder*, 1998-1999.

Scott-James, Anne, *The Cottage Garden*, Allen Lane, London 1981.

Stearn, W T and Davis, P H, *Peonies of Greece*, Goulandris Natural History Museum, 1984.

Stearn. F, *The Genus Paeonia*, RHS, 1946.

Thomas, Graham Stuart, *Perennial Garden Plants*, Dent, 1982.

Wister, J C, *The Peonies*, The American Peony Society, 1995.

IN FRENCH:

Bonpland, Aimé, *Description des plantes rares cultivées à Malmaison et à Navarre*, 1813.

IN JAPANESE:

Ryoji Hashida, *A Hundred Tree Peony Flowers*, 1986.

Ryoji Hashida, *The Illustrated Book of Modern Japanese Tree and Herbaceous Peonies*, 1990.

ACKNOWLEDGEMENTS

THE FOLLOWING BOOKS have been invaluable sources of information, and I would like to thank the authors for permission to quote from them: Ryoji Hashida, *One Hundred Tree Peony Flowers*; Martin Page, *The Gardener's Guide to Growing Peonies*; Allan Rogers, *Peonies*; Wang Changzhong and others, *A Treatise on the Mudan Peony of Luoyang*. I must also thank Mr Hashida for his informative correspondence, and Mr Wang for finding time to meet me during the very busy Luoyang Peony Festival.

Time is a precious commodity, and I am very grateful to peony experts for giving theirs to help me with my research. For their shared knowledge, their infectious enthusiasm and in many cases their kind hospitality, I would like to thank the following people:

In the UK Mrs Margaret Baber, Mr and Mrs John Berkeley, Mr and Mrs Robert Mitchell. In China Mr Song Qinghai in Heze, Shandong. I want specially to thank Mr Zhang Shengli, our guide and interpreter in Luoyang, for his help in making our visit so delightful and memorable. In New Zealand, Julie and John Allan for much useful information and Dorothy and Bruce Hamilton for kindly lending photographs. In the USA, Roger Anderson, Don Hollingsworth, William Seidl and especially Kasha and David Furman who gave me much useful information about Chinese tree peonies and were extraordinarily generous in lending photographs. Photographs were also kindly lent by Roy Klehm, and the commissioned pictures were taken by Ann Hyde.

For permission to photograph their peonies I thank Mrs Margaret Baber at Green Cottage, Mr John Berkeley at Spetchley Park, Lord de l'Isle at Penshurst Place, the National Trust at Hidcote, Mrs Faith Raven at Docwra's Manor and the Borough of Worthing at Highdown. The biggest single source of photographs was Kelways Ltd. and I thank them for their generosity. I would particularly like to thank David Root at Kelways for selecting the photographs and for allowing me access to Kelways' archives and to Peony Valley.

Finally, I thank Tom Graves for finding most of the other illustrations, Nigel Soper for his dedicated work on the design, Helena Attlee for her tactful and skilful editing and Susan Haynes for seeing the book through from start to finish.

PICTURE CREDITS

Every effort has been made by the publishers to obtain copyright clearance for the photographs reproduced in this book.

AKG LONDON 103 (Kunsthalle, Bremen)112 (Museé National d'Histoire Naturelle, Paris)

HEATHER ANGEL/BIOFOTOS 28, 29, 57, 123, 141, 164, 167

BRIDGEMAN ART LIBRARY, LONDON endpapers front and back, (Fitzwilliam Museum, University of Cambridge; half-title (School of Oriental and African Studies Library, University of London); 11 (Private Collection); 12-13 (Victoria and Albert Museum, London); 33 (Victoria and Albert Museum, London); 40 (Victoria and Albert Museum, London); 46 (Private Collection); 49 (Private Collection); 64-65; 67 (British Library, London); 68 (Private Collection, London); 72 (British Library, London); 75 (British Library, London); 76 (Ashmolean Museum, Oxford); 77 (Private Collection); 78 (Allans of Duke St, London); 85 (Belvoir Castle, Leics); 109 (Museé des Beaux-Arts, Lyons); 113 (Wallace Collection, London); 126 (Private Collection); 127 (Cleveland Museum of Art, Ohio); 153 (Mallett and Sow Antiques, London); 154 (Christopher Wood Gallery, London); 195 (Private Collection); 197 (Ackerman and Johnson Ltd, London); 193 (Kunsthistorisches Museum, Vienna); 200 (Private Collection); 204 (Fitzwilliam Museum, University of Cambridge); 206-207 (Private Collection); 336-337 (Private Collection); 351 (John Spink Fine Watercolours, London)

CHRISTIES IMAGES LTD, LONDON 71, 128-129, 194, 202

E.T. ARCHIVE, LONDON 89 left, 124

FINE ART PHOTOGRAPHIC LIBRARY, LONDON 45, 104, 160-61

KASHA and DAVID FURMAN, CRICKET HILL, CT, USA title page, 53, 143, 144, 187 (both), 188, 190, 236 below, 344 (both), 347 (both), 348 (both)

HARPUR GARDEN LIBRARY 168, 180

HULTON GETTY, LONDON 4, 62, 82, 94

ANNE HYDE 15 above and below, 18, 22, 31, 35, 38, 42, 90, 98, 100, 117, 147, 165, 171, 172, 175, 176, 199, 222, 233 below, 258, 284 below, 318, 329, 340 above right and below

KELWAYS LTD 21, (three), 27, 59, 61, 86, 121, 132, 133 (both), 139 (both), 181, 182, 183, 184 (both), 211, 212, 225, 227, 233 above, 236 above, 241, 244 (both), 247, 253, 256, 260, 263, 264, 267, 268, 270 (both), 271, 274 (both), 276, 277, 281, 282, 284 above, 287, 290, 294 (both), 297 (both), 302 (three), 307, 315, 333, 340 below

ROY KLEHM NURSERY, ILLINOIS, USA 131, 136 above, 273

ANDREW LAWSON 118, 156, 157 above and below, 189, 231

NATURAL HISTORY MUSEUM, LONDON 8, 39, 89 right, 114

NATIONAL TRUST PHOTO LIBRARY, LONDON 163

NATURAL IMAGE 36

THE PEONY GARDENS, QUEENSTOWN, NEW ZEALAND (Dorothy and Bruce Hamilton) 60, 136 below, 148, 151, 239

ROYAL BOTANICAL GARDENS, KEW 93 left and right, 97

WEIDENFELD ARCHIVE, LONDON 106

WERNER FORMAN ARCHIVE 81 (METROPOLITAN MUSEUM OF ART, NEW YORK)

JANE FEARNLEY-WHITTINGSTALL 50, 54

INDEX